THE SMUGGLERS

by the same author
THE WORLD OF GOLD

THE SMUGGLERS

An Investigation into
the World of the
Contemporary Smuggler

TIMOTHY GREEN

WALKER AND COMPANY   NEW YORK

First published in the United States of America in 1969 by Walker and Company, a division of the Walker Publishing Company, Inc.

Library of Congress Catalog Card Number: 77-86407

Printed in the United States of America.
Typography by M. Cook and T. Roxburgh

for
SNOWBALL

Preface

A couple of years ago I journeyed through the Middle East, India, and the Far East as part of my research for a book on gold. During my travels I gained some firsthand impressions of the enormous scale of international smuggling today. At that time I was specifically concerned with gold smuggling, but intriguing information about contraband watches, diamonds, and drugs kept cropping up everywhere. I have now retraced my steps through these areas and visited many other countries, trying to piece together the great sprawl of modern smuggling which has been changed so radically by the long-range jet and modern communications. En route I have been helped and encouraged (and once or twice discouraged) by many people— customs officers, policemen, airline security officers, bankers, gold dealers, and, of course, the smugglers themselves. I would like very much to be able to name them all in expressing my thanks for their aid, but because of the nature of the business, that is not possible. I have talked to most of them in confidence.

However, I would like to express my special thanks to Patrick P. O'Carroll, assistant to the commissioner at the United States Bureau of Narcotics and Dangerous Drugs, and to

Lawrence Fleishman, the assistant commissioner in charge of the United States Customs Agency Service, both of whom gave me invaluable guidance and introductions to their colleagues in the field. The members of the United Nations International Narcotics Control Board and the Commission of Narcotic Drugs in Geneva were also of great assistance. But any errors or misinterpretations are of my own making.

As always, my wife has done a professional job of reading and commenting on every chapter. The typing of the manuscript has been done with quite remarkable speed and precision by Kathy Young. I am more than grateful to both of them.

TIMOTHY GREEN
Dulwich, March 17, 1969

Contents

PART THREE
The Luxury Trade

FINALE

INDEX

Profit for Sure

I

Profit for Sure

A smuggler works from inclination, from passion. He is on one side an artist. He risks everything, runs terrible dangers; he is cunning, invents dodges, and gets out of scrapes, and sometimes acts with a sort of inspiration. It is a passion as strong as gambling.

—Dostoyevsky, *The House of the Dead*

Smuggling is often called the world's second oldest profession. While the transaction involved in the oldest profession of all has not altered over the centuries, the smuggler is a chameleonlike character changing his disguise and his contraband cargoes with never-ending fickleness.

The eighteenth-century smuggler cut a romantic figure, slipping up the English Channel on a dark night with a rich cargo of wines, spices, and silks in the hold of his schooner, offloading them at some lonely pine-fringed creek, dallying briefly with a flaxen-haired maiden, then vanishing into the dawn before the Preventive men had brushed sleep from their eyes. The modern smuggler is rarely dashing. He may be that man sitting glumly over his paperback on the flight to New York, apparently just another harassed businessman, with nothing to suggest that he has enough LSD for 100,000 trips concealed in his after-shave

3

lotion; or he may be a poor student earning a quick four hundred dollars by carrying thirty-kilo bars of gold from Geneva to Bangkok in a special vest beneath his shirt; he may be a wretchedly seasick Pakistani shepherding a small boatload of illegal Asian immigrants across the English Channel from Belgium to Britain.

There are the swashbuckling stories, of course, like that of the girl who lost an eye in a car accident and then took to smuggling diamonds in the cavity behind her glass eye, but the romance in that little episode depends rather on your sense of humor. Yet one thing smugglers have always had in common—the desire to make money. Today they are even more successful at that than three hundred years ago. "I assume," said an American narcotics agent a trifle bitterly, "that you will call this book *Profit for Sure?*"

The smuggler's turnover is certainly on a level with the high finance of modern industry. The annual volume of smuggling in drugs, gold, and diamonds and the rate of growth of these rackets would hearten any legal board of directors and win shareholders splendid dividends. The value of drugs smuggled into the United States each year is now over one billion dollars at wholesale prices; gold smugglers are among the best customers on the free gold market, buying up over three hundred million dollars' worth a year, while at least fifty million dollars in rough diamonds is mined illicitly in Africa each year and smuggled out of the continent to the diamond markets of the world.

The smuggler's catalog extends far beyond these best-selling lines. He is in business to supply whatever his client requires, be it parrots, sex hormones, butter, Peking duck, lipsticks, or orangutans. Indeed, in some countries it is hard to work out what is *not* smuggled in. In the Philippines, which may well boast more smugglers per head of the population than any other country, it ranges from spices to cement mixers, from diamonds to cigarettes. Even a wife preparing a dinner party needs her smuggling contacts. "If you ask your hostess for a recipe for some marvelous meat sauce," said the wife of a Manila banker, "she will write it down for you willingly, but she will put brackets around one or two spices to indicate they are obtainable only from smugglers." Smuggling reached such proportions in the

Philippines by 1967 that President Marcos embarked on a nationwide advertising campaign of billboard signs along the nation's highways showing a determined President sternly wagging his finger, while the slogan reads: "Help stop smuggling and make this nation great again."

The ingenuity of the smuggling mind is unending. Apart from the conventional smuggling vest with rows of pockets stitched by a wife or girl friend and worn beneath the shirt, smugglers use everything from hollowed-out teak logs to the compartments behind car headlights; from the ventilator shafts of ships to the toilets of aircraft. Cannabis has been carried in the handles of tennis rackets and beneath the skin of an African drum. Hashish smugglers in the Arabian Gulf recently came up with the idea of molding the drug into balls the size and shape of a lemon, covering them with a yellow membrane taken from toy balloons and passing the lot off as lemons. Coconuts provide excellent concealment once the milk is drained out, but it is essential to put in a little pouch of water so that the nut sloshes genuinely, should any customs man shake it. Two men arriving in New Orleans from Yucatán had nearly five pounds of marihuana concealed inside the air tanks of scuba-diving gear; it took customs men three and one-half hours to ease the drug back out through the half-inch air-valve holes—but a diary found on one of the smugglers showed it had taken seven and one-half hours to put it in. Then there was the miniskirted girl who had diamonds in a pink-suede tassle dangling from her garters. And some kind of prize should go to the American soldier in Vietnam who shipped home, through the mail, a seven-foot python labeled as a table lamp.

All this subterfuge inevitably lands the smuggler with a heavy expense account, which can eat swiftly into his profits. The most expensive racket to run is, undoubtedly, the drug traffic, but the profits are so great that any payoff is justified. One kilo of heroin increases in price from a few dollars paid to a Turkish peasant farmer for his raw opium to over $225,000 as the retail price for diluted heroin on the streets of New York. An illegal commodity can, of course, command premium prices. The cigarette or whiskey smuggler must work to lower margins of profit, for the essence of his business is to undercut duty. In gold and diamonds, the rewards are not as rich as might appear at first glance. Although gold bought in Geneva at forty dollars an ounce can be sold in Bombay for seventy dollars an ounce, the expenses involved in getting it there reduce the profits to a mere four or five dollars an ounce. "We hope to make an average profit of eight to nine percent over the season," said a gold smuggler in Dubai, the little sheikdom at the southern end of the Arabian Gulf, which is the jumping-off point for gold-bearing dhows bound for India. "But," he added, "at one time last year the profit margin was down to two or three percent." The return on diamonds smuggled from, say, Tel Aviv to New York is not much greater. Suppose the smuggler has contracted to carry $100,000 worth of diamonds. The duty payable on that shipment is $8,000, so the smuggler, to be competitive, has to undercut this substantially. His commission, therefore, can be only $4,000 to $5,000. If the diamond dealer himself, or his wife, brings in the diamonds, then the full $8,000 is saved, but most prefer to hire a courier.

Smugglers, just like every other businessman, have their little gripes that things are not what they were and that it is hardly worth staying in business. There is no need for sympathy. Rest assured that the smuggler does not continue either a route or a commodity that is no longer profitable. But avoiding import duty is not the only thing that makes smuggling rewarding. The real benefits of smuggling, in an age of ever-increasing government controls and taxation, can come from dodging income tax or company tax. Indeed, in the United States and in Britain senior customs officials see the prime motive for smuggling as the avoidance, not of import duty, but of internal taxes. The saving of $8,000 duty on a shipment of $100,000 of diamonds may not in itself make the venture worthwhile—given the risk of detection—but the diamond dealer then has $100,000 of diamonds which do not appear at all on his books, so he avoids local sales taxes and income tax on his profit from the sale of those diamonds. This can all add up to a saving, not of $8,000, but of $20,000 or more.

Many poor nations, notably India and South American

6

countries, which are desperately short of foreign exchange, impose either tight import quotas or total bans on the import of many goods. Whiskey, cars, and watches are on quota systems in most South American countries; India bans the import of gold and does not permit the entry of finished watches. Duties may also be so high as to make legitimate import quite impractical. India, for example, charges duty of $7.20 on a kilo of nylon yarn whose actual cost is only $2.40 a kilo. This is an open invitation to smuggle and nylon yarn is one of the biggest contraband cargoes of India.

Indeed, the way to increase productivity in the smuggling industry is very simple: impose high duty or controls, and the smugglers come flocking like homing pigeons. The tight currency regulations imposed in Britain in 1966, permitting everyone only fifty pounds a year foreign-travel allowance, sparked off a wave of currency fiddles. The least sophisticated simply tucked £10,-000 ($24,000) in their underpants and jumped on the plane to Zurich or Geneva; the artful invested in paintings, stamps, or diamonds, which could be exported from Britain quite legally, and sold them the moment they arrived on the Continent. The ultimate destination of every currency smuggler, indeed of every smuggler who is thoughtful of his old-age pension, is Switzerland, that haven of the sacred numbered bank account. The major Swiss banks always hasten to protest that they are not simply drop-offs for every gangster's loot; this is true. The important banks are wary of their clients, but Swiss banking law applies equally to more than three hundred banks great and small; the smuggler is certain to find a friend at one.

Frequently the smuggler does not try to avoid the customs; he simply juggles paperwork to confuse them. This "technical" smuggling, mainly involving underinvoicing, has increased enormously in the last decade. Ten years ago the major problems taxing the U.S. Customs Service were the smuggling in of narcotics, diamonds, and watches (in that order) and the smuggling out of arms. Today the number-one problem is still narcotics, but undervaluation and false invoicing are the second biggest headache and involved more than 2,700 cases in 1968.

The simplest form of underinvoicing is to declare that the

importer paid, say, 50 cents each for 100,000 Christmas-tree decorations, when in fact he paid 75 cents each; he is thus liable to duty on $50,000 worth of goods and not on $75,000 worth. Or an invoice may declare there are 20,000 shoes in a consignment from Italy to New York; really there are 30,000. "They gamble we won't count every shoe," says a customs man. It is a safe gamble for a betting man.

The sheer volume of international trade these days, plus the speed of clearance that is demanded as the air-freight business develops, makes it quite impossible for customs to carry out more than a few token searches. The detection of fraud or of outright smuggling does not rely, of course, on arduously counting 20,000 shoes or having a hunch that a certain passenger has three kilos of heroin taped around his thighs; it depends on good information. The majority of smugglers who are caught by chance are the amateurs, who simply look guilty or make a number of elementary mistakes. The amateur may be too gay and jocular with the customs officer; a husband and wife may opt for different customs inspectors. (They might just have had a quarrel on the plane, but more likely they are halving the risk of being caught.) Or he may select the *longest* line waiting for inspection. The customs' theory here is that smugglers are unconsciously putting off the evil moment of confrontation. However, one amateur smuggler, who had consciously chosen the longest line, said his reasoning was that the customs officer would be moving faster to clear the backlog when his turn came. Amateurs caught by hunches are a good bonus for any customs-service records, but customs priority must always be to detect smuggling on a commercial scale. And this is unmasked only by painstaking investigation and tip-offs. "The best scientific aid I know," says Lawrence Fleishman, assistant commissioner in charge of the U.S. Customs Agency Service, the detective division of customs, "is a good informer."

The value of information is not just that it enables the customs officer to pinpoint a smuggler as he arrives, but it can lead him into the real heart of a smuggling outfit. The man who actually carries the goods is rarely more than a paid courier. A cardinal rule in smuggling everything from heroin to gold is that

8

the key organizers never carry anything. Complete isolation from the physical act of smuggling is all-important. The courier, however, can pick up his package and airline tickets from an unknown man in a hotel room in Paris and simply be told to go to New York and check in at a particular hotel, where he will be contacted. If he is nabbed by customs, the actual consignment is a write-off, but the security of the organization is not breached. It is perfectly simple either for someone quite unknown to the courier to travel with him on the plane to see things go smoothly or to be watching his passage through customs on arrival. At Kennedy Airport in New York—and, indeed, at most airports around the world—there is a viewing gallery where relatives and friends can watch the new arrivals coming through customs inspection. A smuggler's contact man mingles with the cheerfully waving throng and, nose pressed to the glass, watches his man safely through inspection. And at the first sign of trouble, he is off to sound the alarm so that any link is broken. Customs men, trying to preserve that crucial link to bigger fish, will often try to persuade a courier to cooperate with them. They ask him to carry on with his instructions, hoping that his arrest was not observed. Even better, if they are really sure of their man, they will let the courier go through customs quite untouched and trail him to his delivery point.

The structure of a smuggling syndicate is often indefinable. "It's like a plate of spaghetti," a British customs man said ruefully. "Every piece seems to touch every other, but you are never sure where it all leads. Once in a while we arrest someone we are sure is important. Well, he may have been, up to that moment, but once we get him, he suddenly becomes no more than a tiny cog. Someone else important pops up in his place." The close security of a syndicate ensures that if one link breaks, there are six others, probably all quite unknown to each other, to hold it together. A chart trying to pinpoint who's who in the heroin traffic looks like a genealogist's nightmare.

Yet organization does exist and works most efficiently. It is not a matter of one mastermind, or even two, sitting in ivory towers manipulating a global network of chicanery. Rather, there are many intelligent groups of men with a wide range of contacts, each of whom can help them at some stage of an operation. Contacts are as vital to the smuggler as information is to the customs man. He must have a friend or a friend of a friend. Smuggling relies, in fact, on an "old-boy" network as good as that of any English public school. Within this old-boy framework, it is essential to have a friendly travel agent who can make all the bookings as part of his normal business; a foreign-exchange expert or banker who can help with international payments and advise on such refinements as Swiss bank accounts; plus a man who can act as a kind of personnel manager to recruit and brief couriers. A lawyer is also a useful asset to smooth over legal tangles. And the best possible front for the whole operation is an import-export business, which is bound, in the course of its day-to-day business, to receive and dispatch scores of packages, telex messages, and international payments; sifting the wheat of real business from the chaff of smuggling is almost impossible.

Specialization, as in everything today, is essential. The subtleties of each racket are so involved that it demands full concentration. The gunrunner must have an intimate knowledge not only of the actual workings of a myriad of pistols, rifles, machine guns, and mortars, but he must know where in Europe he can find ammunition for an outdated Enfield rifle or a Browning machine gun. He must understand that American 81-mm. mortar bombs will fire from American and Russian 81-mm. mortars, but that for some perverse reason, Russian 81-mm. mortar bombs will fire only from Russian mortars. So if his client has both types of mortar, he must locate American mortar bombs. All of which leaves him no time to speculate in gold or diamonds. Likewise in the frenetic conditions of the gold business, in which a price differential of one or two cents an ounce can mean everything between profit and loss, the gold smuggler buying by the ton on the free market in Geneva, Brussels, or Beirut must hug his telex to glean the latest official prices from the "fixing" ceremonies in London and Zurich. As for diamonds, there is no stricter closed shop in the world, and anyone who gains entry to the sacred portals of a diamond dealers' club must make it the profession of a lifetime.

This specialization is not totally cast iron at lower levels; there is some intermingling of activities in gold, watches, diamonds, and precious stones, particularly in Hong Kong. One import-export outfit there is busy smuggling watches, gold, and emeralds to Japan and bringing back pearls, while also acting as the Hong Kong representative of a small Swiss bank. But there is little cross-fertilization between this luxury trade and narcotics—despite persistent stories of gold for opium. The smuggler of antiques, gold, or fine whiskey is a different species from the narcotics trafficker. The former is a businessman doing a little sleight of hand on the side; the latter is a criminal. The gold smuggler may not be pure as driven snow—some of them are very tough characters—but his moral outlook is quite different. He, and everyone else, despises the drug trafficker. The gold smuggler can plead that although he is breaking the law, he is seeking only to dodge the tax collector; he is not trading in anything which will cause misery or death. As one of them hopefully put it, "Smuggling is not mentioned in the Ten Commandments. In spite of 'render unto Caesar that which is Caesar's,' smuggling is not punishable under the laws of God."

The luxury-trade smuggler often hastens to explain that not only will he never deal in narcotics, but he would not employ a criminal either. "We are very careful not to employ any couriers with a criminal record," said one of the main gold smugglers in Beirut. This sounds a fine moral standard, but is, in fact, more a question of self-preservation. Any criminal is a security risk. Interpol may well have circulated his description around the world. Behind the scenes in any airport these days is a neat filing-card system coupling photographs with cross-references to criminals' descriptions, habits, likely aliases, and specialties. No one wants a courier listed in that black book.

The luxury-trade courier probably breaks the law only in the country to which he delivers the goods. When he embarks from Geneva or Dubai or Hong Kong with his gold, watches, or diamonds, he is not breaking any local laws. The only gauntlet he must run is the customs check on the threshold of the receiving country. The narcotics trafficker, however, attracts the attention of the law wherever he goes: he is equally illegal in Switzerland,

Lebanon, or the United States. And because he trades in human misery, every policeman or customs agent will pursue him with greater zeal than a diamond smuggler with a few undeclared stones destined for the tiara of a beautiful woman.

What unites all smugglers, however, is their need for close family and ethnic connections. Every smuggler is a cautious fellow. He is most reluctant to deal with anyone he does not know personally or with whom he does not share a common language and traditions. Smuggling, after all, demands absolute trust, not only to prevent detection but also to ensure payment for goods delivered. Smuggling, in fact, is most prevalent and best practiced among people who feel outsiders in a community, who have always had to fight hard for survival, perhaps as refugees or immigrants in a new land where they have been able to survive only by outwitting authority. The Mafia in the United States is the obvious example. For years the vital link in the heroin traffic across the Atlantic was sustained by the family ties between Sicily and America. Indeed, it was even strengthened by the Americans deporting their top Mafia criminals back to Italy, where they looked up old acquaintances and plotted revenge. Now, as the first-generation ties between Italy and the United States have weakened and the old friends have died or retired into prosperous old age, the international heroin traffic is moving out of the Mafia's control, into the hands of another bunch of far-flung renegade islanders, the French Corsicans. Like the Sicilians, they hail from a poor, rocky Mediterranean island from which they made a successful leap to France and then to French-speaking Canada. Nor is this only a European phenomenon. In the Far East the Chu Chow Chinese from Fukien province in South China, who were born to the same harsh environment as the Sicilians and Corsicans, have fanned out through the Orient to Hong Kong, Singapore, Saigon, and Bangkok to establish a cousinly network controlling every racket from opium to gold.

The trail of kinship follows every smuggling route. The Sindhi of India, who are wizards at foreign-exchange manipulations and have their little colonies in Bombay, London, New York, and Hong Kong, control much of the financing of the gold and watch smuggling into India. The Armenians, the driving force behind the old Ottoman Empire, were scattered around the globe by massacres in Turkey in World War I, and many have had to live by their wits. They speak Arabic, Turkish, French, and Italian and, like the Lebanese, have the great trading traditions of the Levant as an inheritance. Both groups turn up everywhere from Genoa and Marseilles to New York and Rio de Janeiro.

Trading with those you know is, after all, a basic business instinct. "I find I am most at home in African countries which used to be British colonies," said a London gunrunner. "The chaps I deal with may be Africans, but they were trained by the British. They appreciate how we think, and they speak English. I always wear my regimental tie, because they then know they are dealing with a former British officer. But I wouldn't dream of trying to sell arms in South America. I don't speak the language and don't understand the people."

Overseas roots do not need to be long-established. Two smuggling developments of major importance in the 1960's have followed hard on the heels of new migrations. The movement of thousands of Turks to work in the industrial cities of the Ruhr in Germany has opened up a completely new route for smuggling morphine base, the essential ingredient of heroin, from Turkey into Western Europe. The flow of Pakistani and Indian immigrants into Britain has been followed by highly organized smuggling of cannabis from Pakistan to Britain.

All these relationships have been strengthened enormously by modern communications. The smuggler signals by international telephone and telex today; the building of a network of modern highways throughout Western Europe and America has eased his transport problems; above all, the jet age has made him the most mobile man on earth. In a profession that exists solely to hurdle frontiers, the facilities now offered by the airline business are unparalleled. The introduction of the jumbo jets and, in the mid 1970's, of the supersonic passenger plane will help even more. While police and customs are still hemmed in by their own national boundaries, the smuggler can travel through three nations in an afternoon. True, Interpol can help customs, but Interpol is not an international police force with squads of globe-

13

trotting detectives. It exists purely as a communications link between the police forces of its 103 member countries. If a detective in London believes a man carrying stolen diamonds has hopped off to Antwerp with the loot, he must request the Belgian police via Interpol headquarters in Paris to help him out. By the time they are alerted and in action, the wanted man may have disposed of the jewels and be aboard a jet to Madrid. Interpol works extremely well in certain situations, but the smuggler has a mobility no policeman or customs officer can match. The smuggler is an international man; the customs officer has no authority one inch over his boundary fence.

This new ease in globe-trotting has, however, curtailed sharply some of the smuggler's previous best-selling lines. Above all, the organized watch smuggling within Europe has declined. The Swiss Chamber of Horology estimated during the 1950's that half the watches sold in Britain had been smuggled in by organized teams. Today, partly because of lower tariffs, but more because of the expansion of the tourist business, smuggling of large shipments of watches has vanished. Holiday migrations in Europe have now reached incredible proportions; well over thirty million Europeans go south to the Mediterranean for their holidays every summer. One-fifth of the population of West Germany goes abroad each year; eight million of the French go to Spain and another four and one-half million to Italy; nearly six million Britons cross the English Channel bound for France, Spain, and Italy alone. Most of these holidaymakers can buy watches or perfume at duty-free shops on car ferries or at airports or even in Switzerland itself. Thus everyone becomes his own smuggler. This pattern of do-it-yourself smuggling throughout Europe applies equally to much of the illicit traffic in cannabis and pep pills. A student or a hippie journeys to Tangier or Istanbul to bring back enough "pot" to keep himself and his friends happily turned on during the long winter evenings.

This mass migration across national boundaries in search of sun is a European phenomenon; the Americans certainly travel to the sun, but the majority move within the confines of the United States itself. So outside Europe the need for organized smuggling is as strong as ever, whether for marihuana into the

United States, watches to India, gold to Japan, or diamonds to Indonesia. The jet age has also revolutionized this traffic. No longer does the smuggler have to entrust his goods to some seaman on a slow boat to China and perhaps be forced to wait weeks before they are delivered and he is paid. Now he can deliver anywhere in the world within forty-eight hours. There are four ways of smuggling by air: by bribing a member of the airliner crew; by sending a courier as a passenger; by paying a technician on the ground to hide the contraband in the baggage compartment or the toilets and arranging for another technician to remove the goods when the plane is serviced at the end of the flight; or by careful manipulation of air-freight manifests.

From the smuggler's standpoint, a friend among the air crew is perfect, for he has a genuine reason for popping in and out of a country five times a week. Any ordinary courier, even if he travels on a sheaf of passports, is soon going to be recognized if he flits into a country that often. In the first flush of extensive air travel, many airlines kept their crews on the same run for months on end. Nothing could have suited the smugglers better. They were able to rely on their man going to New York or Montreal or Bombay twice a week for the next six months and plan accordingly. BOAC was plagued for several years by a gold-smuggling ring which infiltrated their crews traveling to India. The stewards, rather than the pilots, are more likely to give way to a smuggler's persuasion. The pilot, after all, is a highly trained man and well paid; he cannot risk jeopardizing his career—and financially he is less hard-pressed. A steward, however, is a different proposition. "A steward," said an airline executive, "is the lowest form of life; he is the worst-paid member of the crew. So if someone in Beirut picks him up from his hotel every time he slips [i.e., has a stopover], wines and dines him, takes him to the Casino, and then says, 'Will you carry gold? It's two hundred pounds into your bank in England, and no questions asked,' he's bound to fall." Many of them have.

Airline infiltration can go far beyond stewards. The most perfect setup ever unmasked was established by French Corsican heroin smugglers on Air France's routes to Montreal and Chicago. The heroin syndicate, apart from corrupting several of the

15

airline's stewards, had also bribed a dispatcher who made up the air-crew rosters, thus establishing control of which stewards were on a particular flight. They even fixed a man in the Air France communications center, so that the airline's telex network could be utilized for the gang's messages to the steward-couriers. A steward arriving in Montreal with a shipment of heroin might find a message waiting for him saying "Rooms available at Queen Elizabeth Hotel," which would appear to be a routine message but in fact tipped him off where to make contact. If the message read, "Bennett's Lodge full," then he would know something had gone wrong with arrangements and he must carry the heroin on to Chicago. If the coast was clear in Montreal, there were two ways of getting the drug off the aircraft: either the steward carried it off himself taped around his waist, or, if more than six kilos was involved, one of the caterers who serviced the planes at Montreal was also in the ring, and he took the heroin off along with the used food trays. The gang had things working so smoothly that frequently they had two stewards carrying heroin on the same flight, although neither knew the other was a courier. When the group was finally detected early in 1965 by the combined efforts of the U.S. Bureau of Narcotics, the Royal Canadian Mounted Police, and the French Sûreté, one of the stewards admitted he had run twenty two-kilo shipments of heroin, worth $800,000 at the New York wholesale price.

Airlines are now more alert to the dangers of penetration by smuggling groups. Most airlines switch their crews to fresh routes once a month and do not permit last-minute swapping around. Most also employ their own security teams, one of whose prime responsibilities is to keep the smugglers at bay. These airline detectives are, in fact, the only investigators who match the smugglers by operating completely internationally, although they have no official police powers. They can carry on inquiries in Beirut today, Bombay tomorrow, and Bangkok or Hong Kong the next day. Their constant traveling makes them valuable aides to policemen and customs investigators fenced in by national boundaries.

Whether he bribes airline crews or dispatches his couriers on flights as passengers, the whole airline and airport business must be an open book for the smuggler. He must understand all the subtleties of ticketing, air-freight and baggage manifests, and crew rosters. He must know all the hotels where the crews stay when they slip, and the bars they frequent. Even more valuable is inside information on the movement of the aircraft themselves—particularly on the transatlantic routes. If an aircraft crosses the Atlantic and then goes on an internal American flight, a courier can hide watches, diamonds, or drugs on the plane while on the Atlantic leg of the trip, then either he or another courier can take them off next day during an internal American flight with no customs controls.

Smuggling syndicates often become an airline's best clients. In the early 1960's, when Beirut was a great gold-smuggling center, the smugglers there were reputed to be buying up to $300,000 worth of tickets a year on jets bound for Bombay, Bangkok, and Hong Kong. The airline offices in Beirut even competed for their business. In Brussels and Geneva airlines also pick up literally hundreds of couriers in the course of a year and may be most reluctant to help investigators looking into smuggling, because they do not want to lose a lucrative slice of business. At peak periods there may be six or more couriers carrying gold on any one flight to the Far East; the record appears to be sixteen gold couriers on a single Pan American flight from Beirut to Hong Kong. Many couriers live in an almost constant state of motion in that unreal limboland of transit lounges. One gold courier posing at the time as a salesman for a Swiss duplicating-equipment firm, who was picked up at Seattle in February, 1968, had airline tickets worth over $2,000 in his pockets, with a routing to Geneva, Frankfurt, Nicosia, Istanbul, Beirut, Vancouver, Tokyo, Hong Kong, Manila, Djakarta, and Bangkok. Another, arrested at John F. Kennedy Airport in New York with $32,000 in Mexican gold pesos in a smuggling vest, had tickets for Zurich to Rio de Janeiro, Caracas, Mexico City, New York, and return to Zurich. Many couriers have a sheaf of passports, enabling them to change names and even nationalities during a flight. "There's nothing easier than getting passports," says a Scotland Yard expert. "You simply go down to the passport office with your picture but someone else's birth certificate and a falsely signed form. And there's always a small market in stolen passports. Housebreakers pick them up occasionally and sell them for twenty pounds. There's absolutely no need to forge passports; genuine ones are too easy to get."

The best credential is the diplomatic passport, giving the courier complete immunity from normal customs procedures. A stolen diplomatic passport is a highly marketable commodity; even better is a genuine diplomat. The French Corsican racketeer sending heroin to the United States employed two diplomats in the early 1960's—Mauricio Rosal, the Guatemalan ambassador to the Netherlands and Belgium, and the Mexican ambassador to Bolivia, Salvador Pardo-Bolland, who between them carried at least five million dollars' worth of heroin under the protection of their diplomatic status. Diplomatic immunity extends, of course, far beyond individuals; the diplomatic bag itself is a most convenient, safe method of transport that has been used over the years for every commodity from gold into India to rough diamonds from West Africa to Tel Aviv. As for official visits by the head of one nation to the leader of another, nothing could suit the well-connected smuggler better. The baggage of the visitor's party is never examined. "You know what those letters C.D. should really stand for?" asked an old smuggling hand in Tangier. "Not Corps Diplomatique, but Contrebandier Distingué."

For the hired diplomat or the ordinary airborne courier there are five key cities around the world for picking up the goods— Geneva, Frankfurt, Paris, Brussels, and Hong Kong. Their importance is determined first by the availability of the contraband in that city and second by their position as major crossroads of international flights. It can become quite a game sitting in the departure lounge at these airports. You can study the passengers fiddling with their boarding cards, sipping lukewarm coffee, or twittering at hostesses on whether their flight is called, and try to figure out which are the couriers. Actually they are probably the ones who look the least anxious and move around least; this is partly because they have done it before and partly because they are all strapped up with gold, watches, or heroin beneath their clothes, which clamps them in a tiring straitjacket. They certainly cannot sprint for the best seat on the plane.

The most nervous person around may be a "station" manager in charge of couriers for a particular city, who may also be at the airport to see a courier safely off. There is a young fellow at Frankfurt, with a small goatee beard, who is often to be seen pacing uneasily up and down the combined transit and departure lounge biting his nails. Frankfurt is a frequent changeover point for couriers with gold or watches; one man comes up from Geneva or Zurich with a smuggling vest beneath his shirt, and instead of going through immigration and customs at Frankfurt, he heads for the transit lounge. There he meets another outward-bound courier. They go into the men's room and lock themselves into adjoining cubicles, which are separated only by a partial partition. One courier strips off his clothes, takes off the smuggling vest, and passes it over or under the partition to the new man.

The no-man's-land of the transit lounge can be the most helpful territory to the smuggler. In Anchorage, Alaska, where many international flights stop to refuel, a passenger, killing time in the transit lounge, can mail a package the size of a shoebox in a domestic U.S. mailbox conveniently provided in the lounge without passing through any kind of customs check. Many gold couriers going into Hong Kong at one time were booked through to Tokyo or Manila with a two- or three-hour layover in Hong Kong; all their baggage remained checked, but the traveler himself, with the gold beneath his shirt, could get permission to go from the transit lounge to the airport restaurant for a quick meal. Instead of eating, he took a taxi to a hotel in Kowloon, dropped off the gold, and was back at the airport in comfortable time for his flight.

The rapid growth of the air-freight business has proved equally convenient to the smuggler adept at juggling cargo manifests, particularly if he is handling bulky contraband that cannot be concealed on a courier or in ordinary hand baggage. Suppose a textile wholesaler in Lima, Peru, wants regular deliveries of $50,000 of material from Europe or America once a fortnight, but he is anxious to dodge the duty. He gets in touch with someone who has a good friend in an airline cargo office, and together they work out a plot whereby the textiles will be dispatched in crates labeled and manifested for Santiago, Chile, via Lima, Peru. During the stopover in Lima, however, the textiles are quietly removed from the transit freight shed, by a prior arrangement with a friendly customs man, while new manifests suddenly appear which neglect to make any mention of the fact that the whole consignment should have gone on to Chile. If all this astute paper fiddling is carried out by one of the airline staff, it can be very hard to detect, and the airline may unwittingly be aiding a smuggler for years on end. One airline, which had been infiltrated by smugglers, was doing such booming cargo carrying to South America and picking up so much business from its rivals, who did not have a smuggler in their midst, that executives in the head office were crowing at their success and planning expansion of their cargo routes—until the whole fraud was unmasked and their business collapsed overnight.

Although the modern airlines have revolutionized the smuggler's trade—as they have most businesses—there are occasions when a good old freighter still has its uses. In the gunrunning racket, weapons are just too heavy to be carried in any practical amounts by aircraft; an intercontinental jet can carry only thirty tons of freight, while the aging Dakotas or Constellations used by most gunrunners can carry less than ten tons. Since it needs 4,000 tons of equipment to put a guerrilla band of 500 men into the field, a boat is the obvious transport answer. Freighters are also used extensively for smuggling everything from jewelry and transistor radios to whiskey and ladies' underwear into South America. These rackets are usually run by one of the officers or the chief steward on a freighter. When his ship is in New York or Panama or Hamburg, he loads up on choice consumer goods for his clients in South America. Then, as his ship approaches its South American destination, he tosses the contraband sealed in rubber bags overboard at a prearranged spot. The trick off Valparaiso, Chile, is to heave the rubber bags over the side at the moment that the Aconcagua River and Mount Aconcagua are in line. This happens when the ship is exactly twenty-two miles out, and the bags splash down into the Humboldt Current, which carries them northward at a steady six miles a day. When the ship docks, the steward reports he put the bags over the side at six o'clock the previous evening. Then it is simply a matter of taking out a fishing boat, lining up river with mountain, and tracking the bags north. "They are easy to see early in the morning or at dusk on an oily sea with a lazy swell," a smuggler explained. "Those dark rubber bags show up clearly in the low light."

The smuggler, of course, is always preoccupied with the most convenient launching pad for his operations. In addition to the five main cities of Geneva, Frankfurt, Brussels, Paris, and Hong Kong, which provide the best jumping-off points for the airborne smuggler, there are four other strategically placed smuggling centers—Beirut, which has the best communications, banking, and international trading facilities of any city in the Middle East; Dubai, the sultry little sheikdom at the southern end of the Arabian Gulf, which has an excellent harbor within easy striking distance of India and a very businesslike sheik, who is making his little country into a first-rate banking and trading center; Panama, a free port, superbly positioned on the west end of the canal, where ships take on water and supplies before heading down to South America; and Tijuana, that raucous Mexican town just across the border from California and within 150 miles of Los Angeles. All of them, except Beirut, are duty-free areas; all practice the spirit of free trade in its fullest sense. And in none of them is the smuggler breaking any local laws—unless he trafficks in drugs.

And where does the poor customs man stand amidst this international avalanche of contraband? Most of them like to claim, officially at least, that they seize up to ten percent of smuggled goods and calculate that if they could improve that average to twenty percent they would knock the profits right out of most smuggling rackets. The latter premise is probably quite correct, but the assumption that they seize ten percent already is overoptimistic. The smuggler is a gambling man, and he would not be happy with odds of losing one shipment in ten. He can tolerate consistent losses of one in twenty or twenty-five, but not much more. The real customs-seizure average is more likely to be under five percent; indeed, some Indian customs officers will admit privately that they catch between two and six percent of the gold, watches, and nylon yarn that are smuggled into India every year from Dubai.

The real test, of course, is whether or not the smuggler can come to a convenient arrangement with customs. This is possible in certain countries of the Middle East, Far East, and South America. The payoffs are normally discreet, but occasionally are quite blatant. Thus an airline pilot presenting his bags for customs inspection at Beirut airport not long ago opened up his suitcase, facing it toward the inspecting officer, with the lid providing a partial shield from the eyes of any curious traveler. A carton of cigarettes lay on top of his neatly folded clothes. The customs officer took the carton, slipped it under his bench, and quickly scribbled his chalk blessing on the case. In Manila a passenger dashing through the swing doors from the customs hall into the main waiting area simply slipped a five-peso note into the hand of the guard on the door.

These two instances have all the hallmarks of the amateur; the professional is more discreet and thorough. He must establish a long-standing relationship with a whole shift of customs men, and if he is using couriers, customs must know how to identify them. Gold couriers to the Far East have been outfitted over the years with a wardrobe of fancy ties, as exclusive as any old-school neckwear, to identify them to officers. This open-sesame plan cannot be employed, however, in Europe or America, where, although the individual officer may be corrupted, a whole shift cannot be bribed to turn a blind eye.

The thoroughness demanded by the professional smuggler, who is concerned with regular patterns and safe routes, not with a spectacular coup, means that he is intolerant of the amateur bumbling through with a few extra bottles of Scotch or a diamond bracelet for his mistress. The professional wants a slice of the 350-million-dollar wholesale heroin market in the United States, or he has a fortune tied up in a fleet of dhows carrying 150 million dollars in gold to India every year. He does not take kindly to any amateur intervening and upsetting his precise plans. "If there is one thing a professional hates, it is the amateur," said a member of the U.N. Commission on Narcotic Drugs in Geneva.

"He will inform on the amateur, and he hates them more than the police."

Between the professional smuggler and the professional lawman there is often a taut love-hate relationship. Each knows the other, and, in an endless game of cat and mouse, they try to fool each other. "We'll go out sometimes and have dinner together and talk about it," said an American customs agent. "The smuggler will know quite well I haven't the evidence to arrest him, so I just buy him another couple of drinks and hope he may help me with a scrap of information about some other smuggler he doesn't like." This gamesmanship is less frequent in the narcotics traffic, which by its very nature is a deadly and dangerous business, but in less lethal rackets, when the lawman finally does get his man, it can be a quite poignant end of a long-standing friendship. Take the time Joe Jenkins, assistant supervising customs agent in Los Angeles, cornered a well-known watch smuggler up from Tijuana, Mexico, whom customs had been trying to catch red-handed for over a decade. The trap was finally sprung in a narrow alleyway just off Wilshire Boulevard in Los Angeles as packages of watch movements were handed over in return for $35,000 in cash. As Jenkins and his men closed in from both ends of the alley and the smuggler realized he was caught, he turned sadly to Joe Jenkins and said, "Joe, how could you do this to me?"

ONE

The Drug Traffic

II

Heroin

The bulky sledgehammer barely left room for the prostitute's feet on the floor of the police car. She sat, thin, hunched up, eyes half vacant, squeezed in between two bulky narcotics-squad detectives, in the back of their unmarked Chevrolet; the inside of the car was lighted only by the stabbing lights from neon signs in the Chicago street outside. "That Azaro, he's rotten, he's selling my husband garbage. I know it must be garbage, 'cause he comes back the other night and tears off all his clothes and his hair is wet with sweat and he's running up and down the room banging his head on the wall and his ass on the radiator. And I can't go near him. He keeps shouting he can't bear to be touched. And my little girl comes in and she wants to get past to go to the toilet. And she says to me, 'Who's that man,' and I says, 'That's your daddy.' And she cries and says it isn't. So I'm going to help you boys get that Azaro, who sold him that rotten stuff. I'll tell you when my husband is there firing up in that house. But you got to promise me you'll just get Azaro and cut my husband loose—and then you got to promise to get him in the Illinois State Hospital. I've been a junkie twenty-two years, and I know this game, but when that bastard starts selling that garbage, I'm going to fix him."

The detectives are patient with this informer, who goes by the unlikely name of Venus. They had raided the house where

27

her husband gets his adulterated heroin a few weeks before. They had battered in one apartment door with the sledgehammer that always lies ready on the floor of the car and found four men sitting around a table cutting up an ounce of heroin. But they had missed the key man. Now Venus tells them, "You hit the wrong apartment. You should have hit the third-floor front and back apartments. Those people got relatives in all those apartments, and they stash the H all over. You didn't know there was relatives there?" "No, we didn't," says the driver wearily. "Venus, we're always behind with the news." "Well, I got news for you boys," says Venus, running on the monologue regardless of their remarks. "I got news for you boys. You got to get up them stairs so fast and hit the second-floor back, and the third-floor front and back all at once. Now, my husband is always there to get fired up between eleven and one and between five and seven. Now, I'll phone you to let you know when he leaves to go there." "What about the search warrant?" asks the senior narcotics man. "I'll sign the warrants for you," says Venus. "I'll sign them with my own name; I want that bastard that bad. But you got to cut my husband loose, even if he's firing up when you get there, and you got to get him in the hospital."

It goes on for half an hour. They go again and again over times, room locations, and telephone numbers. Then Venus slips out of the car and is lost amid the clutter of strollers on the street. A lonely, distraught woman bent on revenge.

"Forty bucks a day—that's the hell of a habit her husband's got," says one detective. "Think of it here in Chicago. At least seven thousand on heroin. Most of them spend twenty dollars a day, some of them forty dollars, or even a hundred dollars, seven days a week. That's the hell of a lot of dough."

It is. Chicago's heroin addicts alone spend at least fifty million dollars a year on black-market supplies of the drug. In the whole of the United States, according to the Bureau of Narcotics and Dangerous Drugs, there are over 60,000 addicts (some sources estimate it at 200,000) spending a minimum of 350 million dollars on heroin every year; adding in cocaine and marihuana, it amounts to an illicit traffic of over one billion dollars annually.

28

For the drug smuggler the United States is, regrettably, the promised land. Although there are more addicts consuming more heroin in the Far East, particularly in Hong Kong, no other black market in the world offers such rich profits. The initial payment to the peasant farmer of Turkey, Mexico, Thailand, or Burma, who sells the raw opium after his poppy harvest, will be at the most $350 for ten kilos. Those ten kilos of opium will produce, ultimately, just over one kilo of heroin. That one kilo of pure heroin will sell, after much adulteration, on the streets of New York or Chicago for $225,000—or more if a shortage pushes up the price.

Such a price spiral can be achieved only when the ultimate purchaser is driven by a compulsion, by a physical craving that removes any shred of inhibition or restraint. The addict has to have his heroin; unless he is being specially treated in a hospital, there is only one place that the American can get it—on the black market. He will beg, borrow, or steal the five or ten dollars he needs every few hours to buy yet another little plastic bag of white powder that will bring him some sort of peace—until the next time.

The smugglers who grow rich catering to this craving are a breed apart from those who deal in contraband watches or gold or whiskey. They are profiting directly from fostering human misery. They meet no sympathy in a hostile world. The German gold smuggler who picks up gold in Switzerland and flies with it beneath his shirt to Bangkok is only likely to fall foul of the law as he passes through Thai customs; if he is caught, he will be fined and perhaps spend a few months in jail. The narcotics smuggler is hounded from country to country as the prime target of police, drug squads, and customs men; if he is picked up going into the United States, he can get twenty years. It is a ruthless, bitter struggle in which neither side is inclined to give any quarter. Not long ago a senior U.S. customs agent working on the California-Mexico border, across which there is a steady flow of narcotics into the United States, received a letter postmarked Mexicali, Mexico. It contained the personal papers of one Robert Corenevsky, a customs informer. There was a terse note with them. "Here is his papers. He made one phone call too much. Our regrets to his widow. Gracias."

The preoccupation with trying to trap narcotics smugglers becomes almost an obsession for many law-enforcement agencies in the United States. Not only is there the Bureau of Narcotics and Dangerous Drugs, known as the Federal Bureau of Narcotics until 1968, whose eight hundred agents around the U.S. and in eight offices overseas (Rome, Paris, Marseilles, Istanbul, Beirut, Bangkok, Singapore, and Hong Kong) have been devoted since 1930 to trying to root out the hydra-headed smuggling syndicates, but the Bureau of Customs devotes almost seventy-five percent of its energies to the illicit narcotics traffic. Indeed, for the majority of customs men in the United States it is their prime topic of conversation. "Narcotics," says Lawrence Fleishman, the assistant commissioner in charge of the Customs Agency Service, "is our number-one problem. Heroin is coming in on an unbelievable scale." In 1968 the combined seizures of heroin made by the customs and the Bureau of Narcotics amounted to 260 kilos. It was a vintage year for seizures, including one spectacular haul of 112 kilos of heroin worth 22.4 million dollars hidden in special traps in a 1962 Citroën shipped on the liner SS *France* from Le Havre to New York. And the bumper total also suggests that the oft-quoted figure of 1,000 kilos of heroin a year consumed by the black market in the United States is a considerable underestimate.

One thing is undeniable—the tenacity of the authorities is more than equaled by the persistence of the smugglers. The bulk of the illicit traffic in heroin to the United States is conducted by a hard core of professional criminals who have both the patience and the financial resources to mount the most complex of smuggling schemes. This is not a business for the amateur; he will either be detected speedily by the authorities or cheated out of business by the smuggling syndicates.

The heroin sold finally in grubby little plastic bags by drug peddlers in bars or drafty, noisy corners of America's cities seems remote from peaceful fields of waving red opium poppies in Afyon (Turkish for "opium") province of central Turkey. Yet it is the harvest there in February and March which yields the best-quality raw opium in the world for reducing into morphine base, the first step in transforming the sticky white gum from the poppy seed into heroin. The bulk of the heroin for the illicit traffic to the United States comes from these Turkish poppies, with the distinctive crenellated cap, like a tiny coronet, to the seedpod. The Turks have cultivated the opium poppy for centuries and now rank third among the seven opium-producing nations who report annually on their opium output to the International Narcotics Control Board of the United Nations. The leading opium-growing nation is India, which produces 56 percent of the world's licit opium; Russia is second, with 26 percent, Turkey third with 17 percent. The four other producing nations reporting to the U.N. are Yugoslavia, Pakistan, Bulgaria, and Japan.* Each year 1,100 tons of legally grown opium are used around the world for medical purposes; nine-tenths of this goes into the manufacture of codeine, the remainder into morphine and similar opium preparations. Since the early 1930's this licit opium growing has been watched with an eagle eye from Geneva, first by the League of Nations, more recently by the U.N. Every nation growing opium should report to the Narcotics Control Board in Geneva precise details of its opium crop and the nations to which it is exported. The board also charts the movement of the medicines made from opium.

The problem is that a nation may report quite accurately on the amount of opium its farmers sell officially, but it is the opium sold by moonlight that feeds the illicit channels. Afyon and the other six provinces where the Turkish government permits the growing of opium are desolate, drought-ridden, thinly populated areas. The farms are widely scattered, the farmers for the most part uneducated, struggling to make ends meet from one year to the next. A good poppy harvest means bread and meat for a few months; a poor one can mean starvation. Officially every farmer must tell the Turkish government opium-buying monopoly, Toprak, in advance how much land he intends to plant with poppies and what he anticipates will be his yield. If he fails to deliver his predicted yield, he can be fined. Naturally, therefore,

---

* Iran also decided in 1969 to reintroduce the legal growing of opium after it had been banned for thirteen years.

he plays safe by underestimating his yield and comfortably fulfill-ing his declared quota, which he sells to Toprak at the stand-ard price of about twelve dollars a kilo. The rest of his crop he disposes of quietly on the black market at prices ranging from five to ten dollars a kilo above the Toprak rate. He has no com-prehension that in doing so he is a cornerstone in a vast inter-national traffic, nor has he any concept of the profits reaped further along the smuggling routes. To him it is an extra few dollars which can mean full stomachs for his family for the next few months. He knows, of course, that he must not talk, but why should he betray the hand that feeds him best?

The harvesting of the opium is a simple process. Two weeks after the petals fall, the remaining pod grows hard. The farmer makes a neat incision in the pod, through which a milky-white latex seeps out. Overnight it hardens around the pod into a brown gum, which can be scraped off in the morning. This is the raw opium, and in Turkey, where the soil and climate combine to produce the finest opium in the world, it will have a high morphine content, ten to eighteen percent. The morphine is the heart of the matter.

The peasant farmer, however, normally sells the raw gum. No one can be sure just how much of it passes into the illicit channels. The U.S. Bureau of Narcotics and Dangerous Drugs has hazarded a guess that it is six to eight percent of the total production. Since Turkey officially produces over three hundred metric tons of opium a year, this suggests a black market in eighteen to twenty-four tons. It is probably much more, for al-though this would yield enough heroin to supply the U.S. market, there is another huge market for heroin right on Turkey's door-step in Iran, which has an estimated 200,000 addicts.

From the moment it is out of the hands of the farmer, the opium traffic becomes big business. Glance at the map of the Middle East and see the richest cities near the opium fields. There are three that matter: Istanbul, astride the Bosporus, where Asia and Europe come face to face; Aleppo, the ancient walled Syrian city that is the focal point of a web of desert trade routes; and Beirut, a cosmopolitan commercial scene that blends French and Arab life, with a potpourri of casinos, nightclubs, and hotels pandering to Arab princes grown too rich from oil revenues.

A handful of wealthy brokers in these cities have taken it upon themselves to speed the opium on the first leg of its journey half across the world. A broker in, say, Aleppo will contract to take five hundred kilos of raw opium from Turkey. He will hire a team of smugglers to trek it down through the Taurus Mountains of southern Turkey and across some byway on the 400-mile-long Syrian-Turkish border. How it makes the crossing no one can predict from day to day; it moves by truck, by bus, by train, by car, by camel and donkey. Syrian border guards who tangle with the smugglers often pitch straight into a gunfight. The Syrian authorities have even laid minefields along the border, but the smugglers round up a flock of sheep or goats and drive these animal mine detectors ahead of them. According to border legends, many a kilo of opium has crossed inside a camel's stomach. At first it was hidden in tin cans inside the camels, until the border guards retaliated with metal detectors that pinged loudly when a passing camel had a load of cans in its belly. That did not trouble the smugglers for long; they put the opium in rubber bags. They kill the camels or give them a laxative to recover the drug.

The most urgent problem for the smugglers at this stage, however, is to reduce the bulk of the opium to the more valuable morphine. This happens either inside Turkey itself or in Syria. The recipe is simple. Take one fifty-gallon oil drum, place in it, say, twenty kilos of raw opium, add one kilo of calcium chloride, cover with water, heat slowly over a fire, stirring with any handy stick. Once the mixture has dissolved in the water, leave for a few hours. The remnants of the opium will settle at the bottom of the drum, along with any stray leaves or other unwanted substances; the morphine, plus a little codeine, remains in the solution. This is poured off and evaporated, leaving the odorless, tasteless morphine base. It is a process almost anyone can do in his backyard—or even in the bathtub.

Chemically this morphine base is now only one step removed from the finished heroin; geographically it has barely started its journey along the smuggling pipelines. The role of the whole-

33

salers in Istanbul, Aleppo, and Beirut is to speed the morphine base westward toward France or West Germany.

Over the years several of these Middle East brokers have achieved international notoriety for their exploits. There was Samil Khoury, a short, wiry Arab who was married to a French cabaret singer and lived in the Rue Badaro in Beirut. He was a constant traveler to France, Germany, Switzerland, and Spain, arranging deals in drugs, arms, counterfeit currency, and anything else that offered a quick profit. He was denounced by the United Nations as the most important drug trafficker between the Middle East and Europe. He was prosecuted frequently but almost invariably released—he had excellent connections in high police and political circles. His chief lieutenant was Mounir Allouei, at one time a narcotics officer with the Lebanese police, who looked after the Beirut end of the business while Khoury was wheeling and dealing overseas arranging, say, a shipment of arms from Brussels in return for one thousand kilos of morphine base to France. But even the most influential of criminals cannot go unscathed forever. In 1965 both men suddenly vanished from the drug scene—indeed from the world at large—and have not been heard from since.

Legend in Beirut has it that Khoury and Allouei were killed for double-crossing a Jordanian hashish dealer. Khoury, the story goes, made a deal with the man to supply him with seven and one-half tons of hashish, which was paid for in advance. Khoury hurried back to Beirut to make the necessary arrangements. While he was lining up the hashish, another of his operations misfired. A cargo of cigarettes being smuggled into Beirut was seized by the Lebanese customs, and Khoury was fined $70,000. He was a little short of cash at the time and was threatened that he must pay or go to jail. He decided to tip off customs about his hashish shipment (since he had already been paid) and then collect their reward money to pay off his fine. Customs duly got the hashish but refused to pay Khoury the reward. Khoury's Jordanian client was not at all amused. Khoury and Allouei met him in a Damascus hotel to try to calm him down, but as they left the hotel they were kidnapped. They were never seen again.

Other dealers in Beirut, however, are as active as ever, although a combination of police pressure and tightened border controls between Syria and Turkey since the six-day war in June, 1967, have meant that less morphine base now passes through Beirut. The Beirut dealers have to travel to Turkey, buy the morphine base there, and arrange for shipment direct to Europe through Istanbul or Izmir.

The preoccupation of both the old and new generation of Middle East smugglers has been to get the morphine into Western Europe, the springboard for dispatching heroin to the United States. For many years the bulk of the morphine base went by sea from Aleppo, Beirut, and, to a lesser extent, from Istanbul to Marseilles, the seaport on the Mediterranean coast which is the headquarters of the French underworld. It was a relatively simple operation to hire a sailor and have him conceal the morphine base aboard his ship. He would be told that once his ship docked in Marseilles he should go to a particular bar or café in the Panier quarter near the docks. The seaman might be given a torn visiting card or Lebanese pound note; his contact would identify himself with the matching half.

This link between Beirut and France was quite predictable. Lebanon is a former French protectorate, and in language, culture, banking, and the underworld, the ties have always been very close. The drug traffic fell into this historic pattern. France, moreover, has a criminal group as tough and ruthless, if less publicized, as the Mafia—the Corsicans. It is these Corsicans, rather than the Mafia, who are the linchpin of the international heroin traffic.

Curiously, the origins of both these criminal organizations have been poverty-stricken islands in the Mediterranean; they even share a language, for most Corsicans speak Italian as well as French. While the Mafia spread to America through emigration, the Corsicans extended their grip to France by taking the ferry to Marseilles in search of fame and fortune. There is an old saying in Corsica that when a boy is born, his father flips a coin; if it comes down heads, his new son will become a policeman, if tails he will become a criminal; if it falls on its edge, he will work. In the last few generations there has been a run of coins falling tails up in Corsica. The French Corsican gangs have become the most powerful element in the French underworld, running protection and prostitution, organizing everything from armed bank raids to art robberies.

Given France's close ties with Lebanon, it was natural they should step in for a piece of the action in the 1950's as the drug traffic from the Middle East to the United States fell into its postwar pattern. Initially the Corsicans were middlemen, acting between the Lebanese and the Mafia, or Cosa Nostra, who were then largely responsible for both the smuggling into and distribution of drugs within the United States. The Corsicans, having gained a toehold in such a profitable business, strengthened their position to such an extent that since the mid-1960's they have been primarily responsible not only for operating the clandestine laboratories turning the morphine base into heroin but also for organizing the smuggling into the United States and even acting as wholesalers from their own depots or "plants" there. The Mafia's role has been reduced, for a variety of reasons, to distributing within the United States.

The predominant reason for the change is an aggressive young element among the Corsicans fighting to expand their power at every opportunity, whereas the Mafia both in the United States and in Sicily has aging leaders. "The Mafia here is now a little bit impotent," said a narcotics man in Rome. Moreover, the original close ties between Sicily and the United States, fostered by the great waves of emigration in the early part of this century, have weakened as the exodus from Sicily has slowed and the family connections between the two countries have become more remote. Thirdly, the leaders of the Cosa Nostra within the United States, although themselves extremely well insulated from prosecutions for drug offenses, have been irritated by the incessant pressure from law-enforcement authorities. During the 1960's a clear Cosa Nostra policy of gradual disengagement from the high echelons of the drug traffic has emerged. The heads of the Cosa Nostra "families" in the United States are so rich anyway they can ignore the profits to be made in drugs, but also they have realized there is as much money to be made from protection, loan-sharking, and gambling rackets within the United States without attracting nearly so much attention from the law. This is not to say the Cosa Nostra have abdicated from the drug business; they are simply not pushing for a larger stake. The French Corsicans are.

The Corsican drug activity centers, obviously, on Marseilles. There, in the low dives of the Panier district, the runners for the Corsicans who specialize in importing morphine base establish contact with the sailors from the Middle East. The dealers themselves keep carefully out of sight, making all their arrangements by phone and coded cable. They prefer to hang out in two high-class bars just around the corner from the back door to the American consulate. They will meet strangers only after very careful introductions through the grapevine. Some naïve amateurs from the Middle East, who think they will slip over to Marseilles with a nice little load of raw opium or morphine base, are completely ignored and may even be denounced to the police.

In 1965 a Turk in Istanbul named Mehmet Yardimci hit on what he thought was a bright idea of concealing one hundred kilos of morphine base inside several tons of marble, which he planned to ship to Marseilles. He dispatched an advance man, Yilmez Turker, to France to find a customer for the marble and the morphine. They lacked only the right introductions. The French showed no interest in buying marble, and even less in morphine. Several French traffickers shied away from this little Turk, who spoke practically no French, trying to sell them morphine base. Before long the French police picked up Yilmez Turker, who was running short of ready cash, and then the whole plot came tumbling out.

Any newcomer attempting to buy heroin in Marseilles without the right friends is equally cold-shouldered. "Suppose I had a million dollars," said one American narcotics agent, "and I wanted to get into the drug business and went to Marseilles. Now, what do I do? Ask the concierge at the hotel? Grab someone in the street and say where are the drug operators? Perhaps I even start frequenting shady bars and restaurants and someone points out a local criminal. If I walk up to him, he'll look at me as if I am an idiot. You must have that common denominator; you know someone, and he knows someone else."

37

Even the initiated, of course, can make spectacular mistakes. Take a Turk called Hasan Sahin, who drove up in a closed truck with Turkish registration plates to a French customs checkpoint on the Swiss-French border at St.-Julien one day in September, 1966. The customs men asked what he was transporting from Turkey to France. "Two and a half tons of watermelons." Watermelons? From Turkey to France, just when the French watermelon crop was ripe and was piled high by every roadside for passing motorists to buy up cheap? This Turk was taking a spectacular loss on his watermelon load. Or was he? The customs men began poking around the juicy melons and chanced on a neat compartment up in the roof which contained five hundred kilos of opium and fifty kilos of morphine base. That morphine base would be worth anything from $1,500 to $3,000 a kilo on delivery in Marseilles, quite enough to subsidize the export of watermelons.

The truck driver, Hasan Sahin, it turned out, was the brother of Mustafa Sahin, who was already being shadowed by French, German, and Turkish police as a suspected international drug smuggler. Mustafa was dealing with another Turk, Abdul An, in Nice, who was a known intermediary in speeding morphine base from Istanbul to Marseilles. All three were arrested.

The morphine among the melons is a clear example of how the drug traffic between Turkey and Western Europe is now developing. No longer is it simply the Syrians or the Lebanese dispatching drugs to Marseilles. The whole network has broadened. The Turks themselves now take a much larger hand in the export business from their country; Istanbul is putting up much of the capital and the organization that came originally from the criminals of other nations.

As the Turks have become more ambitious, two other quite independent developments in Western Europe have come to their aid. First, the great improvement of the highway network between Italy, Germany, Greece, and the Near East over the last ten years has made it more practical for drugs to be moved by road. The increasing movement of tourists and commercial traffic along these new roads also makes it easier for trucks or cars with concealed drugs to blend into the busy traffic scene. In the summer, especially, customs men have no time for more than a cursory glance at most vehicles. The morphine base can be transported swiftly from Istanbul through Turkey into Bulgaria or northern Greece, then up through Yugoslavia and into Italy or Austria. A clue to the volume of the traffic was gained in August, 1967, when a German courier was picked up with thirty-three kilos of morphine base hidden in his car at the Turkey-Greece border.

The second change in favor of the Turks has been the great wave of Turkish emigrant workers who have gone to West Germany and, to a lesser extent, to Belgium to work in the factories. This extensive movement of population (West Germany estimated that 50,000 Turks moved there to work in 1966) has provided the Turkish smugglers with a constant stream of potential couriers to carry opium or morphine base right into the heart of Western Europe. Much of this traffic is unorganized, in the sense that a Turk going to work in Western Europe talks to his friends before he leaves and is told that if he takes along a little opium or morphine in his luggage, it will be a useful nest egg for him to sell when he is a little short of cash while getting established in his new job. So he packs a few ounces. Once in Germany or Belgium, he hears quickly of dealers in Cologne, Aachen, or Liège who will buy his little cache of drugs. "There are two or three loan sharks in these towns," a narcotics agent explained, "and the Turk goes to them when he needs money." The volume involved is immense. In the summer of 1968 narcotics agents were trying to pin down rumors that there was a store of 1,000 kilos of morphine base up in the industrial belt near the Belgium-Germany border.

This hideaway remained elusive, but all the small seizures made in Belgium and West Germany in 1967 and 1968 were ample evidence of the existence of the traffic. A Turkish miner, Mehmet Bozkus, was arrested at Eisden, Belgium, in August, 1967, with 6.6 kilos of raw opium stuffed into a tin. At Mannheim, Germany, two months earlier, a Turkish second-hand car dealer attempted to sell twelve kilos of morphine base for $22,-500 to two other Turks. He had purchased the drug in Istanbul, brought it into Germany by car by way of Munich and Stuttgart.

39

German police arrested all three as the drug was handed over. A few weeks later, German customs in Munich seized 4.8 kilos of raw opium which a Turkish worker had cut up, put in cans labeled as vegetables, and resealed.

The French Corsicans, naturally, are right on top of this new source of supply. They have branched out from Marseilles and established contact with all the dealers buying from the migrant workers. But the real enigma is whether this morphine is being smuggled back into France and processed in existing laboratories on the Riviera or whether a brand-new clandestine laboratory has been set up in Germany to handle it on the spot.

Throughout 1968 police and narcotics agents were chasing every clue that might lead them to a German laboratory. But every trail went cold. Some experts suspect the laboratory is near Hamburg, but it is no more than a hunch. This German-laboratory theory gained considerable support from the fact that the leader of one of the French Corsican gangs—the Lyons gang— was living in Frankfurt.

The Lyons gang, the newest and most aggressive addition to the French underworld, was spawned, as its name implies, from Corsicans frequenting the bars of Lyons. Its young, high-spirited members could not find enough criminal activities to satisfy their talents within the confines of their adopted city, and they spread out through France into Germany. They were even bold enough to challenge some of the older Corsican groups based in Marseilles by hijacking heroin from them. Their best haul was one hundred kilos of pure heroin stolen from the main Marseilles mob. The heroin at that time was being moved from Marseilles to Paris by car. The driver was instructed that when he arrived in Paris he should leave the car in a certain street, take out the rotor arm to immobilize the vehicle, and return later. When he returned, the street was deserted. An enterprising member of the Lyons group had come along with a duplicate rotor arm and absconded with car and heroin. The incensed Marseilles gang realized that someone within their own organization must have tipped off the Lyons mob, ferreted him out, and instead of tossing him into Marseilles harbor, took the more financially astute course of fining him $100,000 to cover their loss.

Despite this rivalry between the Corsicans, their narcotics operations overlap, particularly in the most crucial of all stages—the clandestine laboratory. While the transforming of raw opium into morphine base is an easy operation that almost anyone can perform, the processing of morphine base into heroin calls for much more patience and skill. High-quality heroin can be made only by someone with considerable chemical skill, for there is a danger of explosion.

The full transformation takes several days. There are two crucial stages. First, heating the morphine with a salt called acetic anhydride—a chemical widely used also in the making of perfume and textiles—to produce diacetylmorphine, which is the chemical term for heroin. This, in turn, has to be blended with hydrochloric acid to transform the heroin into a salt which will be easily soluble in water for injection. It is in this later stage that highly toxic and inflammable fumes are given off, and a stray spark can lead to an explosion.

"The chemist must work very carefully and conscientiously," a French narcotics agent explained. "You need a quiet lab in the country, away from the noise, distraction—and police—in town. It requires much more skill than making bathtub gin." The Corsicans either employ professional chemists or train their own. The chemist is provided with a peaceful villa along the Riviera, in the suburbs of Paris, or even in Corsica itself and left to get on with the job. Much of the Corsicans' success in the drug traffic has resulted from their insistence on chemists turning out very high-quality heroin. The American market demands first-class heroin and prefers the French brand. "The French stuff is the champagne of heroin," a connoisseur explained. It invariably commands a premium price over the inferior heroin produced in Mexico. The Lebanese have tried to produce their own heroin from time to time, but it has never matched French standards. The trouble with the Lebanese, it seems, is that they are always in too much of a hurry. The labs have been in Beirut, and the traffickers have harassed the chemist by repeated phone calls or visits demanding to know when the heroin will be ready for shipping. High-quality heroin is not produced under such pressure.

The illegal laboratories are the prime target of narcotics agents. This is the most effective link in the chain that they can snap. Couriers or even organizers can always be replaced, but the loss of a laboratory producing one hundred kilos of heroin a month can disrupt the whole scheme. Experienced chemists are hard to come by. The security around a lab is, therefore, extremely tight; a mere handful of individuals within a gang know precisely where it is. Each one who does will have some special responsibility. There will be one man charged with supplying the acetic anhydride. It must be purchased very discreetly, since a careful check is kept on the destination of all orders. Normally he will get the supply by arranging for a perfume maker or small textile firm to overorder. A second specialist will be responsible for collecting the morphine base from the various "brokers" who receive it when it is first smuggled into France. Most of these brokers will be funneling supplies to the contact men for two or three laboratories.

The finished heroin will be disseminated to the groups handling the transatlantic smuggling by intermediaries. Thus each individual knows little of the complete plot. The whole structure resembles the electrical system of a house, with a main switchbox (in this case the laboratory) radiating power to all the rooms. If something goes wrong in one of those rooms, a fuse blows between it and the main switchbox, to isolate the troublespot from the rest of the supply; the remainder of the system continues to function normally. It is very rare that a main fuse blows, blacking out an entire house; it is equally rare that a lab is seized.

Each of the main groups actively smuggling to the United States has ready access to at least one laboratory. If the Lyons gang is setting up a shipment of one hundred kilos for America, they will obtain as much heroin as possible from a laboratory operated by their closest criminal associates. But if that source can muster only seventy-five kilos, they will shop discreetly around the underworld to determine if someone else has an extra twenty-five kilos available from another laboratory.

Thus far along the pipeline the drug has traveled by moderately conventional smuggling methods—hidden in ships, cars, or trucks. It will have run several customs gauntlets in Europe, but to European customs men it is not the number-one priority it is in the United States. Europe, mercifully, does not have a major consumer black market in heroin. Addicts are counted by the hundred rather than by the tens of thousands and throughout most of Europe can obtain free heroin on prescription from clinics or doctors. Although this system can be abused, it always provides the addict with a free and secure source of heroin. It eliminates all the crime forced upon addicts in the United States, who so frequently must steal to obtain cash to buy the next fix. It also keeps the prices in the small European black market, which is supplied mainly by heroin stolen from drugstores or through overprescription, so low that there is no incentive for criminal groups to move in. Consequently the authorities in Europe, although fully aware of the drug problem (and particularly alert for cannabis, as we shall see in Chapter 4), are not chasing the traffic with the energy of the U.S. Customs or the Bureau of Narcotics.

Once the heroin starts on the final lap of its journey across the Atlantic to America, where an army of law-enforcement men are waiting to keep it out, the cunning of the smuggler must really come into play.

During the 1950's it was the Sicilian end of the Mafia that shouldered the main responsibility for running this gauntlet. They had not only contacts, but cousins in the Cosa Nostra in the United States. Old family ties were strengthened when such American underworld figures as Lucky Luciano were deported to their native land. The Mafia bought its heroin from the laboratories in France and dispatched it, mainly by sea, across the Atlantic. One of the simplest methods was to use innocent emigrants from Italy or Sicily. The prospective emigrant from, say, Palermo would seek out a local travel agent to initiate him in the mysteries of foreign travel. The agent, bristling with timetables, brimming with ideas, was charming. Leave everything to him: reservations, tickets, documents all would be forthcoming in a trice. On the day of departure he would even hurry down to the pier to wish the traveler "*buon viaggio.*" He would bring with him a suitcase or even a trunk and say at the last moment, "Could you do me a great favor and take this one extra piece of baggage with you; it's some old suits I promised to send to my uncle in New York. He'll meet you at the pier to pick it up." The confused emigrant would be only too happy to oblige the agent, who had been so helpful. Thus many a newcomer to America arrived unwittingly lugging a suitcase with a false bottom packed with heroin. "Uncle" duly met him at the pier, making sure, however, that he kept well out of sight until the baggage had cleared customs, and then courteously explained the mysteries of dollars and cents, saw him into a taxi, and relieved him of the extra case.

The Mafia also used their connections with the Cosa Nostra in Montreal and Toronto to channel the heroin into North America through Canada and then down by train or car over the land border into the United States. It was not all smooth smuggling. By 1960 the Bureau of Narcotics was really pushing the Cosa Nostra within the United States hard, and in a significant conspiracy case that year, secured long terms of imprisonment for senior members of three of the five Cosa Nostra families who run the New York underworld. This case was triggered by the arrest in Canada in 1959 of Giuseppe Cotroni, an important Cosa Nostra figure in Montreal, and the seizure of six kilos of heroin. Cotroni's arrest led to twenty-nine Cosa Nostra associates in New York being charged with narcotics conspiracy. They included Carmine Galante, the chief lieutenant of the Joseph Bonanno family; John Ormento and Angelo Loiacana of the Thomas Lucchese family; and Carlie di Pietro of the Vito Genovese family. Ormento was jailed for forty years, the others for twenty years.

While this case and a batch of other stiff jail sentences over the same two-year period did not lead to Cosa Nostra bowing out of drugs, their enthusiasm was markedly cooled. Almost all the major smuggling cases since 1960 have involved the French Corsicans directly, and during the sixties a completely new smuggling pattern has evolved.

Within France itself there are now three main groups mounting the actual drug-running into the United States. First there is the old hard-core group based in Marseilles. Most of the heroin that passes through their hands is moved on, either by ship or plane, to Spain or to South America, where it is redirected toward the United States. In Spain a group of expatriate Frenchmen, who were formerly members of the OAS during the Algerian rebellion in the 1950's, are buying from Marseilles and making their own smuggling arrangements.

They are frequently dealing direct with Cuban or Puerto Rican narcotics traffickers from New York who fly to Madrid, where they feel reasonably at home with Spanish as a common language.

The South American smugglers, based in Buenos Aires, are Corsicans who immigrated to Argentina shortly after World War II. Their specialty is recruiting poverty-stricken Argentinians, Brazilians, and Chileans, normally men and women in their fifties and sixties, and offering them a couple of hundred dollars in return for taking a package to the United States. These bewildered couriers accept gratefully the prospect of the money and have no notion of the severity of the penalties they face if caught. In December, 1967, U.S. Customs and the Royal Canadian Mounted Police in Canada arrested no fewer than thirteen couriers working for this group. Most of them held Spanish, Italian, or Argentinian passports, all of which had been granted U.S. B2 entry visas at the American Embassy in Buenos Aires. Most of the couriers had up to five kilos of heroin each either taped to their bodies or hidden in false-bottom suitcases. They were coming in so thick and fast that some must have escaped the net. But the moment the common factor of B2 visas issued in Buenos Aires was noted on the first few arrests, a blanket warning went out to all customs officers at points of entry to pay special attention to travelers with this visa stamp. In less than a week the arrests totaled thirteen, with couriers turning up in Boston, Montreal, the crossing from Canada to New York State near Lake Champlain, and John F. Kennedy Airport in New York.

This technique of sending in a team of couriers, each with a few kilos of heroin, over a period of two or three days is favored not only by the Buenos Aires group but by the Lyons gang in France. They feel that with a one-hundred-kilo delivery to make, it is safest to divide it among many couriers to split the risk of the whole shipment being caught. Some of the couriers are bound to

45

get through, and the resulting profits compensate for losses en route. There may even be two or three couriers on the same plane, none of them known to each other. If one is nabbed by customs, the others may pass through safely in the general confusion. In fact, at major U.S. airports, if one courier is caught, the customs shuffle him, with the minimum of fuss, into a side room and try to grab every other passenger on the plane for a thorough search.

There is rarely such an obvious pointer among the couriers as the spate of B2 visas which clearly identified them as all working for one outfit, but the heroin itself can yield valuable clues in the laboratory. Just as a batch of raw opium can be pinpointed as a product of a specific region by comparing its characteristics with a master file of data on opium from every corner of the world, so a few ounces of heroin can normally be identified as forming part of a single batch from a clandestine laboratory. It is frequently possible to determine that two or three seizures made at widely differing points were all of identical heroin. This immediately links all those caught to one group of smugglers.

The method in which the heroin is packed and concealed on the courier can give other clues. One evening in May, 1968, a Frenchwoman was caught at Boston airport as she came off a flight from Paris with three kilos under her clothes. The following night a young Frenchman was seized at John F. Kennedy Airport, New York, with three kilos of heroin taped around his waist and a half-kilo package attached to each leg under flesh-colored leotards. The tape used on both couriers was from the same roll.

The couriers, once arrested, can rarely give the customs or narcotics agents any valuable information to lead them to the key men in France or the United States. The courier meets only the person from whom he picks up the heroin; he probably knows only this man's first name and will have met him momentarily in a hotel room. He will have been briefed to check into a particular hotel when he arrives in New York or Boston and wait for instructions. Customs men always try to persuade a courier to keep any prearranged rendezvous in the hope that they can pick up the trail in the United States. Couriers, hoping for a lighter sentence if they cooperate, sometimes agree. The trap rarely succeeds. Almost invariably there is someone on the flight with the courier or meeting the plane in New York just to keep an eye on things; he will not carry any heroin. At Kennedy airport in New York, for example, it is quite simple for the contact man to mix with the jumble of visitors penned in behind the glass screen that looks down onto the customs area. As everyone else waves frantically to friends, he can quietly watch the scene and see if the courier is picked up. If he is, the contact man vanishes, and that shipment is written off as a loss.

Not all the Corsican groups in France favor this method of flying in couriers almost by the planeload. The third major gang, based in the northern French seaport of Le Havre, specializes in trying to sneak the occasional large shipment of fifty or one hundred kilos past the customs. They put all their eggs in one basket—or more often one car. One scheme of theirs unmasked in January, 1962, was to secrete fifty kilos of heroin in special compartments behind the bumpers of a Buick belonging to the French TV entertainer Jacques Angelvin, who was embarking on a tour of the United States. A Corsican named François Scaglia saw Angelvin safely aboard the liner *United States* at Le Havre and watched the car swing into the hold. Then he went ashore and returned to Paris, where he hopped on a flight to New York. When the liner arrived in New York, Scaglia was waiting patiently to see the car got safely through customs. Angelvin drove over to the Waldorf Hotel, garaged his car, and checked in. As the entertainer settled into the comfort of his suite, a New York operator named Pasquale "Patsy" Fuca, who had been given the all-clear by Scaglia, stopped by the Waldorf and picked up the car. He whisked it up to a quiet garage in the Bronx and set to work with an acetylene torch cutting out the heroin which had been welded in behind the bumpers. All this under the patient eyes of U.S. Customs and the Bureau of Narcotics, who had shadowed the car every inch of the way. The heroin they ultimately seized was worth at least eleven million dollars at the retail level in the United States. (Angelvin put his five-year

47

prison sentence to some use by keeping a careful record of the six prisons in which he stayed and then writing a Michelin-type guide to *My American Prisons* when he was released.)

But the seizure from Angelvin's car paled by comparison with the greatest narcotics coup of all in April, 1968. Narcotics agents in France had been interested for some time in the peregrinations of a metal-gray 1962 Citroën convertible which had made a number of trips to the United States, always registered under the name of a different owner. On April 18, 1968, Sûreté narcotics agents were right on the trail of the Citroën as it left a Paris suburb and headed toward Le Havre. The Citroën was driven by Jacques Bosquet, a wealthy Paris contractor, and was followed by another Citroën carrying Nissim Guigui and Paul Mestressat, who had accompanied the car on at least two previous Atlantic crossings (for which each had been paid ten thousand dollars a time). On this occasion, however, Bosquet delivered the first Citroën aboard the liner *France* at Le Havre and saw it safely consigned to travel to New York. The name given for the consignee in New York was fictitious. Two Sûreté men went along on the voyage to watch the car. Two days later, while the *France* plowed steadily westward, Bosquet and an associate, Eugène Malibert, flew from Paris to New York, where they spent a day making final plans for the reception and distribution of the incoming shipment. They then returned to Paris by the roundabout route of Montreal and Geneva. On April 24 the *France* docked in New York. The Citroën was unloaded and pushed to a corner of the pier to await collection. No one came. All through that day and the next, customs men and Bureau of Narcotics agents hung around the pier in a multitude of disguises. Finally at 3 A.M. on April 26, two mechanics from the New York Police Department were brought along to take the car apart. Working through the night, they soon found heroin all over the car. It was tucked into special compartments under the front and back seats and behind a sheet of metal in the spare-tire well. The largest cache was in a false gasoline tank. The real tank had been removed and replaced by a large compartment to hold the heroin, with a tiny tank holding a mere two gallons tucked into one corner. In all, there were 224 hermeti-

48

cally sealed glassine bags, each containing a half-kilo of heroin, hidden in the car; 112 kilos in all, worth 22.4 million dollars.

At dawn the police reassembled the car and left it for another three days. Still no one came to collect it. Finally it was towed away to storage. Someone at the New York end had been alerted, and the delivery was never completed.

The French police, however, who had followed the Citroën so closely that they even released later photographs of it being slung aboard the *France* at Le Havre, moved in and arrested Bosquet and his colleagues in Paris. In terms of the quantity of heroin seized, it was a spectacular coup; in terms of personalities, it was rather less successful. Bosquet, a public-works contractor of fifty-five, was rated fairly highly in the echelons of the Corsican underworld and was, police believe, very close to one of the clandestine laboratories in France. The others were much smaller fry, although Eugène Malibert did admit that he was Bosquet's lieutenant. Malibert claimed to be a real-estate agent living frugally with his wife and six children, but the police alleged he had secretly kept up a $120,000 villa and a stable of race horses. They had certainly been smuggling enough heroin to pay for such luxuries. The narcotics squad of the Sûreté claimed that Bosquet admitted the Citroën had made a total of seven trips across the Atlantic in a period of three years and had carried, in all, 730 kilos of heroin—enough to supply the entire U.S. black market for between four to six months. Bosquet and his associates were lucky in one way: They were arrested in France. The maximum penalty there for narcotics offenses is five years in prison; in the United States they would almost certainly have got twenty years.

It could be argued that the authorities should have detected such a simple trick as heroin under the seats long before the Citroën made its seventh trip. But that, in many ways, was the beauty of the scheme; cars are such old hat for smuggling these days that many customs men assume the smugglers have graduated to more sophisticated techniques. Many of the schemes are now extremely ingenious.

One of the neatest tricks, unveiled through information from the French Sûreté National in the spring of 1967, was to hide the

49

heroin inside oscilloscopes (instruments which measure a fluctuating electrical current in visible waves on a cathode-ray tube) when they were exported from France to the United States. The scheme was the brainchild of a Frenchman named Paul Chastagnier, who had previously been convicted in the United States of counterfeiting. Posing as an export agent, he approached a small electronics firm in a small town near the French-Swiss border, explained that he was highly impressed with the quality of the oscilloscopes they made, and would like to place a substantial order for five hundred oscilloscopes, which he proposed to export to the United States. The firm was beside itself at the prospect of such a handsome contract and made plans to expand its facilities to cope with such an order. They took extra pains with each oscilloscope to make it to perfection, then shipped them off to Paris. There, Chastagnier and his gang, with complete disregard for the meticulous handiwork, ripped out all the internal wiring, leaving only the cathode tube and screen. In the space left by the wires they fitted boxes full of heroin. The oscilloscopes were then dispatched to Foreign Trade Representations, Inc., of New York City. The first two shipments of ten oscilloscopes in all got through safely in December, 1966. But in March of 1967 the Sûreté got wind of the scheme and warned U.S. Customs that a new batch of six oscilloscopes was en route to New York. When they arrived in New York, the authorities quickly found and removed two half-kilo bags of heroin hidden in each oscilloscope; six kilos in all. The oscilloscopes were then repacked for delivery to Foreign Trade Representations, Inc., and duly taken there by narcotics agents. Foreign Trade's export manager, George Varsa, signed for them. Meanwhile, back in Paris the Sûreté had moved in and arrested Chastagnier at Orly airport with another six oscilloscopes packed with six kilos of heroin all ready for air-freighting to the United States. Word of this arrest leaked out to the French press, and just after Varsa had taken delivery of his oscilloscopes, a call came through to him from a French newspaper asking what he knew of the affair. Varsa did not wait to explain. He grabbed his coat and beat a hasty exit from his office—into the arms of narcotics agents waiting outside.

The early tip-off from France was a lucky break in the oscilloscope affair. Without that information, the stratagem might have been successful for years. It is patently impossible for customs to poke inside every single package imported to the United States. Unless they receive specific information, they must rely on occasional spot checks.

The methods and the routes at the smugglers' disposal are endless. Drugs can be in cars or electronic gadgets, carried by airline crews, tourists, or emigrants, seamen, or diplomats. The diplomatic passport constitutes perhaps the best immunity from customs and immigration problems around the world. It did not take the Corsicans long to realize the potential of that avenue of entrance to the United States.

The first clue to the flourishing business of drugs under diplomatic immunity came from the Bureau of Narcotics' Beirut office in the early summer of 1960. The agent there reported to Washington that a Frenchman named Etienne Tarditi, already suspected of organizing the smuggling of morphine base from Lebanon to France, was also handling shipments of heroin to the United States. Not much to go on, but a couple of months later the Paris office of the bureau learned that Tarditi had just arrived in Paris from a visit to the United States. In New York agents started checking airline manifests to determine the flight he had taken, and when they pinpointed him they found a traveling companion listed simply as M. Rosal. Further checking with the airline quickly revealed that M. Rosal had been accorded VIP treatment and was none other than Mauricio Rosal, then Guatemalan ambassador to the Netherlands and Belgium. Their curiosity now fully aroused, the narcotics agents began to build up a careful file of the movements of Rosal and Tarditi. They found that the ambassador made frequent transatlantic trips, and invariably Tarditi arrived in New York two days before him. Even more interesting, the ambassador's checked baggage weight fluctuated alarmingly. On one occasion coming into New York it was 180 pounds; when he flew out two days later, it was only 80 pounds. He could hardly have left 100 pounds of suits at the cleaners. At the beginning of October, 1960, word came from Paris that Tarditi was booked on yet another flight to New York. Would the ambassador show up true to form two days later?

Sure enough, there he was at Idlewild, boldly claiming diplomatic immunity as he explained courteously that he was stopping over briefly in the United States en route from the Netherlands to his home country of Guatemala. He checked into the hotel where Tarditi had already registered. It was a touchy situation, for he was protected by diplomatic immunity as long as he claimed to be en route to Guatemala. Two days later, however, he canceled his onward flight to Guatemala, and that, the narcotics men felt, removed his diplomatic cloak. Shortly afterward Rosal and Tarditi came out of their hotel with four large suitcases and took a cab uptown to Lexington Avenue and 72nd Street. There they were joined by an airline purser from TWA, Charles Bourbonnais, who worked the New York–Paris flights, and their New York underworld contact man, Nicholas Calamaras. The agents surrounded the cab and found over fifty kilos of heroin in the suitcases, along with $26,000 in cash. This, Ambassador Rosal later explained, was his fee for each trip.

The Bureau of Narcotics felt pleased with themselves. "We felt we had really thrown a monkey wrench into this diplomatic operation," George Gaffney told a Senate subcommittee afterward. But they underestimated Corsican ingenuity. Their pride was deflated a few months later when an informant hinted, "Well, you got one of them, but you haven't got the other one. There is another one even bigger than he is." So began another ambassador hunt that was to last three years.

In the first diplomatic case, there had been suspicions that Rosal was connected with French narcotics trafficker Gilbert Coscia, operating out of Marseilles. During a previous investigation in Marseilles the Sûreté had screened some 1,200,000 cables coming into that seaport from America, Cuba, and Beirut. Some of the discreetly worded cables to narcotics traffickers had mentioned a courier called Lambo. At the time, that meant nothing. But during a further careful scrutiny of cables, airline manifests, and hotel registers in Paris, Marseilles, and New York, a pattern began to emerge. Coscia, it turned out, had made four short trips to the United States; in each case the Mexican ambassador to Bolivia, Salvador Pardo-Bolland, had been in New York about the same time. His movements often also coincided with Coscia's in Paris, Montreal (he had formerly been attached to the Mexican Embassy in Ottawa), and Nice. The name was fascinating; in French it would be *l'ambassadeur* Pardo-Bolland, easily corrupted to "Lambo" for short.

So far, however, the evidence was purely circumstantial; just a matter of overlapping travel schedules. Then, in February, 1964, Pardo-Bolland turned up in Nice traveling on a false Uruguayan diplomatic passport which identified him as Lorenzo Suarez de Mendoza of Montevideo. On the Riviera he was observed in earnest discussions not only with Gilbert Coscia but also with a Uruguayan diplomat, Juan Arizti. Investigation revealed that Pardo-Bolland and Arizti had known each other since they had been diplomats in the Middle East in 1953, meeting frequently in Beirut. After four days by the Mediterranean in February, 1964, Pardo-Bolland left Nice airport en route for Paris and New York. Arizti booked himself onto a flight to Paris, then on to Montreal. When he left his hotel, Arizti had two suitcases, but at Nice airport he presented baggage checks for four more suitcases at the left-luggage office. He checked all the bags to Montreal. When he arrived in Canada, with the Royal Canadian Mounted Police and Bureau of Narcotics men in unobtrusive attendance, he waved his diplomatic passport and was whisked through customs untroubled. He took a taxi to Montreal Central Station, placed the four extra suitcases into two luggage lockers, and went across to the Queen Elizabeth Hotel, where he stayed for three days. As he slept peacefully at night, the Mounties opened the lockers with a skeleton key and took a look at the suitcases. Sure enough, they were crammed with over fifty kilos of heroin in quarter-kilo packets. The Mounties quickly substituted identical packets of flour for all except two of the packets of heroin and relocked the lockers. In the morning Arizti came bustling down to the station to make sure his luggage was safe. Reassured, he waited for the all-clear from New York.

On the evening of February 17 he reclaimed his bags from the lockers and took the night train to New York. Early the next morning he checked the bags in lockers at Pennsylvania Station in New York and took a taxi to the Elysée Hotel, where Pardo-Bolland awaited him. Pardo-Bolland then telephoned the Americana Hotel and asked for a Mr. Blanc, who should have checked in. The Americana had no one of that name registered. A puzzled Pardo-Bolland sent a Western Union cable to Carmen Lopez (an alias for Coscia), Hotel Maryland, Cap d'Antibes, France: "Cousin could not be located at indicated address. Lorenzo." Clearly Coscia was very good on his security. Although Pardo-Bolland had been a courier for years, Coscia still gave him an initial false contact in New York, just in case he was picked up. Now that he had double-checked, Pardo-Bolland was advised that the man he really wanted was Jacques Leroux at the Americana. The two diplomats called on Leroux the next morning and handed over the keys for the luggage lockers where Arizti had left the four suitcases.

Mission completed, Pardo-Bolland and Arizti booked themselves on flights out of New York. Leroux, by this time identified as René Brouchon, a renowned French narcotics smuggler, also booked a flight to Switzerland and checked out of his hotel. He was arrested in the street. He tried unsuccessfully to throw away the baggage-locker keys. The diplomats got word of Brouchon's arrest almost at once and rushed to airline offices to try to book earlier flights out of the country. They were not quick enough. In June, 1964, Pardo-Bolland was sentenced to eighteen years in prison, Arizti to ten years, and Brouchon to fifteen years, sentences which have clearly made diplomats since think twice about misusing their privileges to smuggle narcotics.

Smuggling the heroin is only half the battle; getting paid for it can be equally hazardous. By the time the heroin enters the United States, the staggering price spiral is well advanced. The $350 for ten kilos of raw opium in Turkey will have risen first to about $700 for one kilo of morphine base bought in Lebanon for export to France; the price is $1,500–$3,000 on delivery in Marseilles; the finished heroin direct from the clandestine laboratory will fetch $7,000–$10,000 a kilo, while the importer into the United States will pay somewhere between $10,000 and $18,000 a kilo. The final stages of the spiral to $225,000 or more occur within the United States as each kilo is adulterated more and more, until heroin that may have been ninety percent pure when it arrived will be five percent or less on the streets. These later

54

payments are all within the U.S. distribution network. But the amount that must be paid to the Corsicans and others overseas to pay for importation is staggering in itself. Assuming an absolute minimum of one thousand kilos a year smuggled in and an average import price of $15,000 a kilo, this means that 15 million dollars a year must be moved secretly out of the United States to pay for the heroin. Financial transactions on such a scale call for considerable manipulation. Narcotics agents admit that, in many ways, they know far less about how payments get out than they do about how the heroin gets in. The couriers who bring in the heroin are only rarely involved in taking cash back out. The average courier is simply paid $2,000 as his fee for the trip. Even Ambassador Rosal, who had $26,000 on him when he was arrested, confessed that it was his own pay for the assignment; it was not payment for the heroin itself.

Part of the money is certainly moved by the other couriers who are specifically hired to take cash from the United States to Switzerland. One Corsican arrested in New York as he boarded a plane for Switzerland was carrying $247,500 in U.S. currency. He declined to say how he got it or what he intended to do with it. A much more reliable method, however, is to transfer the money to Europe through the normal activities of a holding company operating under some legitimate front. Ultimately most of the money ends up in the anonymous safety of numbered Swiss bank accounts.

But that depends on whether anyone intends to pay in the first place. The smuggler can lose either because his shipment is seized by customs or because the importers in the United States do not honor their commitments. Joseph Valachi, who finally spilled all the secrets about the internal workings of the Cosa Nostra at Senate hearings in Washington in 1963, described how he knew of one example of the Corsicans being cheated by the New York Cosa Nostra in the mid 1950's. According to Valachi, he borrowed $8,000 from one Anthony "Tony Bender" Strollo, his lieutenant in the Genovese family in New York, as a down payment on fifteen kilograms of heroin to be imported from a French supplier he knew as Dominick (almost certainly Dominick Albertini, one of the most notorious French smugglers and laboratory operators of the 1950's). The full payment was to be $37,500, the balance being paid after delivery. Valachi said it cost him an extra $15,000 to smuggle the heroin in, plus $1,000 in incidental expenses. The heroin duly arrived, but he never paid Dominick the balance of $29,500. This shady dealing by Cosa Nostra encouraged the Corsicans to develop their own direct connections with the North American market. They found, for example, that the French Corsicans in the Montreal underworld were much more trustworthy when it came to paying.

Relations inevitably become even more strained when a shipment is seized. Who will be footing the bill, for example, for that 112 kilos of heroin found in the Citroën at New York in April, 1968? Assuming the French export price to have been $7,000 a kilo, that means a direct loss of $784,000, which is bound to hit the pocket of even the most affluent criminal. As a precaution against such loss, the importer into the United States is, as Valachi's evidence demonstrated, normally required to pay a percentage in advance to cover some of the costs at the French end. But someone must lose. The acrimony is often stirred by the fact that no one can agree who was responsible for the heroin at the moment it was seized. The French could argue that they had safely fulfilled their part of the bargain by delivering that Citroën to New York, so New York should pay up. Disputes about it can go on for years.

New York, with the Cosa Nostra network of five families dominating the underworld, together with Negro and Puerto Rican gangs controlling their own special domains, is inevitably the focal point of the heroin scene. There are, at the most conservative estimate, over 31,000 addicts in the city—just over half the total of addicts in the United States. But New York is also the distribution center for black-market heroin destined for the majority of other addicts in the United States, particularly those in Detroit, Buffalo, Philadelphia, and Chicago. Seventy-five percent of the supplies for Chicago's 7,000 addicts pass through the New York pipeline. They are either picked up from New York by couriers from the Cosa Nostra family that runs the Chicago scene, or, increasingly, by agents from the main Negro mob on the South Side of Chicago, which has an agreement with the

Cosa Nostra in the city that it can pick up its own heroin whole-sale from New York in return for a ten-percent royalty.

With New York the main market—and the prime target for the smuggler—the most obvious routes in have always been through the port or airports of the city or via Boston or Montreal. These are the points that have always witnessed the most important seizures, and it makes sense geographically, since they are facing Europe. However, the pressure from law enforcement has been strong in such obvious ports of entry, and the smugglers, who must always keep one jump ahead to stay in business, have clearly been hauling out their atlases and studying them in conjunction with airline timetables. As more and more international flights plunge direct into the heart of America to Washington, D.C., Detroit, or Chicago, it makes sense for the smuggler to use these new openings.

In February, 1968, three elderly Spaniards, two women and a man, were picked up at O'Hare International Airport, Chicago, with a total of ten kilos of heroin taped in crude corsets around their bodies. They had picked up the drug in Brussels, flown to London, and boarded a BOAC flight straight to Chicago. They should have been met in Chicago by a contact man from New York. Instead, the customs, acting on a tip-off, picked up all three. "If I was a smuggler," said a Chicago customs agent recently, "I'd be looking into places like Winnipeg and Calgary and then come down through the back door overland to somewhere like Minneapolis."

The New York distributors now seem willing to range far afield to pick up supplies coming in. They have even been known to make a special sortie to Anchorage, Alaska, to take delivery from couriers passing through that airport. In the Air France case (see Chapter 1), the stewards had been able to drop off the drugs at Montreal, Chicago, or Alaska according to prevailing circumstances.

The most tempting route of all, however, is through Mexico. Quite apart from the flights north from Mexico City to all major cities in the United States, the two-thousand-mile border between Mexico and the United States, stretching from the Gulf of Mexico to the Pacific, runs through desolate country much of the way; the smugglers can cross the Rio Grande River at shallow points or toss contraband over the fence that strides through the desert to mark the frontier. Small private planes can flit back and forth almost unchallenged, while one of the armada of yachts that set out from California harbors on weekends can easily slip south to a Mexican port.

Mexico is important for two reasons. First, it is a stepping-stone for European heroin, which is flown into Mexico City and then distributed through an endless series of channels to all points in the United States. Second, Mexico is itself a producer of illicit opium, which is quickly processed into heroin. The volume of Mexican heroin does not rival the amount produced illegally from Turkish opium, but it is estimated that up to twenty-five percent of all the heroin entering the United States is derived from Mexican poppies.

Officially Mexico is not an opium-producing country. The illicit production started in a curious way. During World War II the Chinese in San Francisco found themselves cut off from their traditional (but illegal) supplies of opium from the Far East. So an enterprising Chinese, realizing that the opium poppy would probably flourish in the Mexican climate, went down there with poppy seeds. He found the Mexican peasant farmers in the hills of Sinaloa province inland from the cities of Culiacán and Mazatlán on the Gulf of California only too happy to oblige in return for a few dollars. For the rest of the war the Chinese on the West Coast smoked their opium contentedly.

With the growth of the international heroin traffic after the war, it was all too easy for other dealers to move in, buy up the raw opium, and convert it to heroin. The Mexican heroin, produced in laboratories far less sophisticated than in Europe, is brown rather than white, for it is only sixty to seventy percent pure and contains much foreign matter. But it is a marketable—and cheaper—alternative to the European drug, especially in California, which is beyond the Cosa Nostra's normal American distribution network. The main traffickers in Los Angeles can buy Mexican heroin for about $12,000–$13,000 a kilo, compared to the $30,000 that dealers at the same level in New York would have to pay. The European smugglers, directing their heroin

58

through Mexico City, give little attention to this brown home-grown rival and have made no attempt to move in and control the traffic. The Mexican heroin-smuggling system developed, therefore, on a much more casual, hand-to-mouth basis. It has never been controlled by large organizations. There are a hand-ful of dealers, mainly living in Culiacán, who encourage the growing of opium in the remote mountain valleys of Sinaloa, Durango, and Chihuahua provinces. The terrain is rugged, most of the valleys almost inaccessible, and the peasant farmers live in poverty, bypassed by the twentieth century. They eke out an existence growing a few gourds or a little corn in haphazard plantations along the edge of streams. To them the opium dealer is simply a man who appears in spring with poppy seeds, tells them he will return in a few months for the *goma* (gum), and pays them a few dollars—perhaps ten or twenty dollars for their crop. That cash, however, can represent their entire income for the year.

The Mexican government, encouraged by the Americans, does attempt to root out this illicit poppy growing, but given the harsh countryside, some stout resistance from the farmers, who have no hesitation at sniping at troops grappling through the mountains to burn their crops, and the casual approach to life in Mexico, the poppy farms flourish. From time to time the Mexi-cans put on a stout performance for visiting politicians or jour-nalists and burn a few token fields, yet there is little sign that the annual crop is diminishing. To be fair to the Mexicans, it is an unenviable task to expect them to spend precious money and risk the lives of their soldiers solving what is essentially an American problem. Some narcotics agents, however, are very bitter about the situation. They argue that given a free hand they could go down to Mexico and sort the whole thing out overnight. The Bureau of Narcotics is more prepared to live with a difficult situation. Clearly, from a political point of view, the United States cannot engage in a major row with Mexico on the issue of smug-gled heroin. It has to be content with giving maximum assistance to the Mexicans as they chase the heroin dealers in their own time and at their own pace. So the heroin flows over the border.

The dealers in Culiacán have laboratories tucked away in the mountains near the farms and bring the finished heroin into the city. Smugglers from all over Mexico fly down to Culiacán to haggle prices with them, and then direct the heroin in two main directions. First over the border through El Paso, Laredo, and Brownsville in Texas and thence north by road to Chicago. About a quarter of Chicago's heroin supplies originate in Mexico, and its distribution there is handled quite independently of the Cosa Nostra or Negro mobs. Many Mexicans travel to the Midwest to work on the farms in the summer and gravitate to the city in the winter. They form the nucleus of the heroin network. Casual workers going north are provided with a cheap car, with the heroin hidden in special compartments, and are told to leave it in a certain street in Chicago. There is little formal organization; it is much more a matter of a family or group of two or three friends getting together to move a little H.

The pattern is much the same in California, which has 7,000 addicts, according to the Bureau of Narcotics; nearer 20,000, according to the California Bureau of Narcotics Enforcement. "There is no monopoly on narcotics in California," says John Storer, chief of the California bureau. "Anyone with a car can become a narcotics peddler by driving down to Mexico and buying any amount he wants. It's easy."

Mecca for the California narcotics peddler is Tijuana, that bawdy, boisterous town just across the Mexican border from San Diego. Tijuana has a splendid race track, gambling casinos, brothels, and some of the most wide-open narcotics dealing anywhere in the world. It is almost impossible to stroll down the street (keeping a very firm hand over your wallet) without being offered anything from someone's young sister to a few ounces of heroin or marihuana (which, as we shall see in the next chapter, crosses the border by the *ton*). Amid the garish glow of neon lights at two A.M. a couple of men may be beating each other's brains out on the street and no one pays the slightest attention. "That's Tijuana for you," says the American undercover narcotics agent, skillfully steering his Buick Riviera around the tumble of bodies. He has casually tucked a .38 into his trouser band before setting out for the evening from a motel in San Diego. "Always have my gun handy in Mexico," he admitted. He also has his car resprayed a fresh color every three months to make it less easily distinguished—with good reason. A few months earlier, a Tijuana heroin dealer, annoyed by his inquiries, had set up an ambush to have him blasted by shotguns as he drove into Mexico one evening. A rival dealer learned of the assassination plot and, by frantic telephoning, managed to locate the agent and warn him. He fully realized that if the plot had succeeded, the resulting heat from Mexican and American law would be far worse than even the most probing of normal inquiries.

There are some things that cannot be fixed, even in Mexico. But it is a rough-and-tumble scene. Most of the dealers have their *pistoleros*, trigger-happy fellows who act as their bodyguards. American narcotics men, of course, have no authority in Mexico. They can simply cooperate with and advise the narcotics agents of the Mexican federal police—an overworked, underpaid group of men. In fact, the American agents are right in the thick of the fray, but they must always vanish smartly at the moment of the arrest, if it is made on the Mexican side, so that they cannot be implicated.

On hectic weekends, some 200,000 Americans bent on having fun raising hell may descend on Tijuana, streaming through the San Ysidro border control in 80,000 cars. It is physically impossible for the U.S. Customs to make any kind of search of this deluge of travelers as they sweep through the eighteen lanes of the checkpoint. They can make a few spot checks and hope for the best. It is in circumstances like these that Tijuana's three main heroin dealers slip most of their supplies into the United States, in one-ounce, double-sealed polyethylene bags. These men are well known to American narcotics agents and customs men, who may even have an occasional drink with them. One agent even delights in telephoning one dealer at three A.M. and saying, "I'm going to bust you, I'm going to bust you," just to let him know the pressure is there. This dealer, who runs a thriving business in conjunction with his brother (they are known as Little Brother and Big Brother) and his common-law wife, is unperturbed. He knows that as long as he stays in Tijuana he is safe. Every lawyer in Tijuana makes his living from defending narcotics cases. "If you live in Mexico City," explained a young Tijuana lawyer who drives an E-type Jaguar, "you make a name as a lawyer defending murder cases. If you are a lawyer in Tijuana you make your name through defending narcotics cases."

While the casual heroin buyer from Los Angeles or San Francisco can come down to Tijuana and pick up his heroin from one of the two thousand street peddlers or one of fifteen small wholesalers, the more professional peddlers in California deal with one of the big three, each of whom maintains a permanent "plant" of heroin already inside the state. The arrangements are easily made. A Los Angeles peddler wants three ounces of heroin. He goes to a Western Union office and sends a money order for one thousand dollars (the largest amount the company transmits) to the Western Union office in Tijuana addressed to his dealer. He signs it with a false name, which the dealer will recognize. Later that day he will get a call from the dealer himself or his agent, telling him to go to a certain gasoline station or snack bar in Los Angeles, where he will find his heroin hidden behind the washbasin or the toilet in the men's room. The peddler drives over and picks up the drug. The dealer's Los Angeles man will have planted it there just before he arrives and will be waiting nearby to see that the pickup is made successfully. It is an almost foolproof scheme. The main dealer stays safe in Tijuana; his Los Angeles man plants the drug before the peddler is told where it is. At best, the police, if they watch every known peddler in Los Angeles, and follow him day and night into every washroom he visits, can eventually get him with the drug. They get nowhere near the other links in the chain with any hard evidence. "What do you do?" asked a California narcotics agent sadly. "Arrest a washbasin for illegal possession of drugs?"

Yet the background is quite clear for all to see. In January, 1968, for example, heroin dealers in the Los Angeles area alone sent money orders to the value of $35,875 addressed to Big Brother and Little Brother in Tijuana. There were fifty-six separate orders, mostly for one, two, or three ounces of heroin. The price fluctuated slightly, but was normally around $325 an ounce. Most of the peddlers were ordering once a week, although it was hard to determine exactly how often because of the variety of aliases with which the money orders were signed.

The three main dealers in Tijuana were apparently first introduced into the heroin business by a millionaire dealer in Mexicali, a hundred miles to the east. This man was already very rich before he bought heroin in Mexico City for the first time. He took it to Tijuana, where he sold this first shipment cheaply at $5,000 a kilo to give the others a head start and get the market going.

Now the four of them, apart from handling Mexican heroin, have a nice corner in the purer European heroin coming through Corsican channels to Mexico City. They have a standing order in the capital with the three or four main sources for European heroin. If eight kilos are available, one of them will fly down to conclude the deal and arrange delivery. Once the heroin is on the border, each of them will take two kilos. This pool arrangement is designed to keep other dealers from challenging their control of the business by preventing any newcomers from getting their hands on the premium-quality European drug. It is a profitable arrangement. One of the Tijuana dealers, who has a weakness for no-limit poker, has no hesitation at gambling $50,-000 a night.

Since these men are so impregnable from legal assault, provided they never stray over the U.S. border, where there are arrest warrants out for most of them, there is only one practical way to undermine them—seize as much of their heroin as possible. This can put them in severe financial trouble. In 1967 Big and Little Brother lost fifteen kilos of heroin through police raids of their plants in Los Angeles and Fresno. This represented an outlay of at least $100,000 on their part (heroin is slightly cheaper on the Mexican route, since there are fewer big-gang payoffs), which even in their profitable position they could ill afford to lose. For a while they were complaining around the underworld that they were really broke. But, unlike some of the other dealers, the brothers do try to pay their debts—and look after any of their couriers or plant men who are caught. If one of their men is arrested, they will call their lawyer. "How much will it cost to fix it?" And they foot the bill. If he does go to prison, they look after his family.

This ample and relatively cheap supply just down the road across the Mexican border has meant that the smuggling of heroin into California from the Far East is negligible. It is not worth the professional going to the trouble and expense of setting up a complicated transPacific smuggling route. Seamen bring a little heroin or opium from Hong Kong into West Coast ports occasionally, but this is normally on their own initiative or for a specific friend in, say, Chinatown in San Francisco. Undoubtedly some Far Eastern morphine base travels west to Beirut, where it is blended with the supply coming out of Turkey and thus enters the French Corsican trail to the United States.

The one important exception to this pattern was revealed when a completely new smuggling route developed by a group of Australians was detected in 1967. This Australian syndicate was headed by two former members of the Sydney police force. They had carefully cultivated contacts with a New York Negro gang at the racetracks in New York and offered to supply them with heroin at $30,000 a kilo—more than the normal import price into the United States, but cheaper than the heroin would be when it filtered down through Cosa Nostra distribution to the Negroes. The deal was arranged, and the Australians lined up a team of their fellow countrymen as couriers and equipped them with false passports. The couriers would fly from Sydney to Hong Kong, where they were supplied with heroin at $1,000 a kilo. They carried it in specially made vests beneath their shirts and entered the United States by air through Seattle, San Francisco, or Los Angeles or traveled west to London and picked up flights to New York.

The Bureau of Narcotics heard rumors of this Australian ring, which was operating completely outside the sphere of their normal informants, in 1966, but were unable to pin the operation down. It was nearly a year before the Australian police, investigating false passports, came up with information which pointed to the drug couriers. One of them, Roy L. Peake, traveling under the name of Glenn Gibson Reid, was picked up in

Honolulu on January 8, 1967, with twenty-six ounces of heroin. He agreed to cooperate with narcotics agents in an attempt to complete delivery in New York. The agents "convoyed" him via Seattle into New York, where they arrested five of his associates, who were waiting for him, quite unaware that anything had gone wrong. The two leaders of the gang, however, fled in a wild chase over fences and up back alleys in New York and vanished. The Bureau of Narcotics ran them to ground a few days later, but they promptly jumped bail and have never been seen since. Back in Australia, meanwhile, police arrested five other members of the gang and thus in one swift operation knocked out a complete syndicate.

This Australian ring, however, was the exception, not the rule. The Orient's heroin is essentially for the Orient's addicts.

Their opium poppies, the white petals tinged with violet, are grown by the hill tribes of northern Thailand, Laos, and the Shan states of Burma, for whom the sale of opium is the only source of cash income. These hill people, particularly in Laos and the Shan states, have little contact with the outside world and have never been brought under any real rule of law. Along with a little maize and rice, the poppy has been their main crop for centuries, and their whole year is planned around the collection of the raw opium in December and January, when the entire family works ceaselessly in the fields slitting the pod and scraping off the gum. The United Nations International Narcotics Control Board estimates that this eager cultivation yields up to one thousand metric tons of raw opium a year—enough to supply several million addicts. There is little sign that it will decline in the near future. A special U.N. survey team that studied the Miao, Yao, Lahu, and other hill tribes of Thailand in 1967 came to the dismal conclusion, "Our examination of the subsistence and cash economy of the hill tribes, coupled with their ingrained social habits, leads us to conclude that under present conditions there can be no short-term practical overall solution to the problem of finding an economically viable substitute for opium."

Apart from this known opium production, the great bogeyman of the Southeast Asian drug traffic is opium from Communist China. For generations Yunnan province of China was a major opium-growing area. Ever since the Communists came to power, politicians from both East and West have found opium growing a handy stick with which to beat the Communists. Since their split with Chairman Mao, the Russians have been as vociferous as anyone in condemning the Chinese. In September, 1964, *Pravda* carried a widely publicized article from its Tokyo correspondent that accused the Chinese of financing their propaganda campaigns around the world with the ill-gotten gains from opium sales. "About half a billion dollars a year comes into the hands of the present leaders of China from the illicit sales of narcotics," *Pravda* claimed, suggesting that perhaps eight thousand tons of opium a year filtered out of Yunnan province into Thailand and thence to Hong Kong and other Asian markets. "The great sums derived from it are spent for anti-Soviet propaganda, and are used to pay for the services of puppets of the Peking splitters. Apparently in Peking they consider that any means are all right for the attainment of these goals."

Good stirring polemics from the outraged Russians—the words themselves are remarkably similar to those of Harry Anslinger, formerly director of the Bureau of Narcotics in Washington, who has frequently charged the Chinese Communists with actively aiding the opium trade to undermine the morale of America and the noncommunist world.

In fact, there is very little evidence to support all these wild allegations about the Communists. Aerial reconnaissance of Yunnan province has shown, apparently, little sign of poppy fields; United Nations observers and journalists who have penetrated into the wilds of Laos and northern Thailand have found no suggestion that the abundant raw opium passing through the region originated in China. Indeed, the most active participants in the whole business appear to be, not the Communist Chinese, but a scattering of Chinese Nationalists, old soldiers of Chiang Kai-shek, who have carried on their own rebel domain in the north of Burma and Laos for the past twenty years. There they still provide an unofficial guerrilla buffer against Communist incursions. Initially they were supplied by the American Central Intelligence Agency, but when that aid stopped, many of them resorted to opium-running as an alternative profession to soldiering. When the poppies bloom in December and January, they channel the raw opium down from the Shan states and the interior of Thailand and Laos to border villages. It is, at best, a haphazard operation—simply a long file of tribesmen walking by night for up to a week, each carrying perhaps twenty-five kilos. If they come from the Shan states, they dump the opium in the Thai border villages of Fang and Mae-Sa and are paid from five to twelve dollars a kilo—probably their only cash income of the year.

Prepared opium has been smoked in Asia for centuries, particularly by the Chinese. Its effects are far less damaging than addiction to the concentrated morphine or heroin; indeed, throughout Asia there are thousands of opium "users," as distinct from addicts, who smoke it occasionally but are able to continue with perfectly normal jobs. Many of the Chinese coolies working in the harbor in Hong Kong are users, but because they also eat regularly, their strength is not unduly sapped. The disturbing trend, however, over the last twenty years has been for fewer and fewer to smoke opium; instead they smoke the more concentrated morphine or a cheap heroin. In Bangkok, Singapore, and Hong Kong, up to seventy-five percent of the users now smoke morphine or heroin—with all the attendant dangers of addiction. (Very few, however, inject heroin. The Chinese apparently do not like to stick the needle into themselves.)

This developing taste for the concentrated opiate is, of course, most convenient for the drug traffickers. Opium is bulky and has a telltale sweet, oily aroma. Morphine, as the European traffickers also appreciate, is far less cumbersome and can be made from the raw opium in a few hours in any handy backyard. Thus, in the towns of Chiang Mai, Chiang Rai, and Lampang in Thailand and of Ban Houei Sai in Laos, much of the opium is swiftly reduced to morphine, which is pressed into tight little bricks. Some years ago a Chinese smuggler, to emphasize the quality of his morphine blocks, took to stamping them with a 999 brand (rather like gold bars being stamped 999.9 to confirm their purity). The notion caught on, and now morphine blocks all through the Far East bear similar attestations to their quality—O.K., AAA, 1A, Dragon, and Two Tigers are among the popular brands. The names and the packaging often suggest that some smuggler missed a vocation in advertising. The O.K. brand of smoking opium comes in a gay, multicolored wrapping showing a crane, perched on a willow tree, gazing down on a junk with yellow sails that cruises on an azure sea; in one corner is a red stamp showing a thumbs-up sign and saying O.K. Madison Avenue could hardly do better with the launching of a new cigarette brand. The coarse Number 3 heroin smoked by the majority of addicts in the Far East is equally seductively packaged; the well-known trademarks are Strong Lion, Single Dragon and Pearl, Double Dragon and Pearl, and Golden Deer.

Thus prettily packaged, the drug is ready for the addicts. It moves south toward Bangkok either by truck or, more frequently, by air from Ban Houei Sai or Vientiane in Laos. In Laos itself no one has ever bothered to make the smoking of opium or its derivatives illegal. No one hinders the export trade of the drug either. Indeed, early in 1969 it was widely alleged around Southeast Asia that a senior Laotian official was growing rich on the trade which proceeded with his blessing. The drugs are flown south from Laos by a little fleet of Beechcraft and DC-3's known as Air Opium. Air Opium pilots are mainly former French Foreign Legionnaires, who stayed on in Laos after the French evacuation and carried on a boisterous existence tackling any job that came to hand. (They once hijacked one million dollars in American greenbacks from Vientiane airport, but it was so obvious who had done it that the money was quickly recovered.) The pilots are well paid; one American adventurer in Singapore, who was offered a job with them in 1968, was wooed with offers of a salary of $2,200 a month. But these men are merely convenient pawns in the traffic and are not the organizers. Their task is simply to drop the packages of drugs into the Gulf of Siam just south of Bangkok, where they are recovered by Thai fishing boats and spirited into the city up the river Chao Phraya, which plunges through the heart of the city in a muddy torrent alive with river craft night and day. A procession of little tugs, looking just like houseboats, churns upstream towing unwieldy convoys of three or four overloaded barges behind them. Off the mainstream is a quiltwork of canals and waterways called *klongs* with little huts of wood and corrugated iron along their banks and teeming floating markets of sampans loaded with bananas, pineapples, bamboo shoots, and every kind of vegetable. Even the most effective police or customs service in the world could not hope to ferret out the drug-carrying boats from this river armada.

Bangkok itself has, regrettably, one of the largest addict populations in Asia. No one knows the real extent of the problem. The director of the Thanyarak Hospital for Addicts estimated there were 400,000 heroin users in 1963; the United Nations survey team in 1967 could get no more reliable estimate. The majority of the Bangkok addicts smoke a coarse purple-colored heroin called Number 3, which is made in the city from the smuggled-in morphine bricks.

Bangkok's influence spreads far across Asia. Just as the Mafia and the Corsicans have been closely involved in directing the traffic between Europe and America, here it is a renegade sect of Chinese called the Chu Chows who are in control. The Chu Chows come from Fukien province in the south of China, opposite Formosa. It is, like Sicily and Corsica, harsh, barren country. The Chu Chows lived by their wits and became over the years a kind of Chinese Mafia. They migrated widely throughout Asia to Hong Kong, to Penang, Bangkok, and Singapore in search of a better life, but the essential family ties, so important in almost all organized criminal activity, remained. "They are very close, and they don't betray each other," said a Hong Kong police officer, with the resignation born of years of trying to make them crack. It provided a perfect network for drug smuggling.

The main traffic is in smoking opium, morphine bricks of the 999 variety, or cheap smoking heroin; relatively little of it is processed into the pure white heroin of the European trade. However, both in Bangkok and in the Hong Kong–Macao complex there are excellent Chinese chemists who can turn out the finest heroin on demand. Six kilos of first-rate heroin were seized by the Japanese authorities in the autumn of 1968 from three Thai students who were acting as couriers for a very well-run Chinese drug group operating out of Bangkok. This Chinese team was using an elaborate code, and the leader, who has not been arrested, was commuting between Bangkok, Manila, Hong Kong, Singapore, and Kota Kina Balu, Borneo.

The drugs fan out from Bangkok in two main directions. By land, they go down the long arm of the Malaysian Peninsula to Penang, Port Swettenham, or Singapore, both for the addicts in those ports (Singapore has 8,000 addicts) and to be smuggled aboard ships that carry them around Asia. By sea, they are secreted aboard oceangoing Thai fishing vessels heading out into the South China Sea and setting course northeast to Hong Kong.

Prior to shipment the drugs are carefully wrapped with up to four layers of polyethylene sheeting and then packed into empty kerosene drums, each holding sixty pounds. The tins are double-sealed to resist erosion by seawater for twenty-eight days; a ring is fixed to the top of each tin. When the fishing boats near Hong Kong, they jettison the tins in neat rows, like a minefield, in shallow water around the Lema or Ladrone islands, which are strung out like a necklace of pearls just south of the mainland. It is then a simple matter for a Hong Kong fishing boat, armed with a grappling hook, to come out and hoist them to the surface.

Four or five main gangs of Chinese are responsible for importing opium and morphine base into the colony, which has, according to the official police estimates, up to 80,000 users (of which 60,000 smoke heroin and 20,000 smoke opium). They stockpile the drug in enormous quantities on lonely farms out in the New Territories up near the Chinese border; from there it filters out as required into Kowloon or onto Hong Kong island itself. The reserves appear to be so extensive that even major seizures by the authorities do not result in any rise in price in the colony at either the wholesale or retail level. (Prepared opium costs about $1,600 a kilo in Hong Kong, morphine $3,600 a kilo, high-quality white heroin up to $9,000.) Hong Kong holds the dubious world record for the three largest drug seizures ever made. In 1960 the authorities discovered one and one-fourth tons of 999 morphine and 768 pounds of raw opium packed into the middle of a shipment of teak logs aboard a freighter from Bangkok. The logs had been hollowed out in the center, the packages of morphine inserted, and the logs nailed back together. There was a variation on this theme in 1965, when over two and one-half tons of raw opium and 400 pounds of morphine were found concealed inside bundles of bamboo, also imported from Bangkok. The following year over a ton of opium and 269 pounds of morphine worth 1.6 million dollars turned up inside five refrigerators from Malaysia.

Trying to contain the drug traffic among the four million people packed into this British toehold on the mainland of China is like trying to catch a mole in a field full of molehills; as fast as you poke into one burrow, he is off down his tunnels and flinging up three more hummocks behind you. Quite apart from the myriad of fishing junks flitting through the islands, over five hundred ships a month call at the port, and it is a physical impossibility for the Hong Kong Preventive Service to make a proper search of all of them. They compromise by having a list of "suspect" ports of origin—Bangkok, Singapore, and Penang, among many in Southeast Asia. Any vessel coming in from these ports is considered suspect; the Preventive Service will go carefully over her crew list, her cargo manifest, and the list of consignees in Hong Kong to see if any of them match their own extensive intelligence files. They have also waged a campaign to encourage shipping companies and ships' officers to police their own vessels, rather than run the risk of the ship being impounded if drugs are discovered. They have prepared an engaging little pamphlet, complete with color photographs of packages of drugs, called "How Ships' Officers Can Help to STOP Drug Smuggling." It advises, for example, "Drugs are most likely to be brought on board vessels in large quantities in Penang, Singapore, and Bangkok. All of these are river or roadstead ports, and it follows that sampans may easily slip under a ship's counter at night unseen and wait for an accomplice on board to lower a rope. This can be stopped by ensuring that your vessel is as brightly illuminated as possible and that some illumination is directed under the stern and over the bow, preferably by cargo clusters having several bulbs."

The Preventive Service's attention is devoted chiefly to checking the flow of drugs into Hong Kong. The colony is also a convenient transit point for drugs bound for the Philippines, Formosa, Japan, and Australia. Japan, in particular, has an increasing problem of addiction to high-quality heroin. The price there is almost on the scale of the American market; it is $27,000 a kilo wholesale, $83,000 to $280,000 retail. This kind of price spiral is more than enough to foster an organized traffic in heroin from both Hong Kong and Bangkok. Hong Kong is highly sensitive, understandably, about its position as an international staging post for narcotics. The authorities constantly try to play down its role. Yet at the same time they are curiously proud of the quality of heroin that their chemists can produce on demand. One well-known operator, One Arm Yip, operated an excellent laboratory in Macao for years, and his heroin was well up to the European standard.

There is very little evidence, however, to support frequent rather wild claims that Hong Kong is a major staging post for heroin bound for the United States. The single major case was that of the Australian policemen in 1967. It is important to realize that there are far more addicts in Southeast Asia than there are in the United States. The traffickers have quite enough on their hands supplying the local markets; after all, Hong Kong, with a population of four million, has 60,000 heroin smokers, which is just about the same number as the official total of heroin addicts in the United States, with a population of 200 million. Adding in the Thai, Japanese, Malaysian, and Australian markets, the total demand for the drug far outweighs the American requirement.

Also the vital ethnic link is missing between the higher echelons of American crime and the Far East. The Chinese communities in America keep very much to themselves, and although they may arrange for occasional imports of smoking opium or even heroin, it is essentially for their own consumption. Organized crime in America is oriented toward Europe, not the Orient. The Chinese mind is something the average American criminal does not entirely understand or entirely trust. Thus, as long as heroin can be imported from French Corsican or Italian contacts in Europe, he is happy to leave the Far East well enough alone.

However, while the production of opium continues on such a vast scale in the Far East, the danger is constantly there that if the Turkish supply could be dried up by concerted government action, then the American traffickers would be forced to look for their drugs elsewhere. Bangkok and Hong Kong might provide a handy supermarket. "What we fear for the future," said a narcotics expert in Thailand, "is a breakout from Asia to supply Europe or America."

III

Cocaine

The cable from New York read, "Regret to inform you your sister very ill. Your presence requested immediately. Forget bags and come at once. Margot." It was delivered to Delia Morales in Santiago, Chile, just before Christmas, 1964. Clearly a cable that called for swift action. Delia Morales was on her way out of the door without bothering with her luggage when the Chilean police arrived. They too had heard about her sister's misfortune and had come hurrying around—though not to offer sympathy. They were rather interested in the bags Margot was so anxious for Delia to forget. A perfectly justified interest, as it turned out, for the suitcases had packets of cocaine concealed in false compartments, which could be opened by pushing a hairpin into a little hole in the bottom and releasing a hidden spring. Delia's sister had been accompanied by three identical suitcases when she arrived at John F. Kennedy Airport, New York, the previous day. The customs inspector thought she looked a little nervous as she came off the flight from Santiago. A search of her luggage quickly revealed why; there were twenty half-kilo bags of cocaine, worth around $250,000 on the wholesale black market in New York, in the false bottoms. It was the largest single cache of cocaine ever picked up from a smuggler coming into the United States. Delia's sister was in fact no relation at all, but a woman

74

called Juanita Bradbie, whose specialty, when she was not smuggling drugs, was shoplifting fur coats. She was one of a number of women Delia Morales had recruited to carry the drug into the United States. As for Margot, who signed the cable, she sometimes went by the name of Margot Moore, but was better known as Lillian Santana, wife of Ralph Santana, the leader of a Puerto Rican gang of cocaine smugglers.

It took quite a while to work out all the relationships, but the seizure confirmed the steady increase in the amount of cocaine being smuggled into the United States. In the 1950's there was very little illicit use of the drug; in 1956, for example, a mere ten ounces of illicit cocaine was picked up in the United States. Since then, however, the market has blossomed. Seizures were eighteen pounds in 1963, fifty pounds (including Juanita Bradbie's consignment) in 1964.

The arrest of Ralph Santana and his gang was little deterrent—although Santana himself was sentenced to fifteen years in prison. Indeed, since 1965, according to George Belk, the New York district supervisor of the Bureau of Narcotics and Dangerous Drugs, "The traffic in cocaine to New York has increased tremendously. It was not a major problem until 1965; now it is."

In the twelve months preceding June, 1968, ninety-eight pounds of illicit cocaine were found—an increase of 143 percent over the previous year. These figures must not, of course, be treated as an exact measure of the increase in illicit traffic; customs have lucky years and unlucky years. One major confiscation can throw statistics for the year completely lopsided. However, a steady rise in seizures over a period of five years is a good indication that business is expanding—as might be expected in an increasingly affluent society.

Cocaine is the drug of prosperity; it is frequently christened the Rich Man's or the Society Drug, apart from its slang description—a Coke, Charley, Snow, or just C. It sells wholesale in New York at between $10,000 and $13,000 a pound, and it is too expensive for the average addict on the street. It becomes, therefore, the drug that is chosen by the wealthy—some people in show business have a particular taste for it. Many addicts inhale it as they would snuff, taking a pinch out of a little box, closing one nostril, and sniffing it up the other. It may look more elegant than the heroin addicts' sordid hypodermic; its effect can be even more dangerous. It damages the flesh and will perforate the nostril partition of habitual sniffers. Initially it gives a quick "kick" to the brain, mental powers increase, and any feeling of fatigue vanishes. It may cause hallucinations. The immediate danger is that too strong a dose can stimulate the spinal cord, leading to convulsions. Many addicts develop a paranoiac belief of being threatened and, as a result, carry weapons. Addiction will also lead to sleeplessness, nausea, and general mental deterioration.

Cocaine is frequently blended with heroin into a fearsome concoction called a speedball, which is injected; the boost from the cocaine offsets the numbing effect of the opiate (rather like drinking strong black coffee laced with whiskey). Addicts who can afford both drugs often prefer it. In Britain, for example, in 1967 out of 1,729 heroin addicts, 413 were addicted to a mixture of heroin and cocaine, while a further 39 used a triple blend of heroin, cocaine, and a synthetic drug methadone. In the United States, where there is (as with heroin) by far the largest black market, there is no official breakdown of cocaine addicts, but the Bureau of Narcotics and Dangerous Drugs estimates the total may be ten thousand.

Cocaine comes from the leaf of the coca bush, which grows exclusively in western South America, the only exception being an insignificant plantation in Indonesia. The coca leaf has two legitimate uses: first, the extraction of cocaine for medicinal use (it has been widely used as a local anesthetic since the 1880's); and second, as a source of non-narcotic flavoring extracts for such drinks as Coca-Cola.

This legitimate coca-leaf traffic is closely watched by the International Narcotics Control Board of the United Nations from Geneva, under the terms of the Single Convention on Dangerous Drugs. All international movements of the drug are recorded, right down to the last leaf. In 1966, for example, the United States imported 264,964,851 coca leaves, all for medicinal use.

76

But the problem, as with the opium poppy, is one of over-production. The demand for coca leaves for medicine and fla-vored drinks is, at the most, 500 tons a year. In Peru and Bolivia alone, the two prime producing countries in South America, about 13,000 tons of coca are produced each year, according to figures reported by those governments. A more realistic figure worked out by the International Narcotics Control Board is around 35,000 tons a year, because government statistics do not allow for the bush growing wild. This means that a mere trickle of just over one percent of coca-leaf production is needed for legitimate use. The rest is dumped right in the lap of the black market.

The main coca-growing region is high in the Andes Moun-tains beyond the cities of Cuzco in Peru and La Paz, Cocha-bamba, and Sucre in Bolivia. There is little other cultivation, and the Indian peasants rely on their meager income from selling the coca leaf to survive. And to help make survival a little more palatable, they and millions of other poverty-stricken South Americans chew the leaf. It has a pleasant, pungent taste, pro-duces a sense of warmth in the mouth, and swiftly anesthetizes the stomach—thus eliminating pangs of hunger or thirst. Peru alone estimates that 800,000 of her people are habitual leaf chewers, with an average daily consumption of one ounce. It is a habit that is hard to uproot. Few regard chewing as illegal.

Ideally, alternative crops must be found, but it can take a generation to persuade peasants to plant them. In the meantime they are caught in a vicious circle: they are cold and hungry, so they chew the coca leaf for comfort; this undermines their health further, so they are quite unable to make the concerted effort to create a better life for themselves, so the only thing to do is chew more coca leaf.

Either encouraging a new agriculture or trying to police the lonely regions where the bush flourishes is a wretched task. "It is impossible country to police," says a former South American Interpol representative. "It is so high that your nails and your lips turn blue, and you can hardly speak."

The International Narcotics Control Board has been urging the Peruvians and the Bolivians to take more positive steps to replace the coca crop, and an Inter-American Consultative Group on Coca Leaf Problems was held in Lima in 1964. But the climate—both geographic and political—does not make for speedy solutions. Bolivia is still not a party to the Single Convention on Dangerous Drugs; Peru is, but has been scrambling for a loophole which allows a twenty-five-year period for changes to be made. "Peru and Bolivia will do nothing," said a disillusioned United Nations official, "but one can hardly blame them. You need a terrific social upheaval first. The coca bush is the only cash crop, and until the social and economic position improves, there will be no change."

And until there is change, the illicit traffic will flourish. While the peasants in the hills chew the leaf by the ton, much of it also moves along the back trails down from the Andes into Brazil, Argentina, and Chile. Many Bolivians and Peruvians who have gone to work in these countries have taken their chewing habit with them. This source of supply is all too easy for the international traffickers to tap. Few of the growers or the local dealers have any notion of the value of cocaine on the North American black market. The smugglers can pick up the leaf for a few centavos a pound. They have their contacts in all the little towns where the coca leaf first emerges down from the hills—in Arica, Viña del Mar, and Santiago in Chile; in Lima in Peru; in Corumbe and Guajara-mirim on the border of Brazil and Bolivia. Since the leaves themselves are bulky, the traffickers arrange for them to be macerated and the cocaine extracted as near as possible to the source of supply, to cut down transport costs and the risk of detection. Frequently the leaves are macerated high in the hills, and the pulp is then smuggled down to coastal towns like Arica, where clandestine laboratories extract the crude cocaine, refine it—and then possibly adulterate it with boric acid, tartaric acid, and sodium bicarbonate.

The leaf or the paste travels by whatever means of transport is going. Roads are rare, so it is often wrapped around the backs of mules and concealed under a load of supplies. Going east into Brazil, it travels by boat down the tributaries of the Amazon or the Paraguay river. Along the Pacific coast it is secreted on trucks or trains. Occasionally there are macabre twists. The leaf was once found packed into the coffins containing the bodies of young Bolivian children who had died in their own country but were being taken into Corumbe in Brazil for burial.

Until the mid-1950's the illicit traffic was largely an internal one in South America. Then, between 1954 and 1956 a number of Puerto Ricans and Cubans appeared in Peru and Bolivia and began building up contacts among local dealers and establishing laboratories. The timing of their arrival is important. This was the period in which Puerto Rican and Cuban immigration into New York was increasing. True to form, as we have seen with heroin and will with cannabis, an illicit traffic can emerge from a wave of immigration.

In the 1950's Batista still ruled in Cuba, and the island provided an ideal jumping-off ground for both marihuana and cocaine smuggling into the United States. The Cubans and their neighbors the Puerto Ricans spoke the same language, had the same history and culture as the people of South America. It was natural that the traffic should evolve around them. There are even the neat stepping-stones of the islands of the Caribbean up from Venezuela and Colombia. Miami is an ideal landing point and has, over the years, seen more cocaine through its doors than any other city in the United States. The early development of the traffic was greatly aided by one or two very senior Chilean and Bolivian police officers, who became deeply involved in the racket. In Chile, at one point, police vehicles were even being used to move the cocaine around.

The initial pattern of the cocaine traffic was, of course, considerably upset by Fidel Castro's victory in Cuba. It deprived the smugglers overnight of their most convenient stepping-stone into the United States. But the Cuban expatriates living in Miami and New York never for a moment lost their grip on the traffic; they adapted to a web of new routes.

The Cuban and Puerto Rican smuggling groups are much less complex than the spider's web of the heroin syndicates. Each important cocaine trafficker will have his own little team. The couriers will vary, but otherwise the whole operation can be mounted by fewer than half a dozen people.

Indeed, it is often as much a family affair as the corner grocery store. In August, 1965, for example, Lucy Ibáñez de Franco, wife of a well-known dealer in La Paz, Bolivia, was singled out by customs at Miami airport. They found she was carrying two ounces of cocaine. This, she explained, was merely a sample for a notorious Cuban trafficker in Miami, just to show the quality of cocaine her husband's outfit could offer. In her luggage was a return airline ticket to La Paz in the name of another woman. Who was this woman? None other than Mrs. de Franco's daughter, who came winging into Miami an hour later. She had a woman companion with her, and between them they were carrying fifteen packages of cocaine worth $200,000 in three false-sided suitcases.

Ralph Santana's outfit, betrayed so completely by that nervous courier Juanita Bradbie in New York, was an equally intimate little group. Santana had two chief henchmen, Lionel Marquez and Frank Serrano. Serrano specialized in coordinating the activities of the couriers abroad. He fixed the precise details of a shipment coming up from South America and might be on hand himself in, say, Santiago or Valparaiso to pack the cocaine into the false-bottomed suitcases and brief the courier. Once in New York, the courier rendezvoused with Lionel Marquez and Santana at a prearranged motel or hotel. Santana and Marquez then distributed the cocaine among their clients. They preferred women couriers, on the assumption that the authorities were less likely to scrutinize women travelers. Santana's wife, Lillian, and Delia Morales recruited them. They normally picked out someone with a criminal background, for, as with heroin, the conventional businessman, taxi driver, or student type of couriers found in gold, watches, and diamonds will not carry drugs, partly for very sound moral reasons, partly for fear of the penalties. Juanita Bradbie, the courier who gave the game away, had a record for shoplifting fur coats (indeed, while she was out on bail pending trial, she was arrested for fur-coat stealing in Augusta, Maine, and given a two-to-four-year prison term). Another of their couriers was Sybil Horowitz, a flim-flam expert who successfully came through with a large consignment of cocaine about six weeks before Juanita's ill-fated flight. That load had been distributed from a Long Island motel by Santana and Marquez. And Marquez' wife, Lisa, had been used as a courier from Chile on at least one occasion.

All their cocaine had been purchased from a Valparaiso dealer, René Hard-Huasseff. He slipped through the net cast for the Santana gang, but was caught eighteen months later because he had lost his best customers and was eager for new clients. Shortly after Santana was arrested, a Bureau of Narcotics agent based in Mexico City sent a letter to Hard-Huasseff in Chile saying he had been working with Santana, and wasn't it just too bad about the arrest. He would like to take up where Santana had been forced to leave off. Hard-Huasseff was interested, but cautious. It was not until the summer of 1966 that he seemed satisfied with the agent's reliability and delivered eleven pounds of cocaine to the agent from Mexico City—all under the watchful eyes of the Chilean police.

The simplest thing is just to put the cocaine aboard a plane from South America to Miami or New York and hope the courier gets through, as Santana did. Others prefer greater subterfuge. The nitrate boats heading north out of Lima and other Pacific ports offer a thousand hiding places. Much of Peru's cocaine production also goes north by mule or truck up the Pan American highway into Ecuador and is then either shipped or flown out of Guayaquil. Ecuador and its neighbor Colombia both ban the growing of the coca bush, but there is considerable illicit production by the Indians in the Andes, which is fed into the mainstream of supplies coming up from Peru. Part of the Colombia production filters down into San Cristóbal and Caracas in Venezuela, which offer easy access by sea to Puerto Rico and direct flights to Miami. In fact, the customs at Miami pick up a steady stream of couriers from Caracas and Guayaquil.

One of them, Roberto Prado, from Ecuador, was picked up at Miami International Airport in June, 1968, as he flew in from Guayaquil with $75,000 worth of cocaine taped around his body. He said innocently that he was supposed to deliver the cocaine to someone who would make contact with him on the main street of Miami. A rather unlikely story, but, as he was ready to cooperate, the customs men decided he should keep the rendezvous. Sure enough, on Flagler Street, another Ecuadorian, Calo Grijalva, from Guayaquil, came bustling up to Prado. Grijalva, it turned out later, had given Prado the cocaine in Ecuador and had come along himself to make sure the shipment was delivered without a hitch. For a while the two men strolled along the street talking. Then along came another courier, also from Guayaquil, Luis Sánchez, making the same rendezvous. Now that both his men had arrived, as he thought, safely, Grijalva took off to report to Pedro Dante, a Cuban trafficker living in Miami, that he was all set to deliver. Prado and Sánchez, meanwhile, continued wandering around the streets, but finally went back to the Ponce de Leon Hotel, where Sánchez had already booked himself into Room 419. As both men went into the room, the customs pounced. Inside the room they found a pair of undershorts with pockets sewn into them, containing eight packages of cocaine; eleven more packages had been stuffed underneath the mattress on the bed; in all, Sánchez had brought in over $60,000 worth of cocaine.

The other cocaine trail is through that highway of the drug traffic, Mexico. It arrives in Mexico City by air or is landed at one of the small ports on the west coast and smuggled up to Guadalajara. Most consignments are of refined cocaine, but a clandestine laboratory processing the leaves was discovered in southern Mexico in 1965. Its supplies were coming up from Lima in false-bottomed steamer trunks. From Guadalajara the cocaine is distributed along the heroin network on the Mexico–United States border; most of the main heroin dealers in Tijuana or Mexicali look on it as a profitable sideline. They handle perhaps one pound of cocaine for every ten of heroin. The price is around $10,000 a pound for high-quality cocaine—which is $2,500 under the New York price. Couriers picked up on the border are often carrying cocaine and heroin. One young Mexican woman picked up at Calexico in 1968 had 130 ounces of heroin and 20 ounces of cocaine in a special compartment in the gas tank of her car—the handiwork of those "upholstery" specialists whose signs are so prominent on the main street of Tijuana.

While the mainstream of the cocaine traffic is from South to

North America, there is a side tributary to Europe and the Middle East. Most addicts in Europe, who like to blend a little cocaine with their heroin, obtain it through the black market in drugs stolen from drugstores or pharmaceutical firms. But people with the right contacts, particularly in the south of France and Lebanon, get their cocaine direct from South America. This pipeline is directed by the Lebanese, a tradition begun by the notorious smuggler of the 1950's and early 1960's, Samil Khoury. He had a nice little racket in cocaine from Brazil. Since he vanished without trace, others have picked up his connections. Most of the consignments arrive in Beirut by air from Brazil, but some also cross the Atlantic in private yachts. In the summer of 1968 many law-enforcement authorities on both sides of the Atlantic were keeping a watchful eye on one particular luxury yacht, which makes a round-trip voyage from Florida to Brazil to the Mediterranean once or twice a year. Its main cargo was reported to be counterfeit currency, but on the Brazil-to-the-Mediterranean leg of the trip, cocaine was almost certainly taken as a bonus. After all, it can be bought for as little as $2,000 a pound in Brazil and sold wholesale in Beirut for $12,000. Ten pounds would help to make it an extremely profitable voyage.

Although the picture today is of an expanding illicit traffic in cocaine, there is some reason to hope that within a generation it could be curtailed by a really imaginative program in South America to provide an alternative crop to the coca bush. The habits of centuries and emotions and politics do not make this easy, but at least the growing area is confined to part of one continent—albeit into many thousands of square miles. The opium poppy and cannabis unhappily flourish on every continent except Antarctica. If Peru, Bolivia, Colombia, and Ecuador can gradually persuade their peasants in the hills to plant an alternative crop and can come to terms with the social and economic problems which result in millions chewing the coca leaf for comfort, then there is a chance. These countries have already discovered that leaf chewers from poor areas who are fortunate enough to be able to move to towns and secure steady employment drop the habit once they are adequately fed and housed. The international traffic will flourish just so long as there is the local demand in these countries which produce plenty of leaf at cheap prices. But without that easy source of supply and without the connivance of some police officers, which has continued on and off, particularly in Peru, in recent years, the international trade might well dwindle.

A simple combination of circumstances makes it a profitable drug to smuggle at the moment; but if supplies became much harder to obtain, the smugglers might turn their attention to other, and less dangerous, things. This is little consolation in the present context, but it is one of the few chinks of light for a better future. And a few rays of hope are needed, for even if every field of coca bush, opium poppy, and *Cannabis sativa* were burned tomorrow, this would not solve the newest problem—synthetic drugs from the chemist in the laboratory.

IV

Cannabis

No one is ever likely to enter *Cannabis sativa*, as the botanists call it, for a flower show. It is a singularly uninspiring plant, straggling like an untidy beanstalk to a height of six or eight feet, its narrow, spiky leaves covered with a fuzz of tiny hairs, its flowers small and anemic. Yet this plant has become a symbol of a social revolution. That Latin tag *Cannabis sativa* is, of course, much too much of a pompous mouthful for the millions who seek simple euphoria from eating, drinking, or smoking the dried leaves or the resin that is distilled from the unfertilized female flower.

The Egyptian prefers to call it hashish (the best of all herbs), the Moroccan knows it as kif (peace and tranquillity), the Turk calls it esrar (secret preparation); to the Indian it is charas, to the Brazilian maconha, to the South African dagga, to the Mexican marihuana, to the American or the Briton it may be Indian hemp, grass, tea, weed, or, simplest of all, pot. And pot has been catapulted into the consciousness of every parent and teen-ager in Western Europe and America these last five years. "Legalize pot," some of the teen-agers cry. Most of their elders shrink back bewildered and are inclined to side with a doctor who called it "the weed of the brutal crime and the burning hell."

Yet, like it or not, the pot revolution is upon us. As *Life*

85

magazine observed of the American scene in 1967, "Almost overnight the U.S. was embarked on the greatest mass flouting of the law since Prohibition." Europe was not far behind. In Britain there were over 2,393 convictions for cannabis offenses in 1967 (compared with 274 for heroin), which was more than twice the previous year's total. The number of convictions for actual cannabis smuggling almost quadrupled from 1966 to 1968. Oxford undergraduates were sent down, public-school boys at Blandford and Lancing were expelled, and pop heroes Mick Jagger of the Rolling Stones and John Lennon of the Beatles were hauled into court and fined for possessing a few meager grains. The authorities estimated in 1968 that perhaps 300,000 people in Britain had sampled the drug at least once; other calculations suggested 40,000 took it regularly. In Geneva the United Nations International Narcotics Control Board conceded that "Millions, perhaps even tens of millions, indulge in the consumption of cannabis."

This, of course, is nothing new. In many countries the drug has been an essential part of the social scene for centuries. As far back as the seventh century B.C. the Assyrians adored the drug's euphoric effect. Herodotus, writing in the fifth century B.C., reported that the seeds of the plant were roasted on hot stones and the fumes inhaled. In India cannabis has been used for two thousand years as a narcotic and is widely used even today as a medicinal drug in the Ayurvedic-Unani system of medicine practiced by thousands of village doctors in India and Pakistan.

While the poor in Europe and America have often attempted to forget the miseries of poverty, starvation, and disease by drinking alcohol, the Muslim, forbidden to touch strong drink, has sought a little peace amid a haze of hashish.

Indeed, whether one is for or against cannabis, it must always be seen in the context of its social role. It has been and still is the drug of the dropout, the misfit, the outsider, or the rebel. There is a remarkable similarity today in the social background of the main growers, smugglers, and consumers of cannabis. They are all slightly outside the mainstream of the community in which they live—or they are rebelling against that community. The smuggling, as we shall see, is carried on almost entirely by immigrant groups, who have carried a long-standing habit with them to their new homeland, where they often feel lonely and unwanted; or it is done by hippies and students. The smuggler himself is often closely involved. Unlike the professional heroin smuggler, who will not be an addict, indeed, who would not dream of getting a fix, the pot smuggler often enjoys turning himself on and may disseminate the weed partly because he wants more people to share in what he considers a delightful experience. Cannabis smuggling may be against the law of the land; it is not necessarily against the social habits of many inhabitants of that land. It must not be viewed as darkly as the illicit traffic in heroin. The heroin smuggler, quite rightly, has been labeled the merchant of death; the cannabis smuggler will argue that he is the merchant of happiness.

The real problem, as the "legalize-pot" campaign gathers momentum, is that opinion is divided over the merits and the dangers of the drug. It is not an addictive drug physically. The young argue that smoking pot is no more dangerous, maybe even less so, than smoking tobacco or drinking alcohol. If it is all right for their parents to get nicely plastered on martinis, surely they cannot refuse their children the right to get turned on smoking pot? Back comes the reply that pot can be a stepping-stone to much more dangerous hard drugs like heroin or cocaine and that, although not physically addictive, it can lead to a psychological dependence and seriously undermine a person's ability to work. Professor William Paton, F.R.S., of the department of pharmacology at Oxford University said, "I am still waiting for a Benjamin Britten or a Henry Moore among the ranks of cannabis smokers. The evidence I have from deans of faculties in universities is that the habit of using cannabis, far from improving performance of students, is more likely to cause your dropout from college and life."

In fact, far too little is known about the effects of cannabis for any firm stand to be taken by either side. "Cannabis has not really been scientifically investigated yet," says Dr. Olaf Braendon, who heads the United Nations Narcotics Laboratory in Geneva. "We don't know what happens in the body when it is used. We haven't isolated the essential parts of the drug. At the moment there is no way of even determining if a man has taken it; there is no urine or blood test. Even if it isn't harmful to the individual, what about someone who takes it and drives a car? Cannabis distorts the senses, it gives a feeling you are a superman. That's okay if you are an Arab on a camel in the middle of a desert, but not at Piccadilly Circus or on Fifth Avenue driving at sixty miles an hour. It would be very dangerous for society to allow the free use of cannabis until we have found out much more." For the moment, therefore, cannabis remains sternly forbidden.

Most nations agreed to outlaw it as far back as 1925 at the Geneva Convention on the manufacture, sale, and movement of dangerous drugs. This international agreement was polished up by the Single Convention of 1961, which stated that the use of cannabis for other than medical (it is supposed to be good for corns) and scientific purposes must be discontinued as soon as possible, but in any case within twenty-five years. The Single Convention has had singularly little effect in stemming the onrush of people anxious to get "turned on." Police and customs men admit they are almost completely overwhelmed by the expansion of the illicit traffic in the 1960's. A recent U.S. Customs report noted, "Time was, and not long since, when a hundred-pound seizure of marihuana was regarded as an event. During 1966–67 there were eighty-seven such seizures."

In just three years the American haul of contraband marihuana jumped from five tons in 1965–66 to thirteen tons in 1966–67, then spurted ahead again to thirty-five tons for 1967–68. That is enough to make seventy million joints (marihuana cigarettes) selling for one dollar each. Applying the normal ratio of confiscation, representing ten percent of the total illicit traffic, this suggests an American retail market of $700 million a year for marihuana; even allowing that customs had a bumper year, it indicates at least a $500 million market—an extremely profitable smuggling business, although the price spiral is much less spectacular than with heroin. In the interior of Mexico, marihuana can be purchased for one to four dollars per pound; on the Mexican border it is twelve dollars per pound; one thousand cigarettes can be made from every pound, giving it a retail value of

88

one thousand dollars. The markup in Europe parallels this. Joints sell for up to ninety cents in Britain and between twenty-five cents and $1.25 in West Germany; the hashish, or cannabis resin, from which they are made will have been purchased initially in North Africa, Lebanon, or Pakistan for prices varying from $2.50 to twenty dollars per pound.

Yet, for all its profitability, the smuggling of pot has never tempted the higher echelons of organized crime. The riches to be gained are still small beer compared with heroin. Look at it from the standpoint of a French Corsican or Mafia gangster. He can buy one pound of heroin from a clandestine laboratory in France for $3,300, he can sell it in New York at the American wholesale level for up to $9,000. If he buys a pound of marihuana in Tijuana for twelve dollars, the best he can hope to get at the wholesale level in Los Angeles is one hundred dollars. It is not worth his time or the risk.

But just as heroin is under the wing of those two maverick groups of islanders, the Sicilian Mafia and the Corsicans, the organized international cannabis traffic to Europe and the United States is directed largely by immigrant groups who initially brought to their new homeland a habit which they had indulged in for centuries. Thus the Pakistanis, Indians, West Indians, and Turks are important in Europe; the Cubans, Puerto Ricans, and Mexicans in the United States. Apart from these immigrant groups, a host of freelancers pervade the cannabis scene. Many of them are hippies or students traveling with their own supplies; some are individuals who see cannabis as the best-selling line of the moment and move in for a quick profit. One young Mexican picked up at San Ysidro on the Mexico-California border with 480 pounds of marihuana in his car told the customs he had driven down to the Mexican city of Culiacán and purchased the drug at ten dollars a kilo. He was on his way to San Francisco, where he hoped to rent a room and look for customers.

The professional smuggler or the hopeful amateur who wants to earn a fortune out of cannabis must quickly come to terms with two problems. The first is the sheer bulk of the drug. There are essentially two by-products of *Cannabis sativa*: the dried leaves, which are marihuana, kif, or pot; and the resin, extracted from the unfertilized female flower, known as cannabis resin, hashish, or chavas, depending on where on the globe it is encountered. The leaves are pressed into one-kilo (2.2 pounds) blocks by a gadget like a hay press and packed in polyethylene bags about the size of a two-pound bag of flour. This presents a considerable transportation problem; couriers with pot beneath their shirts are useless unless they are just carrying a little for their friends at a party. The dried leaves, therefore, travel by car, pickup truck, yacht, truck, or private aircraft in shipments of one hundred pounds up to half a ton. The second smuggling hazard is that pot has the aroma of a rich pile of new-mown grass clippings, which is guaranteed to set the sensitive noses of authority twitching.

The resin, on the other hand, is a much more practical smuggling proposition. It looks like brown oatmeal and is the drug in concentrated form (rather like a packaged soup); it is less cumbersome and has little smell. The majority of international cannabis smugglers, with the exception of those organizing the transportation of marihuana across the Mexican border into the United States, naturally trade in resin.

Since *Cannabis sativa* is an uncomplaining plant, which will flourish in any warm climate, and will even grow in stunted form as far north as the Arctic Circle, there are supplies conveniently at hand for most of the markets. In Africa, for example, there is little active smuggling across borders, because cannabis can be grown easily in any quiet backyard or valley. Most of South Africa's dagga is grown in the northern and eastern Transvaal, Natal, and the African reservation of the Transkei. Africans, who find the drug some consolation against the harshness of apartheid, particularly in the shanty towns around the larger cities like Johannesburg, carry it with them when they go to work. This traffic is a casual one. It is an African bringing along a little for his relatives and friends.

This is the pattern throughout most of Africa, the Middle East, the Far East, and South America, where the drug is grown locally. The United Nations Commission on Narcotic Drugs noted in the report on its twenty-second session, held in January,

1968, "Much of the cannabis traffic appears to be local and on a small scale, being carried out by individual cultivators who consumed it themselves or passed it on over short distances within their country." Some governments do take a stern line even with this local traffic. In Nigeria, where in 1966, before the civil war broke out, twelve tons of illicit cannabis was seized, the penalty for trafficking the drug can be life imprisonment or even death.

Not everyone, however, has cannabis growing down a quiet lane nearby. For them it must be imported. The major cultivators are often rebels in their environment, just like those who smoke, chew, or drink the drug. The four main growing areas for the international traffic are the Rif Mountains of Morocco, the mountainous Hermel and Baalbek regions of Lebanon, the remote valleys of the foothills of the Himalayas in the north of Pakistan, and the desolate interior of Mexico. In each of these inaccessible regions the local inhabitants are outside the mainstream of progress and have a long history of resisting the incursions of colonizers or their own governments.

The Berbers in the Rif Mountains have been at war for centuries with the rest of the population of that corner of North Africa and with the French and Spanish, who have tried to administer it. The Danaji in Lebanon have maintained the same spirit of independence from the other Arabs and from the French in Beirut. They appear to be brigands, but would argue they are fighting for the integrity of their own domain. Their very isolation from central authority makes it easy for them to grow cannabis by the acre. Once it is harvested, it emerges mysteriously in the nearest cities. The farmers who grow it in the fastness of the hills receive very little cash, perhaps five dollars or less per kilo, but that is enough to enable them to maintain their sturdy independence. They treat with disdain earnest emissaries from central governments who try to persuade them how much nicer it would be to plant sunflowers instead. The Lebanese have been attempting to do this with their errant Danaji tribesmen in the hills since 1966. This sunflower campaign is heavily subsidized. The Lebanese are paying sunflower-seed producers prices above the normal market price to tempt them into giving up the cannabis crop. The government calculated at the outset that cannabis cultivation covered 12,500 acres. So they launched their scheme with a token 250 acres of glowing sunflowers in 1966; two years later, in 1968, there were nearly 8,000 sunflower acres.

Although the sunflower fields may look splendid, the tribesmen appear to show little enthusiasm for this new crop. It takes too much hard work. All that was demanded for a handsome hashish crop was a day's work casually scattering seed; then the plants grew without much further attention. Sunflowers need regular hoeing; therefore, although sunflowers may now be blooming gaily where some of the hashish once grew, hashish is now being grown in other less obvious spots as keenly as ever. One U.N. delegation, visiting the area recently to see the progress of the sunflower scheme, was even offered hashish by some innocent who did not realize the nature of its mission.

From Lebanon the hashish filters out all over the Middle East, packaged under such extravagant labels as "Fleur du Printemps," "Atomic Bomb," "Extra Extra," "Sahara No. 1," "Hitler," and "Mussolini." These are heady concoctions for Arabs, particularly Egyptians, who want to escape for a few hours from the harshness of their lives and indulge in dreams of grandeur and power. The hashish seems to have miraculous powers of seeping through the war zones of the Middle East, ignoring armies, frontiers, and nationalist passions. One almost has visions of the pony- or camel-express riders dodging flying bullets; only it is the hashish, not the mail, that must get through. Even in the tense days of January, 1968, as the Israelis and the Egyptians eyed each other uneasily across the Suez Canal, the smugglers were hard at it swimming the canal, laden with nylon sacks of Sahara No. 1. The Egyptian border patrols picked up one band of five smugglers emerging from the waters of the canal near Ismailia weighted down with 488 pounds of the drug, worth up to $221,000 on the retail market in Cairo. An even larger haul of eighteen sacks, worth almost one million dollars retail, was picked up by a fisherman on the Egyptian shore of the Gulf of Suez after it had been ferried across in a small boat from Sinai.

The Egyptians, naturally, often charge the Israelis with conniving with the hashish smugglers, and the Israelis, equally naturally, hotly dispute this slur. The Egyptians, for example, declared that 1,550 pounds of hashish found in a ship near Suez in December, 1967, had come from Lebanon via Israel and Sinai. The Israelis certainly detect a great deal of hashish passing through their territory, but this is understandable, since the quickest route from Lebanon to Egypt is through their land. Indeed, since Israel occupied Sinai during the six-day war in June, 1967, it has become extremely inconvenient to smuggle hashish any other way. The alternative route through Syria and Jordan down to the Gulf of Aqaba is much more complicated. So the hashish flows through Israel—but not with the connivance of the government. They take their drug hunting very seriously. They even have a squad of tracker dogs trained to sniff out hidden hashish, and, to their credit, they nosed up over $100,000 worth of the stuff in 1966.

The Lebanese are content to put most of their energies into supplying the convenient local market in neighboring countries. However, like all good businessmen, they are not averse to selling their product to all comers. But people from farther afield who want the drug must make their own smuggling arrangements. Many do. The pungent fumes curling up from the Lebanese hashish are encountered at parties all over Europe. It arrives in a variety of organized and unorganized ways. The simplest way is through the migrant worker, particularly from Turkey. We have already seen that the Turk going to work in Germany often takes a little raw opium or morphine base with him. Hashish is an acceptable alternative, particularly because the Turk himself can enjoy a quiet smoke if he feels depressed when he is working far from home (whereas he is highly unlikely to use the morphine). The hashish can also be sold for a little useful pocket money. "We find," says one U.N. narcotics observer in Geneva, "that the cannabis traffic often starts from social facts like this. The Turkish worker in Germany is unhappy, he misses his little pipe of hashish, so he sends home for some or buys it from a friend." It is then a natural step for the

Turks to sell hashish to the local German market, and as the taste for it develops, Germans think about importing it themselves.

In fact, Germans, Britons, and Americans have been paying increasing attention to Beirut as a handy source of supply for hashish, and it has been moving west by road and air. The main dealers in the Middle East or Europe never carry it themselves. It is easy enough to find an innocent student. A nineteen-year-old Lebanese student, Georges Nasri Abou Daher, was picked up at London airport in September, 1968, with $8,400 worth of hashish tucked into his suitcase. He had been tempted by the opportunity of a free holiday in Britain with all expenses paid; he will, in fact, enjoy three years as a guest of Her Majesty. A twenty-four-year-old Londoner, David Jones, was arrested by Greek customs men on the Greek-Turkish border with ninety-two pounds of hashish in his car in February, 1967. He explained he had been offered $2,400 to carry the drug from Beirut to London. Another young Englishman, Richard Griffiths, from Hull, was arrested in a bar on the island of Rhodes as he was trying to sell twenty-four pounds of hashish he had purchased in Beirut. He pleaded, "I needed some money, and I thought the sale of hashish could earn me some." Instead he got twelve months in prison. The Swiss police rounded up one group of young Swiss hashish smugglers early in 1968 who were driving through from Kabul, a hippie haven in Afghanistan, via Istanbul with large supplies of hashish. One of the group was the son of a pastor in Basel, and he kept the drug hidden under the floor of his bedroom.

These casual carriers—students, "hippies," people out to make themselves a little easy money—pop up all over the Middle East like mushrooms after a shower. But police and customs officials, who are often inclined to be lenient on their own people for using the drug, will crack down hard on foreigners.

The Lebanese customs seized twenty-three pounds of hashish from two Britons, James Bogan and Robert Harris, in the summer of 1967 after they had journeyed up to Baalbek and bought packets labeled "Fleur du Printemps" at the low price of thirteen dollars a pound. They were each given three years. In December,

1968, at least twenty young Europeans, including seven from Britain, were believed to be in prison in Turkey serving sentences of up to thirty years for hashish offenses. All had been picked up coming through either from Lebanon or along the "hippie trail" from Kabul in Afghanistan, or Lahore in Pakistan. Even the Russians experienced the fringes of the traffic. They handed out sentences of two to five years' hard labor to hashish couriers who were caught in Tashkent while in transit from Kabul back to Europe. During the first half of 1968 two Britons, three Americans, one Canadian, and three Swedes were all jailed there. One of the British smugglers, Michael Parsons, had thirteen pounds of hashish in the lining of a special vest when he stopped in the city overnight after coming up on an Afghan Airlines flight from Kabul. The Russians claimed he told them he hoped to sell it for $72,000 (an extremely ambitious price) on his return to London.

Many of these hashish smugglers from Europe are so amateurish in their approach that they leave themselves wide open to detection. They frequently arrive in Lebanon by sea, bringing with them a car, often a Volkswagen, with European plates. They drive up to Baalbek, purchase the hashish, hide it in the car, and scurry back to Beirut, ready to take the next boat back to Europe. Now, it takes no imagination on the part of a Lebanese customs man to realize it is a complete waste of money to ship a car all the way from Europe for two days in Lebanon; it would be infinitcly cheaper to rent a car in Beirut. Unless, of course, there is a hidden motive in the journey. The smugglers are caught again and again.

The nearest country for the European pot smoker to buy the drug is Morocco, where the locals call it kif. At least 1,500 acres of the Rif Mountains are given over to cannabis cultivation. Indeed, it is one of the last lines left in that faded smuggler's supermarket, Tangier. In the years up to 1957, when Tangier was a free port, it was a happy, busy haven for all kinds of Mediterranean smugglers. There was a small gold refinery in a private house in the center of the city, turning 400-ounce bars of gold into handier sizes for smuggling. A fleet of high-speed launches, guided to their destination by a radio transmitter in the Rue

Velasquez, fanned out all along the Mediterranean, loaded down with cigarettes and whiskey. Today Tangier lives mostly on the memories of those heady days; the gold-refinery chimney is cold, the radio silent. Some of the most colorful characters are dead, including Paul Lund, a self-confessed robber on the run from Birmingham, who was a cigarette smuggler in the 1950's and then retired to keep a bar. He regaled his customers with anecdotes of smuggling derring-do, winking between each story at his friends, from whom he would inquire anxiously afterward, "Did I tell it all right, George?" They assured him that he did.

These days, most of the cigarette and whiskey smuggling is purely local—and it is coming into Tangier from Ceuta, a Spanish toehold on the North African coast a couple of bays to the east. Tangier has only its memories—and a healthy export business in kif.

It filters down by donkey and camel from the high valleys of the Rif Mountains into the maze of tiny shops and cafés of the Casbah. The most immediate customers are the Moroccans themselves, for whom a pipe of kif is as natural as a martini at six. Some of the writers and artists in Tangier's colony of expatriates also find the local permissive attitude to the drug one of the pleasures of living there. The Moroccan police appear to direct far more attention to Europeans visiting the city to pick up supplies to smuggle back home than they do the local citizen quietly turning himself on.

The traffic from Morocco to Europe is a flourishing but casual one, carried on by the legions of Scandinavian, German, and British (the French and the Italians are less keen on pot) tourists and students who flock south to the sun every summer. They buy a few ounces or even a pound or two of kif in Tangier and take it back home for themselves and their friends to dream over in the long, dark winter evenings. Many of those dusty students hitchhiking their way back through Spain in late summer have their private supply in the knapsacks bulging on their backs. Some even take back five or ten pounds and sell it at a slight profit at home to pay for their holiday. "People say, 'Oh, are you going to Tangier? Bring me back a couple of pounds,' " says a Gibraltar detective. Both the Rock and Algeciras, the Spanish port across the bay, bear the brunt of the through traffic in kif. A German couple coming through Gibraltar not long ago had twenty-six pounds tucked into the spare tire. They were detected because they had stuffed the tire so full that stray bits of the dried leaf were trailing out behind them.

The normal tourist souvenirs from Tangier make ideal hiding places, especially the leather pouf which sells for three to ten dollars in the Casbah (depending on how well the tourist bargains). Kif in a pouf is a great favorite. One German tourist on a Mediterranean cruise in the Swedish liner *Kripsholm* borrowed every penny his fellow passengers would lend him and bought 110 pounds of kif when the liner stopped at Tangier. He concealed it in a pouf and his lifejacket, and tried, unsuccessfully, to smuggle it ashore in Hamburg to sell to his friends in his hometown of Hannover. Two Englishmen from Nottingham on vacation in Tangier hit on an even better scheme. They bought kif and patiently inserted it inside colored raffia used to make beach bags and baskets. They then arranged for the raffia to be woven into baskets for them. "It was a masterpiece," said an admiring local detective.

A little kif through the mail also makes an ideal alternative to the souvenir postcard, a gambit that is not confined to Morocco. Little packages labeled "Gift parcels" containing kif and hashish from thoughtful friends in North Africa, and Middle East, and Pakistan turn up all the time in Britain, West Germany, and the United States. U.S. servicemen in Vietnam flood the mails with parcels of the stuff (they also mail home such souvenirs as live grenades, antitank rockets, and shells). The prize, however, must go to the Moroccan who came up with the idea of little honey cakes filled with kif for tourists to carry or post home.

The casual nature of the traffic offers the temptation to a smuggling entrepreneur to try to break in and organize his own rather more formal supply route with the minimum of effort. The main development has been to move kif in bulk to the tourist resorts of the Costa Brava and the Costa del Sol in Spain, where there is an even larger market among the twelve million northern Europeans who flood into the country every summer. But there is also a small organized traffic into the heart of Europe.

One young Welshman, Richard Corbett, from Cardiff, had things down to a fine art before he was arrested in Spain in 1965 with thirty-seven pounds in his car. He bought this kif in the hills outside Tangier, thus bypassing the middlemen in the city and getting it much cheaper; he paid less than $1.20 a pound. He stuck bags of the drug inside the roof of his car and then covered them over with the roof lining. He would then take the ferry to Algeciras, drive up through Spain, and cross into France at San Sebastián or Port Bou. He took care to go through with a convoy of tourist cars so that the customs were too busy to pay much attention to each vehicle. He passed through Paris and Frankfurt, then up to Copenhagen and into Sweden. In every large city he would make for the jazz clubs—"preferably modern jazz." There he would ask around casually if anyone had any pot to sell. Once he made contact with a peddler, he would ask to buy a large amount—much more than any normal peddler in a club would carry. He would then be referred up the line until he reached a local wholesaler—to whom he would immediately offer his own shipment. He reckoned ultimately to sell for $4,800 the kif he had purchased in Morocco for forty-eight dollars. An extremely profitable little racket—until its attractions were tarnished by three years in a Spanish jail.

The large-scale organized traffic in cannabis into Europe comes, however, from much farther afield. Britain is usually the ultimate destination.

Since 1960 the British taste for cannabis has been growing faster than in any other nation in Europe, with the possible exception of West Germany. Until this boom began, there had been a steady but not alarming flow of both cannabis resin and leaf into Britain from a variety of countries. The banana boats from Nigeria had brought the dried leaf into Liverpool in little plastic packets that looked as if they were filled with sage. It was an informal traffic. Seamen working the run knew that it was negotiable, so they would nip ashore at Lagos or Port Harcourt and buy up a few ounces. Once back home, they easily sold it in clubs near Liverpool Cathedral where the local dealers congregated. This traffic continues. One prosperous Nigerian in Liverpool makes it his specialty to buy from the seamen and distribute the drug by car to Bradford and London.

The first large supplier to the infant British pot scene was Burma. The smuggling was operated by six well-organized rings, who used the boats of two British shipping companies on the run from Rangoon to the United Kingdom. Most of these ships docked initially at Tilbury and then plodded on around the coast, dropping off the rest of their cargo at Hull or Glasgow, Liverpool or Avonmouth. The drug was concealed aboard the ship at Rangoon in any one of a thousand hiding places, from the engine room to the forecastle.

The chief smugglers were Indians working in the engine room, who pooled their resources every time they were in Rangoon to buy as much cannabis as possible at $2.30 a pound. When their ship docked at Tilbury, they would meet local contacts to discuss the best port to drop the drug off. If there were rumors that customs were very alert in Hull, they would agree to leave the drug on until the vessel docked at Glasgow. It was an ideal situation, for they could bide their time and, at the right moment, the crewman could slip ashore with the drug. Customs can be alert only when a ship first docks. It is impossible to keep track of comings and goings once loading or unloading starts. A friendly docker is a great ally in sneaking the drug ashore. One Liverpool docker, disguised in a pillowcase, admitted on television that he removed drugs from ships in Liverpool for seventy dollars a time. The profits on the Rangoon run were substantial for the small-time smuggler. The cannabis he had purchased in Rangoon for five dollars sold for nearly one hundred dollars ashore in Britain.

This route took a hard knock in 1959, when British customs seized almost 400 pounds on a ship in Liverpool and, simultaneously, the Burmese authorities arrested half a dozen of the leading dealers in Rangoon. The trade never recovered from the shock. For a time most of Britain's cannabis came from West Africa and from Cyprus—where it was easy to pick up hashish from Lebanon.

Then, in the early 1960's the really hard-core organized traffic began to emerge. It developed, as in Germany, from a special set of social circumstances. The role played by the Turkish migrant worker in West Germany was taken in Britain by the immigrant from the West Indies and Asia. The peak years for immigrations from these countries into Britain were 1960–62, with a maximum of 136,400 in 1961. Many of these immigrants came from an environment where it is as natural to take the occasional whiff of cannabis as it is for the Englishman to nip down to the pub for a beer. Some immigrants, crowded into slum houses in industrial cities in Britain, cold and lonely, naturally looked to cannabis for comfort. Since cannabis was not readily available in the backyard in Britain, nor from any little dealer down the street, the immigrant communities, particularly in the Southall, Birmingham, Manchester, and Bradford areas, began to organize their own supplies. That meant smuggling. Since the vast majority of immigrants to Britain are extremely careful to stay well within the law, the traffic was handled inevitably by a few of the more unscrupulous members of the immigrant community, who again quickly saw the possibilities of even greater profits by smuggling it in, not only for their own people, but for the community at large.

Quite apart from this growing demand for cannabis, there were two other extremely significant problems developing among the immigrant communities which, again, could be turned to advantage by the handful of racketeers. First, the controls that were finally placed on Commonwealth citizens entering Britain by the 1962 Commonwealth Immigrants Act started a growing traffic in smuggling Asians, unable to qualify under the act, into Britain (see Chapter 7). Secondly, those Asians working in Britain wanted to send money back to their families. They could do this through the conventional banking channels, but then they had to accept the official exchange rate of sterling into rupees. In 1968 this was eighteen rupees in India, fifteen in Pakistan. By going to unofficial currency dealers, operating in every city in Britain where there is a large Asian community, they could trade their sterling at an exchange rate as high as twenty-four rupees to the pound for India, and twenty-two to the pound for Pakistan.

The racketeers thus acquire enormous quantities of sterling overseas, with which they can purchase other goods, including gold, watches, and radios, to be smuggled back home. The sale of cannabis from Pakistan in Britain added to this profitable cycle—immigrants and drugs out of Asia; gold, watches, and radios back in.

The traffic from Pakistan is entirely of the concentrated cannabis resin, the only practical way in which the drug can be transported over such long distances. It accounts for eighty percent of the illicit supply to Britain. Since the mid-1960's this resin has been coming into Britain by the hundredweight—a drastic change from the day when customs men or police felt a celebration was called for if they seized one pound.

The importers are Pakistanis and Indians living in London, Birmingham, and Bradford. They commute back and forth between these cities and make regular flights to the East, especially to Lahore in Pakistan, a great town for making deals on immigrants and drugs. Over a period of eighteen months one organizer filled one and a half passports with immigration entry and exit stamps—ostensibly he was selling films. Two of the Pakistanis are brothers, one living in the Birmingham area, the other in Bradford. When the Birmingham-based brother was arrested on drug charges in 1967, the police found a diary which contained a lengthy list of names and addresses of contacts, not only relating to drugs, but also to watch and diamond dealers in London, Amsterdam, Karachi, and Bombay.

The smuggling methods are highly professional, showing that time and patience have been devoted to planning tactics. The most straightforward method is to recruit Asians already living in Britain, who hold British passports, and offer them a free two-week holiday back at home. It is crucial to choose couriers with British passports so they clear immigration with the minimum of fuss on their return; a man carrying a substantial quantity of cannabis must not be caught simply because his papers are not in order. Immigration officers at London airport have noticed a steady flow of Asians with British passports who make these two-week "holiday" trips. It is quite obvious from the work they are doing in Britain that they could not afford the round-trip fare themselves—and, if they could, they would almost certainly spend longer than two weeks in their homeland with their families. Many of these travelers stop off briefly in Brussels or Frankfurt, either to pick up goods to be smuggled into Pakistan or India or, on their return journey, to drop off cannabis. This cannabis can then be picked up by another courier and brought across the English Channel, either by air or by car ferry.

Six hundred thousand cars cross the Channel every year from ports and airfields on the south coast of England. The customs checks on the British side are stiffer than anything usually encountered on the Continent, but in the peak season the examination must perforce be cursory.

Some cannabis comes 4,500 miles overland by car all the way from Pakistan, often in the same vehicles carrying would-be immigrants to Britain. The London *Sunday Telegraph* reported in May, 1968, in great detail one such journey, which took place in the autumn of 1966. Two cars, a Vauxhall Victor and a Mercedes, started from Lahore carrying four potential immigrants, who had each paid about $1,200 in return for a promise that at the end of the trip they would be smuggled into England. What they did not know was that the spare tire on the roof of the Vauxhall was packed almost to bursting point with thirty-one pounds of cannabis; their two driver-guides had neglected to tell them this. All went well until they reached the Bulgarian-Yugoslav frontier. There an alert Yugoslav customs man eyed the tire on the roof of the Vauxhall and realized it was the wrong size for the car. He ordered the driver, known simply to the immigrants as Singh, to take the tire down. It thumped on the road as if loaded with lead. The customs officer pulled out a knife, slashed the tire, and cannabis resin spilled all over the road.

The main staging post along the route both for cannabis and immigrants is Frankfurt. Here many hopeful illegal immigrants are told to wait for instructions—and often have to fritter away weeks of waiting. Cannabis also frequently changes couriers in Frankfurt. It is relatively easy to arrange for someone else to bring a car across on the Channel ferry to pick it up.

West German police have made several large seizures of cannabis from Pakistan as it passed Frankfurt in transit. One raid on a Frankfurt garage in 1967, triggered off by a tip from the British police, yielded thirty-four pounds in the back of a car that had just arrived from Pakistan. In another haul in January, 1968, the police found 176 pounds being carried by two students, one British, one Australian. They had purchased the cannabis for ten dollars a pound in Pakistan, flown with it to Paris, and checked it for a time in a luggage locker at the Gare de l'Est. Then they hired a car and drove with the drug to Frankfurt, where they were trying to arrange for it to be smuggled into England when they were arrested. They had done a previous run in August, 1967, when they had brought twenty-two pounds in from Pakistan and sold it in Frankfurt and Munich.

At Dover the customs keep a wary eye open for heavily laden cars driven by Asians as they come off the Channel ferries. They picked up one from the Ostend ferry in July, 1966, and painstakingly pulled it to pieces. Behind the door panels and the back seat were 119 pounds of cannabis, worth $100,000 on the retail black market. The two Pakistani couriers, one a laborer from Wolverhampton, the other a bus driver from Coventry, pleaded they had only been paid expenses to travel to Ostend to pick up the drug. They were working, in fact, for one of the main smuggling groups importing cannabis for the Birmingham and Bradford areas.

This syndicate suffered two further major setbacks over the next twelve months, but both the new cases revealed they had become far more subtle in their smuggling methods.

The twenty-five crates clearly labeled "Fresh Fruit (oranges)" looked quite innocuous when they were unloaded from a Pakistan International Airlines flight at London airport on an April weekend in 1967. But a customs officer peering among the oranges found an undeclared eighty-nine pounds of cannabis packed in with the fruit (they were Kinnoo oranges, a great favorite with Pakistanis). Shortly afterward, a Pakistani from Birmingham named Abdullah Hamid Butt and an Indian, Muhammad Younas, of Surbiton, drove up to collect the consignment. They saw the customs hovering near the orange crates, fled to their car, and took off at high speed. An airport detective gave chase and finally caught the pair when they stopped for a red light. Butt was given two years in prison, Younas fifteen months. This was merely a foretaste of what was to come. Probing into the activities of Butt and Younas, customs men came up with information indicating that oranges were not the only convenient cover being used for cannabis smuggling. Sam Charles, the customs' senior investigator, flew to Karachi, where he interviewed one globe-trotting Pakistani, Abbass Ebrahim Haji, who claimed to be a film distributor and also ran an import-export business from Walthamstow in the suburbs of London. Customs kept an eye on Haji's wanderings for several months and spotted him in Birmingham in January, 1968, with two Pakistanis, who were later convicted of unlawful possession of drugs. Then, in April, 1968, they received a tip-off about a shipment of mango pickles due at Tilbury on April 7, consigned to Haji. Sam Charles and his men carefully opened every one of the 105 cases of pickles, containing 410 cans, and found nine tins packed with 164 pounds of cannabis beneath a shallow layer of pickles. They took out the drug, replaced it with gravel, and resealed all the cases. The whole shipment was then loaded into a truck and, with Sam Charles in overalls acting as driver's mate, was taken to Haji's home in Walthamstow. There Haji and two other Pakistanis pitched in helping Charles and the driver unload all the cases into the front garden. The job done, Haji offered the customs man a one-pound tip. Charles politely refused and told Haji who he really was. All three men were arrested. When the customs men were carefully sifting through Haji's belongings, they came on a cigarette pack with an address in Slough scribbled on the back. Living at that address was a brilliant Indian-born scientist, Gurdev Singh Sangha, who was working in London on secret projects on laser-beam modulation for the Ministry of Defense and the United States Defense Department. Ostensibly Sangha was living modestly with a $144-a-month grant from his American backers and was busy finishing his Ph.D. thesis. In fact he was operating at least six bank accounts and in between his government work, which was covered by the Official Secrets Act, he was full of bright schemes to fool the customs. When he was arrested, the investigators found in his pocket a tailor's bill with a note about a consignment of "gulkand" (a jam made from sugar

104

and rose-petal leaves) due to arrive at Liverpool a few days later. Sure enough, among the heavily scented jam, they found 250 pounds of cannabis packed neatly into nine tins. The total market value of the two shipments was £150,000. Sangha and Haji were each sent to prison for five years. While Sangha was in Brixton prison awaiting his trial, he painstakingly finished off his Ph.D. thesis on laser-beam modulation—a paper considered so important in scientific circles that he was given special permission to work late at the prison. He was even allowed technical discussions with his professor from London University.

Sangha, of course, fits neatly into romantic conceptions of a shadowy "mastermind" behind the drug smugglers. Customs men admitted at his trial that they had no actual assessment of the amount of cannabis that had been smuggled in undetected since Sangha first gave the smugglers the benefit of his wisdom. But it would be quite wrong to label him as the king of the smugglers. It is, of course, often extremely difficult to say who really is the top man. The whole operation is so hydra-headed. "You think you have an important man," said one investigator, "but the moment you arrest him he becomes singularly unimportant in his organization. Someone else you haven't got takes over."

It is hard indeed. Barely had Sangha been sentenced at the Old Bailey when the court was busy again hearing charges against yet another team of mango-pickle smugglers. This time it was three Pakistanis, one from London, the others from Bradford, who had tried to bring in almost a quarter of a ton of cannabis with a black-market value of almost $750,000. Another shipment even turned up in suitcases in a room at the Hilton Hotel in Park Lane. The undermanager and a hotel detective searched the room one evening because the occupier, an Indian named Mukhter Ahmed, had not slept there for two nights. They suspected he had left without paying the bill. When they opened his suitcases to see if there was anything valuable that might offset the debt, they found no suits, shirts, or socks, just $40,000 worth of cannabis.

This was not the sort of credit the Hilton usually accepts, so the hotel detective summoned the police. They kept watch on the room and arrested three Indians who came by to pick up the bags. Ahmed, the errant hotel guest, was not among them, but he was eventually traced. The key man behind this conspiracy, who was a travel agent, decided not to wait and stand trial. Although his passport had been forfeited to the police, he vanished from the country and later turned up in India back in the travel business. At the trial of the remaining defendants in November, 1968, the defense counsel made the interesting plea that the cannabis was not intended for general circulation. He pleaded it was for use by the Indian and Pakistani community in London and stressed that they did not drink and all their lives had been accustomed to smoking the drug. They did not consider it harmful. The judge was not impressed. "If members of your community," he told the smugglers, "choose to come and live in this country, they must realize they are subject to the same laws as anybody else. You did this with your eyes wide open, knowing perfectly well that the dangerous-drugs laws here are strictly enforced."

Although this judge was stern, there is an increasing undercurrent of opinion in Britain that the law relating to cannabis needs to be revised. There is no question of its use being legalized just yet, but the Wootton Committee, which investigated the whole issue for the Home Office, recommended in 1968 that cannabis should be removed from the same category as heroin and cocaine under the Dangerous Drugs Act. It also suggested that penalties for mere possession of a small quantity should be reduced (at present possession carries a maximum penalty of ten years and a $2,400 fine). The committee argued, however, that penalties for trafficking should be increased. But no action is likely for some years, because removing cannabis from the list of dangerous drugs would entail Britain going back on its agreements to the United Nations under the Single Convention.

One rather unexpected sidelight on the traffic into Britain is that the traditional criminal establishment has reacted against it almost as strongly as the Establishment. The professional criminals are not involved in the business at all. Once the Asians have smuggled it in, West Indians handle most of the distribution network within the country. The old-fashioned British burglar, with a couple of teen-age children, is as perturbed by the whole thing as anyone. "We've had some assistance from downright villains," said a detective superintendent in the north of England. "They say to us, 'I've never grassed in me life, but drugs I don't like.' "

Things may eventually become easier on the pot smoker, but the smuggler seems in for a hard time all around. The 1968 Interpol Conference in Tehran showed that within its member police forces at least there is increasing determination to stamp out the international traffic in drugs.

Yet can it be stopped? The authorities can make some impact on heroin and cocaine, because they are dealing with a traffic for which the community at large has no sympathy. With cannabis the situation is entirely different; here a substantial segment of the population wants the use of the drug legalized and is already challenging the law by using it. The movement of this drug across international frontiers is now on such a scale that the authorities can do no more than nibble at the problem. In Europe the drug now comes in by the hundredweight. In America marihuana arrives by the ton from Mexico.

The dried cannabis leaf from plants growing in Chihuahua, Coahuila, Durango, and Zacatecas provinces in the interior of Mexico makes up eighty percent of the U.S. trade. It comes across the 2,013-mile border into California, Arizona, New Mexico, and Texas in such quantities that it is surprising anyone living down there does not get turned on just from the heady smell of marihuana passing by moonlight. Indeed, step into the customs storeroom in San Diego, and that is almost what happens. The room is stacked from floor to ceiling with polyethylene-wrapped, one-kilo bricks of marihuana. One afternoon in May, 1968, there were twenty tons of the stuff in the room, and the air was so pungent that visitors felt quite lighthearted after sniffing it for a few minutes. Once in a while the customs men have a grand burnup.

From the interior of Mexico, much of the marihuana moves down to the little town of San Luis in Sonora province, which acts as a wholesale market. It is then transported by road up to the smuggling front line at the border towns of Tijuana, Tecate, Mexicali, Nogales, Ciudad Juárez, Piedras Negras, Nuevo Laredo, and Matamoros.

The actual smuggling operation is something of a free-for-all, with a host of amateurs crossing with two or three bricks of marihuana, each weighing one kilo, for themselves and their friends, while the professional groups move anything between one hundred and five hundred bricks at a time. The amateurs are most numerous in California because, as with heroin, it is easiest to jump in the car and drive over the border to buy your own. Supplies for Chicago, Detroit, Cleveland, and New York, all two or three thousand miles by road from Mexico, have to be more organized. The strongest group handling this wholesale traffic to the great cities are the Cubans. Cuba itself had a profitable corner in the marihuana market before the days of Fidel Castro. Once Castro took over, marihuana growing and distributing through the island stopped abruptly, but many Cuban expatriates, weaned on smuggling, started moving it from Mexico. The Puerto Ricans, with good contacts from their island to marihuana moving up from Venezuela and Guiana, also handle a large wholesale business. The Mexicans themselves handle some of their own export trade, particularly to Chicago.

The hippies, the students, and the young men who have deserted from the U.S. Army or are draft-dodging to avoid being sent to Vietnam supplement the professional traffic. For them the marihuana scene is essentially a part of a social revolution; it is a prop and a weapon in defying the established order of which they want no part.

The simplest method for all concerned to obtain pot is to buy an old car for one hundred dollars in Los Angeles and drive down south of the border. There the car is loaded up with the kilo bricks of marihuana. Frequently it is just stuffed in the trunk or under the seats. The professionals, however, usually prefer to hand the car over to one of the "upholstery experts" who thrive in towns like Tijuana, making special compartments to go under seats or the frame in door panels or in gas tanks. Several makes of car even come tailor-made to the smuggler's need. If you take the headlights out of a 1956 Chevrolet, there is a compartment in the wing behind each light which will hold fifteen kilos. The 1959 Ford Thunderbird has two factory-built hideouts measuring 8″ x 8″ x 4″ underneath the back seats, and its fenders are so bulky that they offer ample room for a few kilos. During 1967, when this Ford was clearly the car of the year among smugglers, the U.S. Customs inspectors on the borders learned to look for telltale bolts on the fenders, which indicated a container had been fitted. They picked up eighteen drug-laden Fords in a few months. "Ford," the customs men on the border say jokingly, "is in the smuggling business." Indeed, its Ranchero pickup truck is another smuggling favorite, along with Chevrolet's El Camino pickup. Both these vehicles have a compartment under their bed which is ideal for hiding marihuana.

Some dealers on the border trade in heroin and marihuana, others prefer to specialize. The Mexican reputed to be the main marihuana dealer in Tijuana dispatches two or three cars across the border every day, each carrying an average load of 330 pounds, a total of three and one-half tons a week. He buys his marihuana in Sinaloa at about $12,000 a ton. He sells it to clients in Tijuana at around $25,000 a ton; if they want it delivered in the United States, his prices go up according to the distance. Just inside California, in San Diego, it is $65,000 a ton, in Los Angeles it is up to $100,000, in San Francisco it may reach $200,000. At that rate he can comfortably afford to lose half of everything he ships. The majority of the professional couriers are Mexicans. They make two or three journeys a week, for which they are paid $100–$150 a time, and are very practiced. If an American customs officer waves a courier to one side for a more detailed examination of his vehicle, the Mexican will leap out and run like a frightened rabbit back through the no-man's-land into his own country. Car and drug are abandoned. Such occurrences are so frequent on the border that everyone takes it in stride. In March, 1968, there were eighteen seizures of marihuana totaling 1,299 pounds at the San Ysidro checkpoint alone.

Smugglers who fear they may blush if they pass through the border have a variety of tricks to avoid actually carrying drugs when they face the customs. They will first cross into Mexico and fix the deal with their local contact. He loads his car with marihuana and sets off along Mexico's Route 2, which runs parallel to the eight-foot-high fence staking out the border between the two countries. The American, meanwhile, slips back through the San Ysidro, Tecate, or Calexico border crossing with an empty car and clear conscience. Once in California, he branches off along California routes 94 or 98, which also follow the border. At a prearranged spot the two cars stop, and the Mexican throws the marihuana over the fence. The back-door entry can be arranged, of course, equally as easily over the phone. It is impossible to police every inch of the border all the time, particularly in the lonely high country east of Tecate near the Campo Indian Reservation and the Anzo-Borrego Desert State Park.

The more sophisticated smugglers have long since graduated from cars; they use private aircraft. "We simply can't keep track of them," admitted a border customs agent. "They can land on any level patch of ground or on a dirt road inside Mexico. We know they often use a dried-up lake bed just south of Mexicali or even penetrate farther down into the Western Sierra Madre, where they can pick up the marihuana cheaply for ten dollars a brick." Officially all private aircraft should log their movements and report to customs if they have crossed the border. Most pilots either conveniently forget to comply or land on a back road as soon as they have recrossed the border into the United States and unload before flying on to their home airfield, where they dutifully report empty-handed. This flying smuggler service is especially active on the Texas-Mexico border, over which most of the marihuana for Chicago and New York passes.

In an effort to combat the flying smugglers, the customs bought their own Cessna Super Skymaster in 1968 to enable them to shadow smuggling suspects through the clouds.

A boat is equally handy for California and Texas smugglers. Every weekend a small armada of private yachts and high-speed launches sets off into the Pacific from Long Beach, San Diego, and Chula Vista. Who knows where they go once they are over the horizon? Fishing? More likely the little Mexican port of Enseñada, just sixty-six miles down the coast from the border. Enseñada is a frequent venue for yacht races in which many Americans compete, and if they do not win a sailing prize, what better to take back for consolation prize than a little marihuana? Of course, all law-abiding sailors should report to customs on their return, but who can keep track of the returning flotillas late on Sunday night as they chug into scores of private harbors along a couple of hundred miles of coast?

There are always the unlucky ones. Just before midnight one October evening, a couple of California fish and game wardens were on the prowl along Malibu Beach, just north of Los Angeles, on the lookout for any poachers fishing for lobsters out of season. They stole silently up on a party of men busy ferrying sacks ashore from a yacht moored some way off. Lobster poachers caught red-handed! The wardens moved in to arrest the shore party. They grabbed two men and looked in the sacks. Not a single lobster; just half a ton of marihuana. The yacht, hearing a rumpus on shore, cut its moorings and took off at full throttle. Four hours later a Coast Guard cutter intercepted it trying to slip into Long Beach harbor without lights. The skipper, James Danaher, not only admitted he had picked up his cargo in Enseñada, but confessed to bringing in an earlier shipment of half a ton a few weeks before. One of the gang escaped the dragnet and for months could not be found. Hardly surprising; he was in San Diego jail after being arrested quite independently for trying to smuggle 222 pounds of marihuana in his car.

The border crossing itself is the major hurdle for the marihuana smugglers, but the drug may still be two or three thousand miles from its final destination in Chicago, Detroit, Cleveland, or New York. No one can relax until it is safely delivered. The men organizing the wholesale supplies to these cities know full well that if customs catch one of their couriers coming over the border, they will attempt to persuade him to complete the delivery— under customs supervision. Good security, therefore, is essential. Either the courier is watched by another member of the gang as he comes through the border or he will have to telephone every few hours for new instructions. He must keep to a strict timetable; if his phone call is late, suspicions will be aroused and the trail will go cold.

Ideally, if the customs men have confirmed information that a particular car is carrying marihuana, they will not attempt to' stop it on the border, but will simply trail it. Once, in the autumn of 1967, this paid off spectacularly. Customs agent Paul Martin at Calexico, California, received a hard-and-fast tip from an informant across the border in Mexicali that a 1959 Ford station wagon coming through the border on the evening of September 22 was loaded with a large consignment of marihuana destined for an important Cuban trafficker in New Jersey. The agents prepared to play tag for the 3,300-mile drive right across the United States. Sure enough, the Ford with two Cubans came through the Calexico checkpoint on time and set off up Route 111 with four customs cars as discreet escorts in front and behind. At El Centro, fourteen miles up the road, the Ford pulled into a motel, and the two men rested there until noon the next day. Then they set off on a wandering journey around southern California. Eventually they drove through San Bernardino and struck off northeast on Interstate Route 15 into Utah and Wyoming, where they picked up Interstate 80 through to Chicago. Although they stopped only briefly to refuel, they maintained a leisurely pace, between forty-five and fifty miles an hour. The customs cars kept hard on their trail, all through Chicago and on to Cleveland. There the Cubans took a brief break, then zoomed onto the Pennsylvania Turnpike, where they picked up speed to a steady seventy. The customs cars were now hard put to keep up with them without revealing the trail. Refueling was difficult. The customs men dared not stop at the same service stations as the Cubans in their Ford, so they had to chase on ahead or drop behind to refuel, then race on to catch up. One customs car had a blowout at 105 m.p.h. On the New Jersey Turnpike the Ford pulled into a service area and the driver made a phone call for final clearance for the delivery. Fifty minutes later he pulled up outside a private house in a quiet suburb of North Bergen, New Jersey.

They were welcomed by Angel Roberto Millan, a Cuban well known as a major marihuana wholesaler in the New York area. Millan opened up his garage doors and guided the Ford inside. It was just 8:30 in the evening, almost exactly ninety-six hours since the long surveillance began in Calexico; it was the longest successful "convoy" ever achieved by the U.S. Customs. It was worth it. When the customs men moved in, they found half a ton of marihuana in neat kilo-sized bricks in a special compartment constructed below the bed of the station wagon. It was the second-largest haul ever made in the United States.

For years the great and convenient harvest of pot in Mexico kept concentrated cannabis resin from the Middle East or Asia at bay. However, now that the demand within America has grown so fast that marihuana has to be hauled around by the ton, smugglers are paying increasing attention to the more convenient resin. A bustling young Jewish gang is already hard at work shipping it over from Europe. It is headed by a young man, originally from Baltimore, who now finds it more convenient to live in Europe for the necessary reason that a warrant for his arrest for drug smuggling has been issued in the United States. He buys hashish through Beirut, packs it into false-bottomed trunks, and dispatches it by sea from Le Havre to Montreal, New York, and Baltimore. One of his couriers, a young woman, was picked up with sixty-six pounds in three trunks when she arrived in New York. But that setback was merely a passing inconvenience. The smugglers realize only too clearly that the marihuana, cannabis, hashish, or pot traffic—call it what you will—is definitely a growth business today.

V

Synthetic Drugs

During World War II the British, Germans, and Americans issued their front-line troops with Benzedrine tablets to be taken in moments of extreme physical or mental exhaustion to enable them to keep fighting. The soldiers called the pills "bennies." Today's teen-ager, battling simply against sleep at all-night or all-weekend parties, also gets his overdraft of energy from bennies or one of a host of new stimulants of the amphetamine group, which are known, in the language of the drug scene, as black bombers, french blues, nigger minstrels, dexes, jolly beans, or sweets. For those in search of tranquillity instead of stimulation, there are barbiturate pills, christened goof balls and sleepers. While to top it all off, anyone in search of hallucinations, who is not satisfied with the mild euphoria of cannabis, tries mescaline, psilocybin, or the most powerful of all mind-affecting drugs, LSD (short for d-lysergic acid diethylamide).

Where the natural powers of opium, cannabis, and cocaine left off, the chemist has taken over. All these drugs synthesized in the laboratory have, of course, medical applications. Most of the millions of little tablets flooding daily from pharmaceutical firms are prescribed by doctors. But what about the teen-ager who wants to stay awake for a weekend of fun? Or the long-distance truck driver with a load to deliver? What about the person who wants to escape from what he sees as a drab world around him into the explosion of color and feeling offered by an LSD experience? Unless he has a sympathetic doctor, he has to seek out black-market supplies.

The black markets of Europe and America are discreet, but not hard to find. Unlike the heroin business, where a peddler will probably have his regular little clientele among whom he pushes the drug, the market for pills is more casual, catering to thousands of individuals, who, once in a while, go in search of a few pills. The peddler may be a barman in a bowling alley in a Chicago suburb, a teen-ager gyrating to a Rolling Stones disk in a Soho discothèque just off Piccadilly Circus in London, or a student with a beard and shaggy sheepskin coat standing around on one of the drafty corners of Nikolai Platz in Copenhagen. The price is rarely beyond a teen-ager's pocket. In Britain pills cost from 1/- to 2/6 each, in Copenhagen around two shillings (two kroner), in America they are as little as ten cents each. LSD (known in the business as "zen") is expensive, at four to five dollars for a microscopic droplet on a cube of sugar, but as its users are likely to be seeking an experience only occasionally, this is no strain on their budget.

The low price does not immediately suggest an attractive prospect for highly organized selling or smuggling—until you calculate the odds involved. Pharmaceutical firms count pills by the 100,000; one shipment may comprise 500,000 pills. An illicit dealer in Copenhagen, for example, can purchase 100,000 Preludin tablets in Italy or Switzerland for about $2,600; back in Copenhagen he can resell those pills wholesale to a trafficker from Sweden for $6,500 or dispose of them in small quantities within the city itself for $25,000. The profits in illicit LSD are as mind-stretching as the drug itself. It is so powerful that the normal dose is a tiny droplet of 50 to 200 micrograms; this means that if not one drop is wasted, a single gram of LSD could supply 5,000 doses. In fact, it is not practical for the illicit distributor to parcel the drug out quite so exactly, but the black-market price, nevertheless, runs around $2,000 a gram wholesale, $12,500 retail. The chemist who makes up a batch of LSD could distribute it wholesale for well over two million dollars a kilo. The prospect of such profit must make the heart of any potential illicit drug trafficker beat faster.

Actual smuggling, of course, is not always called for. Unlike the opium poppy, cannabis, and the coca bush, pills (which have been bracketed under the official name of psychotropes, to distinguish them from narcotic drugs) are not dependent on the whim of any climate or soil. They can be made anywhere, and, as far as psychotropes are concerned, there is no need for illicit manufacture. The most immediate source of supply in any major American or European city is pills pilfered from pharmaceutical firms (some of whom apparently reckon on a three-percent loss on their production lines) or stolen from drugstores. In Britain, for example, the black market depends almost entirely on such sources. "It is more profitable to steal a tin of one thousand Drinamyl (purple hearts) tablets, which sell for two-and-six [thirty cents] each on the black market, than it is to pinch a case of whiskey," said a London detective, "and you sell the pills above their normal price, while stolen whiskey has to be sold below the market price." With such a bountiful internal supply, smuggling is isolated, although one haul of 150,000 Dexadrine tablets was picked up at the left-luggage office at Victoria Station in London in 1967; they were part of a consignment of 450,000 tablets smuggled in from Cyprus.

Europe's pill smuggling is, in fact, concentrated almost entirely in Denmark and Sweden. The manufacture and distribution of pills in Scandinavia has long been rigorously controlled, and the black markets of Stockholm, Göteborg, Malmö, and Copenhagen are unable to get their supplies locally. Moreover, these two countries have the most serious problem of drug addiction in Europe; Sweden has over 10,000 addicts, many of them on heroin, methedrine, or amphetamines. Although amphetamines are supposed to be taken orally, some Swedish addicts have been dissolving them and injecting the solution intravenously. Denmark has, according to a special report published early in 1969, 4,000 addicts, the majority of them dependent on amphetamines. Some of these addicts require an incredible 150 Preludin tablets *a day*.

The crossroads of the traffic to supply this Scandinavian

black market is Copenhagen, because it is the best communications center. Its airport handles nearly ten times as much international traffic as Stockholm's, making it harder for the customs to keep an eagle eye open for smugglers. Apart from the local Danish trade, ninety percent of the illegal drug supplies for Sweden pass this way. There is little customs control between the two countries, and Danes visiting Sweden do not even need a passport. It is all too easy for a Swedish trafficker to take the ferry across from Malmö with his car and load up with pills.

Much of the initial bargaining is remarkably open. Stroll any evening along Amager Torv, a pedestrian shopping plaza, in the heart of Copenhagen or through Nikolai Platz, just around the corner, and there are little huddles of young people with long hair, wearing anaraks, jeans, and sandals. One of them sits on a bench right outside the entrance to the Danish Foreign Ministry, casually strumming a guitar. (Ironically, the Danish government's official narcotics representatives to the United Nations Commission on Narcotic Drugs have their offices in this building, and the problem is, literally, on their doorstep.) It is here that pills and cannabis change hands in small quantities; here also that a trafficker from Sweden in search of 10,000 Preludin tablets will make his first contacts. Such large shipments, obviously, will not be handed over in the street, but from this initial contact he can move on to meet the wholesale dealers in one of half a dozen restaurants nearby.

It is a fairly informal business, although some of the dealers have been moving drugs on a vast scale. In May of 1968 the Copenhagen police arrested a group of eighteen pill smugglers, headed by an Austrian and a Swede, who were living in a rented house in Copenhagen. The police seized 100,000 Preludin tablets, plus five liters of amphetamine concentrate from which the gang could have made a further one million pills. The Swede escaped the initial Copenhagen raid, but was arrested a few days later by the Swedish police; he was carrying a further 100,000 pills. Their source of supply was a Swiss pharmaceutical firm near Lugano, which was, unofficially at least, prepared to sell to the black market.

Another Copenhagen dealer was an Italian living with a

Danish girl. His tactics were to phone a friend in Naples and ask him to line up perhaps 35,000 Preludin tablets. His Danish girl friend then flew to Naples with a false-bottomed suitcase to pick up the pills.

So far this illicit drug traffic has been in the hands of young people out to make a quick profit—but those profits are clearly large enough to tempt professional criminals. "What we are afraid of," said Detective Chief Inspector Gauguin (a grandson of the painter) of the Narcotics Division of the Danish Criminal Police, "is that some of our real criminals will see how easy it is to make money. The Swedes have just had a case in Stockholm where a gang of professionals were making pills illegally in Finland and smuggling them into Sweden. Some of the big fish here may be starting soon."

The Scandinavian countries, led by Sweden, have been most active in trying to persuade the International Narcotics Control Board and the Commission on Narcotic Drugs in Geneva to bring dangerous drugs under their supervisory umbrella by bracketing them with the narcotic drugs covered by the Single Convention (the international agreement on narcotic drugs). The Swedish delegate to the twenty-second session of the Commission on Narcotic Drugs, which met in Geneva in January, 1968, argued, "The problem of the abuse of amphetamines is so serious it requires priority. Control of these drugs should be applied immediately under the Single Convention."

However, many other governments, including those of France, the United States, and Great Britain, feel that the Single Convention is tailored too specifically to the problem of narcotic drugs and a much more effective policy is to draft a new international convention on psychotropic substances and LSD. During 1968 the U.N. Commission on Narcotic Drugs worked on proposals for a new convention, which were discussed by the commission members at their annual meeting in Geneva in January, 1969, and sent to their respective governments for approval. At that meeting a resolution also was adopted calling on governments to place amphetamines under the same control as those applied to narcotic drugs under the Single Convention, purely as an interim measure, until the new international convention can be ratified. In recommending this intermediary step, the commission said, "Increasing abuse of these stimulants constitutes a grave danger for the health of the individual and for society. Immediate action is needed to combat this threat to mankind."

The rising tide of pills has also led to new policies at national levels. In the United States, which along with Sweden and Denmark is the main target of the illicit pill traffic, the Bureau of Drug Abuse Control of the Department of Health, Education and Welfare was long responsible for keeping a watchful eye on the movement of dangerous drugs. Then in May, 1968, this bureau was merged with the old Federal Narcotics Bureau (which had previously been under the U.S. Treasury Department) to form the Bureau of Narcotics and Dangerous Drugs under the wing of the Department of Justice in Washington, D.C. This was a logical move, since many of the heroin and marihuana traffickers shuttling illicit consignments over the border from Mexico also handle an extensive trade in pills. The previous year the U.S. Customs, finding that its seizures of dangerous drugs were soaring, started keeping a more accurate track of its arrests and hauls of dangerous drugs. In the first year of this new survey, 1967–68, they made 525 seizures of over 3,900,000 pills.

The main artery through which the pills enter the United States is that same two-thousand-mile-long border between Mexico and California that sees every other kind of smuggling opportunism. These contraband pills come from two sources: first, from Mexican pharmaceutical firms; and second, from U.S. supplies which are exported under license to Mexico and then smuggled back.

There are several sophisticated variations of this technique, whereby the pills appear to leave the United States and then return but in fact never leave the country. The simplest method is for a Tijuana drugstore owner to telephone an American wholesale drug house and order, say, 500,000 Dexadrine tablets. The tablets will be consigned to him at a bonded warehouse just on the American side of the border. He drives across, takes delivery at the bonded warehouse, signs the right forms to say the drugs are being exported from the United States to Mexico, and drives off. Before going back across the border, he delivers the pills to his American client.

A variation on this theme came up in 1967, when a shipment of two million amphetamine tablets destined for export was found to consist simply of bags of dried cement thinly topped with aspirin tablets. The amphetamine tablets had been diverted into the illicit market without bothering to send them abroad first.

Anyone not up to such subterfuge can simply drive down into Mexico and pick up his supplies. Most of the towns on the Mexican side of the border have pharmacies which are only too happy to oblige. In Tijuana the asking price is usually ten dollars for 100 Benzedrine pills; but wholesale the price is as low as five dollars a thousand. Two brothers who run a pharmacy in Piedras Negras, just across the border from Eagle Pass, Texas, think nothing of fulfilling an order for half a million bennies delivered to Eagle Pass or San Antonio, which would be enough to keep all the truck drivers in America awake for a year. Most of the pills cross the border concealed in cars, but light planes are also frequently used. One light plane, flown by the Los Angeles dealers, led the authorities on a wild chase all over southern California in May, 1967. The pill purchasers, Frederick Addi and Gregory Buck, had flown down to Rosarito Beach in Baja California, Mexico, to pick up a mixed load of amphetamine and barbiturate tablets. When they took off again from Rosarito Beach without filing a flight plan, customs received a tip-off; they immediately began watching all local airports in southern California. Sure enough, the plane came in to land at San Fernando airport in the northern suburbs of Los Angeles, but as they taxied to a halt, the smugglers saw police on duty. They turned the plane around, raced back to the runway, and took off, while police and customs cars tried desperately to drive through traffic and keep them in sight. Ten minutes later the plane landed at Van Nuys airport, a few miles to the west. The two men leaped out and began throwing the bags of pills into Addi's sports car. They could not fit them all in, so they jumped in the car and drove off to Addi's apartment near the airport. There they did not even wait to open the door; they threw the suitcases of pills straight through the plate-glass living-room window, hopped back in the car, and raced back for the rest. Police caught up with them just as they stacked the last of the 585,000 pills into the car. They admitted later they had paid a mere $7,000 for the consignment in Rosarito, but expected to gross $116,000 in sales in Los Angeles.

At least pills in such quantity are fairly hefty to move around; LSD, on the other hand, is so concentrated that one man can carry a million dollars' worth as easily as his after-shave lotion. Indeed, a smuggler leaving London airport for New York in October, 1967, was effectively doing just that. He had ten grams of LSD worth over $125,000 retail concealed in three contraceptives packed into a tin of Yardley's talcum powder. The arrest of this courier, Alexander Davison, off on an LSD sales trip to the United States, gave Scotland Yard's drug squad a strong lead to an illicit LSD laboratory in London. A month later they arrested a chemist, Victor James Kapur, and an antique dealer, Harry Nathan, on charges of making LSD at a laboratory at New North Road, in Islington, London. When Kapur was arrested he had in his Jaguar enough packets of ergotoxine, the essential ingredient of LSD, to make over $400,000 worth of the drug. The Kapur case was the first of three major seizures made by the Yard over a period of fifteen months from November, 1967, to January, 1969, which revealed London as a key manufacturing city for LSD. The market for this LSD is, however, America. And it is the prospect of rich profits in America, where far more young people use the drug occasionally than in Britain or Europe, that has tempted a number of Europeans, almost all without prior criminal record, to move into the illicit manufacture of LSD. The smuggling of the drug is very new. The first arrest for smuggling it into the United States was in April, 1963, when two young men were arrested in San Francisco delivering three pints of LSD solution to an undercover agent of the U.S. Food and Drug Administration. They claimed that it had been smuggled in from Israel. But it is the London cases that demonstrate most clearly how Europe is being drawn into the illicit traffic.

The advantage (from the illegal point of view) about LSD is

that it can be made and marketed by a small team. Only two or three people are needed. First, a good chemist is crucial; second, there must be a good salesman, ideally with good connections in the United States, to market the drug; and someone has to put up the necessary cash (this could, of course, always be the chemist or the salesman). It costs between five and ten thousand dollars to get an illicit laboratory started—equipment taking two-thirds of this outlay and the ingredients the other third. The ergotoxine is expensive, and the basic chemicals for one gram of LSD cost about $540. There is also the additional cost of travel to the United States to market the drug. No one has yet determined the exact sources of finance for the London laboratories—there appears to be no connection among the three raided—but there are strong indications that at least one of them was backed by American money. When the laboratory in Cable Street, Stepney, was searched in January, 1969, thirteen thousand dollars in American currency was recovered. The financing of the Kapur laboratory in Islington was more obscure. Kapur was buying his chemicals in Hamburg, where the ergotoxine, which is primarily produced in Hungary and Czechoslovakia, is more easily available than in Britain or the United States. He was paying for it with money credited to him at the American Express office in Hamburg by a Swiss bank. The usual wall of silence from the Swiss bank prevented inquiries into the origin of this money.

But it has been clearly established that all three laboratories were selling, or at least were aiming to sell, on the American market. In each instance either a courier has been caught en route or investigations into the movements of the organizers have confirmed the link. The key man charged in connection with the raid on the second laboratory had just returned a couple of weeks earlier from a marketing trip to New York, San Francisco, and Toronto when he was arrested in April, 1968. (He did not wait around to stand trial, but jumped bail and vanished.)

The European demand for LSD is too scattered to warrant the attention of such an organized team out to make large profits. The small amounts of illicit LSD available on the black market in London, Stockholm, and Frankfurt have mostly been distributed casually through students getting a little bit for their friends. The London laboratories have all been planning on a much grander scale. The largest seizure, in January, 1969, involved eighteen jars, several of them still full of the basic LSD materials, the others bearing traces. The police estimated that if all jars were originally full they would have enabled the laboratory to make enough LSD for five million doses. This is the frightening point about LSD: A little can go such a long way. The first two laboratories seized in London had each made about ninety grams of the drug before they were detected. Yet even ninety grams is enough for 450,000 doses and yields a net profit of $110,000 wholesale.

Without going too deeply into the moral issues raised by LSD, there is little doubt that if the drug is taken without medical supervision it *can* have extremely alarming and dangerous effects on people who may already be on the fringes of nervous disorders. The problem raised by this emerging illicit international traffic in LSD is that a mere half-dozen unscrupulous individuals, tempted by the profits to be made, can manufacture enough LSD to keep everyone under thirty in the United States on a permanent "trip." And inevitably when such handsome rewards are involved, organized crime finds it hard to resist such a rich bait. Their control of the heroin traffic is quite enough of a worry without handing them another field of rich reward in LSD.

TWO

Arms and the Man

VI

The Gunrunners

Arms dealers fight shy of journalists, who tend to dip their pens in a pool of blood when they write about the arms traffic. It all comes out red. The fact that 5,000 people a year die through accidents with electric fires in their own homes is ignored, but if someone sells a few guns and twelve people die, it's all over the papers.

—London arms dealer

Gunrunning is a pretty cold-blooded business. It can lead only to death, but in conversation with a gunrunner that thought hardly ever comes up. He is always far too busy explaining how he "bought" an ambassador last week to provide him with fraudulent end-use documents for a consignment of Browning machine guns and Mauser rifles or recalling his encounter with the buyer for Congo rebels who said, "*Je suis un patriote,* so add on only one hundred percent to the invoice as my commission." Although the gunrunners may try to make it out as a life of derring-do, it is in fact a seedy business, carried on mainly in bars or hotel bedrooms, selling second-hand arms to second-string nations.

Everyone says, of course, that it is not like it used to be in the good old days and talks nostalgically of Sir Basil Zaharoff, the highly secretive international arms salesman who was the confidant of Lloyd George and Clemenceau in World War I, and of Siegfried Wallner, an elderly boulevardier complete with monocle and swordstick who specialized in arms-buying for South America. "It's got dirty and messy recently," lamented a gunrunner deeply involved in ferrying arms to Nigeria. "It used to be a tight-knit group like the Mafia or Masons, run by chaps with a wife and family—not that they were angels. It was cutthroat competition, but once a deal was fixed, we left each other alone. Now it's young charlatans who cut each other's throats after a deal is fixed; racketeers in the true sense."

The gunrunner is very much a breed on his own. Unlike the conventional smuggler, whose task, whether he is running heroin or diamonds, is simply to outwit the authorities for his own profit, the gunrunner, while highly concerned with profit, is also frequently an undercover agent of a government's political interest. The arms traffic almost invariably goes hand in hand with politics. As a London dealer explained, "The amount of purely illicit arms dealing carried on without government connivance for political purposes is very small." Another put it more bluntly: "What are guns for except to change the political situation in a given area?"

Not all arms traffic, of course, calls for the gunrunner's sleight of hand. Many international arms deals, whether arranged directly between governments or by reputable dealers like Interarmco, are perfectly open and above board. Thus Israel will buy Mystère jets from France, Turkey will receive tanks from the United States under a NATO agreement, and Britain gets Polaris missiles from the United States. Similarly, a firm like Interarmco may act as a broker between the Venezuelans, who are anxious to equip their air force with jets, and the Swedes, who are phasing out some of their jet fighters and are looking for a buyer. These transactions may be the subject of political criticism from opponents at home and abroad, but they are not hidden. Indeed it would be foolish to imagine that any major nation could equip its forces in total secrecy by under-the-counter deals.

But there is a no-man's-land between the official arms shipment, openly sanctioned by governments, and straight gunrunning which provides a convenient leeway for a government, which may not want it openly known it is supplying arms to another country, to ensure that the necessary weapons in fact get through. This no-man's-land of "gray" arms transactions tagged with large political labels is a happy hunting ground for the gunrunner, acting unofficially and discreetly as an instrument of someone's foreign policy. His territory is every political cockpit from Africa to the Middle East and from the Far East to Latin America. In these areas of turmoil there is rarely a nation or guerrilla band, however poor, however much an outcast, that cannot find some foreign government to champion its cause by conniving in a discreet supply of arms. If the British and Americans will not oblige, perhaps the French will; if the French will not play, then they can try the Russians or the Chinese. The arms will not come prettily tied in pink ribbon; more likely they will be labeled agricultural machinery or refrigerator parts; they will not be delivered by ships or planes flying the flag of the contributing nation; and the big power may deny in the face of all criticism that it is supplying arms or that it has ever heard of the country or guerrillas at issue. In this arena the gunrunner comes into his own, wheeling and dealing. As one of its exponents put it aptly, "Gunrunning rolls on the ball bearings of bribery."

The real skill of the gunrunning racket is to judge just how much manipulation governments will tolerate and what is and is not illegal. Under peaceful conditions there is rarely much call for the gunrunner; any nation in search of arms can usually obtain them either by direct contact with another government or through one of the twenty main international dealers. The intrigue really starts when it becomes clear that hostilities are about to break out in a particular area or once the first shot is fired. Governments then become hypersensitive about their own international arms commitments and at granting export licenses to authorized arms dealers. So the gunrunner comes into his own.

The pressures of war, with troops at the front burning up ammunition by the minute, can quickly corner a beleaguered nation into paying any price to keep precious supplies coming. The gunrunners know it and charge appropriate prices. European arms dealers have scalped both Nigeria and Biafra unmercifully since that civil war broke out. Their price for rifles virtually doubled in six months. A Biafran agent shopping for arms in London paid a reported £145,000 ($350,000) in 1968 for three former Royal Navy torpedo boats which had been sold off as surplus for £10,000 ($24,000) a few years previously. This latter deal, however, was rather exceptional. The gunrunners' trading is normally limited to light equipment—rifles, machine guns, mortars, bazookas, and ammunition. However good his connections, he is rarely in a position to order up a squadron of jet fighters, a tank corps, or an obsolete destroyer. Governments are most particular about the disposal of that kind of hardware, and there can be no secret about its origin. If Nigeria suddenly has an air force equipped with Ilyushin bombers, there can be no doubt that they came from Russia; but a batch of 2,000 Mauser rifles could have come from almost anywhere. Thus the gunrunner's job is to provide the bread-and-butter equipment for an army, although he may charge jam prices.

Africa, even more than the Middle East, has been the gunrunners' great market for almost a decade. First the long-drawn-out civil war in the Congo, then the African guerrilla campaigns against Angola, Mozambique, and Rhodesia, and finally the tragic Nigeria-Biafra conflict created a nonstop demand for weapons which could not pass through conventional channels.

The shopping center for these arms for Africa and the Middle East is Europe, while the United States is the prime source of supply for Latin America.

Most of the gunrunners have some kind of military background, but they find that almost more important than thorough knowledge of weapons is an understanding of the psychology of their clients, and in this the colonial past of Africa has been most important. Thus the Belgian arms dealer feels an affinity for the former Belgian Congo, the French dealer for the former colonies of Gabon or the Ivory Coast, the British for Ghana or Nigeria. Not only is there no language barrier, but both sides know the other's peculiarities and weaknesses. "I always wear my regimental tie when I'm in Nigeria," said a British dealer, "and that gives them an idea of who they are dealing with." Although that may not appear the best of credentials, it is better than, say, an American whose background would be totally unknown. The Nigerians have years of experience of British officers and can judge them accordingly. In the same vein, most European dealers leave South America strictly to the Americans. "That is their sphere of influence and understanding," explained a European dealer. "I don't know South America, and I wouldn't dream of trying to sell guns there." Anyway, he is not short of clients in his own arena.

Immediately after World War II there was a surfeit of unwanted arms in Europe; rifles and small arms were almost given away. Today there is little World War II equipment floating around the second-hand market, but as NATO forces are constantly modernizing and discarding their equipment, there has never been any real shortage of weapons. Most European forces, for example, calculate they need four rifles per man. Thus, if the West German Army adopts a new rifle, it unburdens itself of 100,000 or more second-hand obsolete ones onto the market. Since most African nations calculate their needs at one and one-half rifles per man, there are plenty to go around.

The only real shortage now is of ammunition. During peacetime the European arms factories find little call for ammunition from their own forces, and so production lines are cut back to a minimum. A sudden demand for ammunition for a war in Africa or the Middle East can now send gunrunners ferreting into every possible supply dump—particularly for ammunition for some of the more dated equipment that may have been phased out completely by European forces.

The hub of the arms traffic is Brussels, where a nightclub in the Rue de Char et Pain has earned itself the informal nickname throughout Europe, Africa, and the Middle East of the "Gun Bourse." Here an African or Arab in search of arms knows he can make his first contact with a European arms smuggler. The Belgians are fairly obliging in their export licenses, so there is normally no problem in completing the deal. Belgium, in fact, is a convenient entrepôt for many arms shipments. "I had one order for sixty thousand rifles for Saudi Arabia," recalled a London gunrunner, who is a regular commuter to Brussels, "but the British government wouldn't let me send them, so I arranged for them to be sent to Belgium, and they were forwarded from there."

The first priority in most gunrunning operations is to fix the necessary documentation, particularly an end-use certificate, issued by the receiving country, confirming the order of the arms and stating they will not be passed on to any other nation. "And that," said the London gunrunner, "means buying yourself an ambassador so you can get your end-use certificates."

This end-use certificate is the passport of an arms consignment; without it the American or European governments will not consider granting the necessary export permit. The certificate merely confirms that country A has indeed ordered 10,000 Mauser rifles or fifty bazookas and seventy-five .762-caliber machine guns, which is no problem if the arms really are destined for country A, but not so simple if they are really bound for country B. Thus a friendly ambassador, who in turn has a good friend in the Ministry of Defense of his home country, can be all-important. This paperwork can be costly. "I had one order for ten thousand rifles," a London smuggler recounted, "which cost me thirty-three dollars each just for paperwork. I bought them for eighty-seven dollars each, but had to sell them for one hundred and twenty each to cover the end-use certificate."

The government accepting the end-use certificate is not necessarily fooled, but it helps to preserve the political niceties, and if someone whips up a storm later, the government can declare, hand on heart, that they approved the arms shipment only to country A; it is not their fault if the arms were reconsigned without delay. It makes a good alibi.

The right documents are one priority; the other is transportation. Diamonds, gold, watches, or narcotics can all be carried by a lone courier beneath his shirt. The gunrunner, however, is not manipulating goods by the ounce but by the ton. As one of them put it, "You can't carry arms in a briefcase." One rifle weighs around ten pounds; 500 rifles weigh 5,000 pounds, which is the payload of a DC-3. A million rounds of small-arms ammunition weighs thirty tons and calls for three or four Constellations or Britannias, which cost at least $12,000 each to charter for a flight from Europe to Africa or the Middle East.

The pilots on these gunrunning flights are an odd bunch. All of them are in it for the money—but it may be money to have a good time with booze and girls or money to enable them to break out and settle down with a wife and family. "I've got a wife and five kids, and all I'm after is the down payment for a house," said one pilot ferrying arms to Biafra. Some of them do two or three trips a year just for the excitement and $5,000 tax-free a time. "Many of my chaps," explained a gunrunner just in from Brussels, "are ex-pilots who have normal jobs as salesmen or in insurance. But they like to go off once in a while for a week and come back with a couple of thousand pounds in their pocket. They just tell their wives they've gone off on a business trip and will be back on Monday." Not all return. They are mostly flying ancient, metal-fatigued planes with worn-out engines. An American Negro mercenary pilot, with his wife, who happened to have gone along for the ride, were killed in Biafra in August, 1968, when their aged Constellation flopped into the forest just short of a jungle airstrip. Many others have had lucky escapes after engine burn-outs or forced landings.

An American international arms smuggler who was heavily embroiled in the Biafran struggle for over a year was lucky to get out of the wreckage of a Royal Air Burundi DC-4 which crashed with a load of arms in Cameroun in October, 1967, after a flight which has become something of a classic saga in recent gunrunning. The gunrunner had a contract with a French arms dealer to ferry seven tons of sub-machine guns from Holland to eastern Nigeria. The consignment called for four trips in a DC-4, for which the gunrunner was reportedly paid $14,000 a trip. His four-engined DC-4 took off from Rotterdam with a flight plan filed for Birmingham just to confuse the Dutch authorities. Over Birmingham he radioed the tower that he had been ordered by his company to divert to Majorca and was proceeding there directly. He flew to Palma, refueled, and headed on south to Hassi-Messaoud in Algeria. After refueling again, he took off on the long flight over the Sahara to Fort Lamy, the capital of Chad, on the eastern border of Nigeria. But the plane ran out of gas after a bumpy fourteen-hour flight across the Sahara, and the gunrunner attempted a pancake landing on a marshy riverbank. The aircraft broke into four sections as it slithered to a stop, but he stepped out, suffering only from mild concussion.

Aircraft are the only way to deliver arms in a hurry or to a beleaguered force, but it is far cheaper and easier to deliver them by sea when practicable. This seaborne gun traffic received an unexpected bonus in 1967 through the closing of the Suez Canal following the Arab-Israeli war. "Now the canal is closed, many more ships are going around Africa," explained a gunrunner to Nigeria, "which is most convenient for those of us with deliveries to make in West Africa. It's important that the country where the ship is officially going is roughly in the same direction as the country where it stops unofficially en route. But a voyage around Africa allows for all kinds of handy deviations."

The gunrunning ships are aging tramps sailing under flags of convenience; their charter rates to gunrunners are, understandably, above the conventional market rate. Although most of them can steam along at only a sluggish eleven or twelve knots, the gunrunner is always careful to charter tramps with their own derricks, so that he can unload his cargo into barges. The gunrunning ship is more likely to anchor off a mangrove swamp than in a modern port equipped with cranes.

In the spring of 1969 one gunrunner was operating an unpretentious fleet of three tramps to West Africa. The oldest vessel was a creaky 9,000-ton freighter built in 1948 and flying the Liberian flag; normally it cost $1,140 a day on a time charter of a year, but the gunrunner was paying a $200-a-day premium for his particular cargo. The second vessel was a 9,300-ton Panamanian freighter built in 1952 costing $1,260 a day for normal cargo and around $1,500 for arms. The fleet was rounded out with a Greek-registered freighter of 5,600 tons at $1,250 a day, again with a $200 premium. "Loyalty," said the gunrunner, reviewing his little armada, "costs money."

But given these freighters at his disposal, he could at least start to move arms on the scale demanded by modern warfare.

The volume—and cost—of arms even for a battalion of five hundred mercenaries or guerrillas is staggering. The following was one gunrunner's assessment of their requirements, together with the prices he would charge, exclusive of the cost of transportation, in 1969. "Payoffs," he noted, "are added in these prices."

750 automatic rifles @ $250 each	$ 187,500
100,000 rounds of ammunition per rifle @ $140 per thousand rounds	10,500,000
150 .762-caliber machine guns @ $1,200 each	180,000
250,000 rounds of ammunition for each machine gun @ $140 per thousand rounds	5,250,000
75 light mortars @ $2,400 each	180,000
1,000 mortar bombs per mortar @ $75 each	5,625,000
150 bazookas @ $1,000 each	150,000
500 grenades per bazooka at $48 per round	3,600,000
150 sub-machine guns @ $70 each	10,500
100,000 rounds ammunition for each @ $48 per thousand	72,000
Five light armored cars @ $5,000 each	25,000
Fifty trucks and half-tracks for troops @ $2,500 each	125,000
100 trucks for ammunition, spares, etc., @ $2,000 each	200,000
plus 10% for spares	2,613,450
	$28,747,950

This armory—albeit a very extensive one—for just five hundred men would weigh almost 4,000 tons, a full cargo for a sizable freighter.

Obviously every unit is not so thoroughly equipped or well supplied, but this breakdown does give a measure of the gunrunner's scale of operations. In a struggle such as the one between Nigeria and Biafra, with many thousands of men involved on each side, this business is enormously increased.

Throughout the 1960's Africa has been the gunrunner's bread and butter. The "wind of change" ushered in, unfortunately, an era of turmoil out of which the unscrupulous could make a great deal of capital. First it was the Congo, then Angola, then the Nigerian civil war.

During the Congo strife the gunrunner with a nose for profits headed direct for Katanga, the richest province of the Congo, and made a deal with Moise Tshombe. The advantage of this alliance was that Katanga embraced the Congo's rich diamond fields, so that payment for the arms was assured. From the moment of Congo independence in 1960 more than half the diamond production began to pass through illicit channels (see Chapter 8). By good fortune, from the gunrunning standpoint, many of these diamonds mined illicitly were snapped up by Belgian diamond dealers from Antwerp, who stationed their buying agents at Brazzaville and in Burundi to tap the outflow of stones. With Belgium also involved as the crossroads of the European arms scene, it made for happy cooperation.

The prospect of profits to be made in the Congo acted like a whirlwind, sucking in riffraff from all over Europe and America. An American, appropriately named John Paul Wilde, was caught trying to smuggle four B-26 bombers out of the United States bound for the Congo. Another American set up shop as a dealer in Khartoum, where the airport often resembled an arms-supply dump.

Even after Tshombe won control of the whole Congo, achieving international recognition so that he was able to negotiate directly with governments for arms, he did not neglect his old gunrunning friends. He continued to pass them business just to keep them happy in case of future, less easy times. As the Congo itself settled down to some semblance of order in the late 1960's, the gunrunners still found plenty of business around its fringes among the African liberation movements operating against the Portuguese in Angola and Mozambique. Here, as in the Congo, the arms were paid for almost exclusively with rough diamonds.

A European dealer who met the leader of the African Liberation Front for Mozambique when he was on an arms-shopping expedition to Europe in 1968 was offered a handful of rough diamonds in a hotel room in Stockholm. He declined them on the ground that, although he could judge a rifle with only half an eye open, he knew nothing of diamonds. He advised the African to sell his diamonds in Antwerp and come back with the cash—which he did.

These liberation fronts, by some artful double-dealing, succeeded in siphoning off several shipments of arms which the Portuguese were sending by sea to Biafra in the early days of the Nigerian civil war. The Portuguese, needless to say, were highly incensed to find that shiploads of weapons being dispatched to West Africa were ending up being used against their own troops in Angola and Mozambique.

Yet in the shambles of the Nigeria-Biafra struggle, no amount of treachery should come as a surprise. According to gunrunners who have participated in the Congo and Nigeria, the Congo arms traffic was relatively straightforward. European governments were officially against giving permits for arms to be exported to the Congo, but manipulation of end-use papers could be arranged quite cheaply. With the Nigerian war, however, both the United States and the European powers are much more sensitive about the illicit arms traffic, and controls are strictly applied. End-use certificates signed by ambassadors are treated with considerable skepticism, and the necessary export papers are often not forthcoming unless the ambassador or his military attaché can answer questions satisfactorily at a personal interview. "This," says one of the leading gun suppliers for the Nigerian federal government, "makes things very expensive. It is one thing for an ambassador or a military attaché to sign an end-use paper; it is quite another if he has to go to the Foreign Office in person to explain the contract. If he will do that at all, you have to pay heavily."

This is the problem nourished by an effective arms embargo. The better the official embargo works, the more the country in need of arms has to plunge deeper into the mire of the black markets. The Nigerians have received large consignments of Russian military equipment for free, but this has chiefly been in the form of aircraft and heavy equipment; they have been forced to shop around every back alley of the illicit market for small arms and ammunition. Their dilemma is heightened by the fact that much of their equipment is outdated, and both ammunition and spares are hard to come by. "I have an order for ten million rounds of .30 Browning ammunition," said an arms smuggler in London, "but I can't find any. It isn't made anymore. The only way to get it is to persuade an arms factory to start up a special production line."

As a result of this Nigerian dragnet for arms, three executives in the Swiss armaments firm Oerlikon Buehrle were charged with obtaining false end-use documents to facilitate the export of arms to Nigeria. Under Swiss law, armaments may be exported only to countries which are not at war and are not situated in an area where hostilities are likely to break out. Government export permits are granted only when there is proof that the consignments do not violate this embargo, and assurances are given that the buyer will not reexport to countries on the embargo list. The Oerlikon Buehrle inquiry, touched off by persistent reports that the federal Nigerians were using Swiss antiaircraft guns, revealed a network of subterfuge involving not only Nigeria, but six nations on the banned list. The Nigerians had received $1,400,000 of arms illegally, mainly antiaircraft guns made and paid for by the Germans at the end of World War II but never delivered before the German collapse. All had been shipped out to Nigeria with false documents. Moreover, Oerlikon had even sent two technicians to Nigeria to train the federal forces in the use of these guns.

Other false end-use certificates had been presented to the Swiss authorities to secure export licenses for 12.5 million dollars of arms for South Africa, over four million dollars in arms to Israel, 1.5 million dollars to Egypt (so Oerlikon had supplied both sides in the Arab-Israeli conflict), with smaller amounts also to Saudi Arabia and Lebanon.

When the whole plot was exposed, the Swiss authorities alleged that a further 2.5 million dollars of fraudulent orders were already in the pipeline. Although this messy affair was eventually cleared up, the Swiss authorities themselves did not escape considerable criticism that they had been turning a blind eye to this illicit traffic for over a year, until persistent press reports and complaints filed by Swiss officials engaged in relief work in Nigeria made it impossible to ignore it any longer.

The Oerlikon Buehrle affair also demonstrated the dilemma facing an arms firm in a small neutral country; it cannot hope to make a profit on the minimal demands of Switzerland's citizen army, so it has to export. And who needs its exports most urgently? A nation at war. But such export is forbidden. It is understandable, although not forgivable, if the arms maker starts searching for loopholes in the law.

The Biafrans, on the other side of this bitter civil war, have been equally dependent on arms from any source. Initially their main supply line was through Portugal. The Portuguese government gave unofficial blessing to the Biafran stand, and an American gunrunner, operating out of Room 228 at the Hotel Tivoli in Lisbon, helped with the arrangements. Every night his Constellations loaded with arms and other supplies took off from Lisbon on a wearying ten-hour flight to Bissau in Portuguese Guinea, then on to São Tomé, the slip of a Portuguese island right on the equator, two hundred miles off the Nigerian coast. After refueling and a change of pilots, they ran the gauntlet of flak over the federal Nigerian positions into besieged Biafra, trying to pinpoint in the dark the tiny airstrips, with such reassuring names as Annabelle, carved out of the jungle and lit by the guttering flame of kerosene lamps. It was a hair-raising lifeline that just kept the Biafrans fighting.

Then, in the autumn of 1968 the American and the Biafrans fell out, reportedly because payments for the arms and airlift fell behind. For a few weeks it seemed that Biafra could not hold on. Gunrunners are rarely sympathetic to a cause when the kitty is empty.

Yet it was not over. Suddenly the African night was alive again with the droning of the engines of a squadron of four DC-4's, three DC-3's, and a single Constellation skimming in over the trees from Libreville, the capital of the former French colony of Gabon. This airlift, flown by an assortment of ex-RAF and French pilots, humped in a weird grab bag of arms and ammunition, which appeared to include equipment from every country in Europe, including Hungary and Czechoslovakia. The guiding hand behind this unexpected build-up of arms was France—although the French government denied any kind of complicity. But, as a gunrunner said, "It's amazing how easy the French have suddenly become over end-use certificates. They are giving them away free." And this, of course, is a convenient way of ensuring that Biafra gets its guns. General de Gaulle's staff did not themselves have to rush around buying up arms and shipping them to Biafra; they just made it easy for the professional gunrunner to get the right documents. This kind of assistance is not given, of course, out of the kindness of a Frenchman's heart; Biafra has valuable reserves of oil. If she were to survive as an independent nation, she would have to remember the French benevolence when oil supplies started flowing again. Guns are the tools of political interest.

And so they are in the Middle East. Here, of course, both the Arabs and the Israelis have been able to achieve their basic arms build-up through direct contracts with other governments. The gunrunner's role has been twofold: first, to fill in odd gaps for spares or supplies not available through conventional sources, and second, to equip the little private armies of wealthy sheiks on the Arabian Gulf and the guerrilla forces everywhere from Kurdistan in the north to the Yemen and Aden in the south.

The gunrunners helped get the Israelis out of a dilemma with their mortars. The mortar, apparently, is a temperamental bit of metal. Although most of them are made to a standard 81 millimeters and should, therefore, fire all 81-mm. mortar bombs, it does not work quite like that. American 81-mm. bombs will plop off obligingly from any old mortar, whether it was made in the United States, Britain, West Germany, or Czechoslovakia. Mortar bombs made in Eastern Europe, however, will fire only from Communist-made mortars, because of some subtle shaping of their firing pin. The Israelis had an international assortment of mortars which they were most anxious should be supplied entirely with American bombs, which would not discriminate in the heat of battle against the nationality of any particular mortar and refuse to go off. American bombs, however, were in short supply; they were all needed by the Americans themselves for

Vietnam. An enterprising gunrunner soon solved that one: get the mortar bombs for Israel from Vietnam.

The pilfering of American military equipment in South Vietnam has been one of the by-products of the build-up of forces there and has reached enormous proportions in everything from motor fuel to rifles and mortar bombs. American M-16 rifles stolen from Vietnam have turned up in every corner of Southeast Asia and even as far away as Algeria. Much of this stolen equipment filters out over the borders of Vietnam to Pakse or Vientiane in Laos and to Phnom Penh in Cambodia. The story in Southeast Asia is that the Israeli need for United States 81-mm. mortar bombs was well satisfied in Phnom Penh, and the bombs were flown into Tel Aviv a few days before the six-day war.

Indeed the airways between Southeast Asia and the Middle East appear to have been especially busy in May and early June of 1967. A cargo plane from one Arab airline made an overnight stop at Singapore the week before the war with a load of what were euphemistically called 1,100 kilos of cotton belt webbing; in fact it was a shipment of Chinese arms, en route from Hong Kong to Beirut.

The growth of El Fateh and the Popular Front for the Liberation of Palestine, both of them guerrilla forces in the Arab states bordering Israel, has also given the gunrunner a new batch of clients. These guerrillas obtain part of their supplies unofficially from their own governments, but they have been scouting for other weapons through the "Gun Bourse" nightclub in Brussels. The arms have been ferried from Europe to the Middle East in some strange disguises. Most of the illicit shipments are organized by an important sheik in Jordan. They have ranged from a consignment of 10,000 9-mm. pistols landed in the desert at dawn near the Gulf of Aqaba by a DC-6 chartered in Europe, to a shipment of Sten guns packaged in crates labeled "Crystal Chandeliers," which were landed at Aqaba. The dockers landing the crates were being told, "Be careful, be careful, they contain glass. The chandeliers are for a very important person." All went well until one of the crates broke open and a shower of Sten guns tumbled onto the quayside. Another sheik tried to bring in two hundred pistols in two suitcases labeled as part of the luggage traveling with an English nanny working in Jordan. A sharp-eyed customs man, realizing that the cases were far too heavy to contain the belongings of a frail English nanny, ordered them to be opened.

Any arms smuggler is advised to make sure that prior "arrangements" with customs have been made. One British gun-runner had a narrow escape when he traveled to Beirut to watch over the safe delivery of twenty-five bazookas and five hundred rounds of ammunition. He was supplying these, through a middleman in Beirut, to a sheik from the Arabian Gulf. The Beirut agent assured him everything was fixed at the customs and that the sheik himself was flying to Beirut to pick up the weapons. The arms arrived at Beirut in late afternoon and were offloaded in crates and taken to the customs shed. "No more worries," the gunrunner was assured. "Let's join the sheik and go to the Casino for a party." Late in the evening, when the party was in full swing, a young Arab came rushing up to the sheik's table and said a few hasty words to the Beirut agent. The British gunrunner, understanding the gist of the heated Arabic conversation, realized that the customs were not as amenable as had been supposed. Down at the customs house someone was asking embarrassing questions about the bazookas. Politely he told his hosts he must go to the men's room. Once away from the table, he jumped in a cab, rushed to his hotel, grabbed his bag, and checked out. "I was fairly tight, but I got to the airport and said, 'When's the next plane?'They asked 'To where?' I said, 'To anywhere.' The chap said, 'There's an Air India flight to Rome on the tarmac.' I put down a fifty-dollar bill and said, 'Get me on it.' Which he did. Everyone else was arrested in the Casino."

One arms pipeline to the Middle East is not strictly political, although ultimately the weapons do end up being used for political purposes. Initially, however, it is a straightforward trade—guns for Turkish morphine base in the illicit heroin traffic (see Chapter 2). The swap takes place in Istanbul, after the guns have been smuggled overland across Europe from France and West Germany. This trail begins in the industrial cities of the Ruhr—Frankfurt, Mannheim, Düsseldorf, and Cologne. The gunrunners either steal or hire a large car, normally a Mercedes SL250, which has a good market value at the end of the line in Turkey. The cars are driven to Lyons, where a garage specializes in respraying them a different color and putting in special compartments for the arms. The arms, usually pistols, rifles, and ammunition, are purchased through the "Gun Bourse" nightclub in Brussels and brought down to Lyons to be concealed in the car. Then it sets off for Istanbul either by way of Switzerland, northern Italy, Yugoslavia, and Bulgaria, or down through Italy and across the Aegean on the car ferry to Greece. When one car on the northern route was involved in an accident in Yugoslavia, its mission was revealed when ammunition spilled all over the road. The cars frequently pause in Sofia to rendezvous with potential Turkish and Arab buyers both for arms and cars at the Berliner Restaurant in the Bulgarian capital. Then they are driven on to Istanbul, where the arms are offloaded. Then, before the car itself can be sold, one sideways shuffle takes place. When the German driver brings the car into Turkey, the fact will be recorded in his passport; the passport must also be stamped for taking the car out. This is achieved by driving to a Turkish border point, getting the passport stamped in, and then, instead of proceeding into Greece or Bulgaria, turning around down a back lane to Istanbul. Once there, the car is handed over to its new Turkish owner, and in turn the German driver picks up a consignment of morphine base, which he takes back with him by plane or train. The guns, meanwhile, will either be distributed among Turks themselves in the remoter villages, where most of the farmers and peasants like to keep a gun in the house, or they are passed on to the Kurdish tribesmen in eastern Turkey and northern Iraq, who have been waging a spirited guerrilla warfare for their own independence against pro-Nasser Arabs in Iraq for years. The link with narcotics originated from the Kurds' search for arms. Since they had no money to pay for rifles and ammunition, the only marketable commodity they could offer was morphine base or raw opium.

The Kurds' quest for arms has occasionally led them far afield—even to Miami, the hub of arms smuggling out of the United States. In July, 1966, two sheiks from Iraq turned up in

Miami and started buying up rifles and pistols from local dealers. Their purchases were so extensive that word of two Iraqi gentlemen amassing a small armory quickly filtered up to the authorities. They kept a tail on the gun-buying sheiks and finally jumped them at Port Everglades just as they were supervising the loading of 500 Persian M98 rifles and 2,623 pistols worth $85,000 onto an Italian freighter bound for Beirut. Taxed with their spectacular failure to obtain the necessary export papers, the sheiks pleaded they were shipping the arms back to the Kurds, "to fight Nasser."

Although they had overlooked their paperwork, the sheiks had certainly picked an excellent marketplace for weapons. Ever since Fidel Castro successfully gained control of Cuba, Miami and the Florida Keys have been a hotbed of Cuban expatriates and American adventurers all bent on mounting their own private invasion of Cuba (to say nothing of odd CIA adventurers with the same aim in mind). Indeed, Miami and the Keys often have more the air of an armed camp than resorts for sun-seeking tourists. Lines for tuna or shark trailing overboard from pleasure craft bobbing in the Caribbean sunshine may mask the fact that the boat is really laden to the gunwales with guns for some new sortie to Cuba or Haiti. In December, 1966, the authorities rounded up one little expeditionary force of eighty Cubans, Haitians, and Americans, all dressed in army camouflage fatigues, just as they were about to set out in a small armada of four launches from Cocoa Plum Beach midway between Miami and Key West. They were equipped with a weird armory including 148 rifles, ranging from a .30-caliber weapon made in 1903 to a Russian-made rifle and 80 .30 M-1 rifles, together with 15 machine guns, 9 mortars, 2 rocket launchers, and 89 bayonets. This expeditionary force was led by an ex-Cuban senator named Rolando Arcadio Masferrer in collaboration with Father Jean Baptiste Georges, a former Haitian minister of education who was to become President of Haiti if this invasion against President Duvalier was successful. It was not the first time that Father Georges had been picked up with enough arms to launch a miniature Latin-American revolution. In 1964 he was stopped in a car bowling through Miami Beach at daybreak by a policeman who noticed a defective brake light on the U-Haul trailer behind the car. What was in the trailer, the policeman inquired? "Household appliances for a priest," said Father Georges. The policeman took a look and found the trailer crammed with rifles, machine guns, explosives, and 25,000 rounds of ammunition. The priest explained he had purchased this "religious equipment" in New York for $8,000 and was planning to ship it to Haiti to help a plot to overthrow Duvalier.

Although most of the gunrunning out of the creeks of Florida is destined for Caribbean adventures, some of it also filters down via Panama to South America as the raw material of revolution. A number of gunrunners operating out of Panama charter ancient B-29's from Miami and fly them down to Panama to pick up arms. The planes then take off down the west coast of South America, often refueling in Santiago, and then drop off the arms in Chile or the Argentine at a convenient ranch with its own private airstrip. Their flight plan, of course, will make no mention of this extra stop en route. But it pays to bribe the right people along the way. One group of gunrunners recently flew in seven loads of arms successfully to a ranch in the Argentine, each time filing a flight plan from Santiago, Chile, over the Andes to Córdoba, Argentina, but never bothering to go on to Córdoba. They had paid off several officials in Córdoba, but not the air-traffic controller. He was quite aware of what was going on and decided, after a while, to make a protest at not getting his slice of the cake. When the B-29 came on its eighth flight and set down at the ranch instead of Córdoba airport, he put out an alert. The plane was overdue, he reported. It must have crashed in the mountains. Aircraft and police all along the route were called out, and a massive hunt started in the hills. Two or three hours later the B-29 calmly winged back into Santiago airport, quite ignorant of the fact that half of South America was looking for them. So that little caper came to an unexpected end. It was a stern reminder of that London gunrunner's axiom that "The arms traffic rolls on the ball bearings of bribery."

145

VII

People Smuggling

Her Britannic Majesty's Principal Secretary of State for Foreign Affairs requests and requires in the name of Her Majesty all those whom it may concern to allow the bearer to pass freely without let or hindrance, and to afford the bearer such assistance and protection as may be necessary.

I, the undersigned, Secretary of State of the United States of America, hereby request all whom it may concern to permit the citizen (or citizens) of the United States named herein to pass without delay or hindrance and in case of need to give said citizen (or citizens) all lawful aid and protection.

Most people probably never take the trouble to read the preamble in the front of their passports. They accept the document as readily as a driver's license or a credit card. Even when they arrive in a new country the immigration officer often appears to give the passport no more than a cursory glance, stamps it, and hands it back. It is a formality—for those who have them. But lack that little blue or green booklet, and you might as well be a man from Mars, unrecognized and unwanted on a hostile planet. Once in a while stories drift to the surface of people in limbo, caught in the no-man's-land of airport transit lounges or condemned to a life at sea, refused entry in every port. In an age of bureaucracy, when everything must be correctly recorded, a person who is not written down scarcely has the right to exist; even the right visa can become synonymous with freedom itself.

Those lacking the essential documents have two choices: stay put where they are or find some method of getting through, over or under the barrier by subterfuge. The latter course either means getting the right documents by bribery, apparently the right documents by forgery, or bypassing authority completely. This is a situation ripe for commercial exploitation, even if the motive for making the illegal crossing is political, as with escapers from Eastern Europe into West Germany and from Communist China into Hong Kong. Several unscrupulous groups in West Germany have made small fortunes charging up to $2,500 to help people breach the Iron Curtain, while the men who run the "snake traffic" ferrying illegal immigrants into Hong Kong charge anything from $130 to $250 for the trip from Canton or Macao.

Leaving aside for the moment the rather special reasons for escaping from Communist countries, there are three main motives for illicit travel. First, there is the criminal on the run who needs fresh papers to move from one country to another. Bruce Reynolds, one of the architects of the Great Train Robbery in Britain, who eluded the police for five and one-half years after the two-and-one-half-million-pound raid, kept moving around Europe and North America with the aid of four passports, all in different names, all with different photographs showing him in a variety of disguises. A man like Reynolds can always pick up an extra passport in a matter of hours through his underworld connections. Housebreakers often steal passports, along with cash and jewelry, knowing full well they will find some eager underworld purchaser who can substitute his own photograph.

The second motive for illicit travel is the desire of divided families, separated by some legal technicality or immigration quirk, to join each other. Finally, and in the vast majority, there are thousands in poor, underdeveloped countries who are drawn by the prospect of prosperity to Europe or America, but denied entry because of quotas or other immigration controls. Any of these people, driven on by fear, love, or the lure of a rich nation, will often pay handsomely in cash or mortgage their future earnings for a chance to run the gauntlet of the forbidden border.

For the lone traveler with the right connections, there is always a floating black market in forged or stolen passports to be found. A spare passport is an eminently marketable property. In South America it is possible to obtain a legal and valid passport for around five hundred dollars. One Latin-American diplomat not long ago absconded with thirty-six and showed up in Hong Kong selling them for two thousand dollars apiece. Nearly five hundred British passports vanished in a weekend raid on the main London Passport Office in Petty, France, in the autumn of 1967 and soon turned up in the illegal immigrant traffic into Britain. Forged visa stamps are equally marketable. U.S. immigration officials detected a neat plot early in 1968 involving a spate of U.S. nonimmigrant visas apparently issued by their consul in Belem, Brazil, who suddenly appeared to be working overtime. The racket turned out to be part of a pipeline to get Hong Kong Chinese into the United States. They traveled first to Colombia on their normal passports. There, for a fee varying between $350 and $500, they handed over passports to the forgers. When the passport was returned a few days later, it had a flurry of new immigration stamps, which indicated the traveler had left Colombia, arrived in Brazil, obtained an American visa through the consul in Belem, then journeyed back to Colombia. All the date stamps were in the correct sequence. Nearly sixty Chinese entered the United States before the authorities tumbled to the trick—and then only because the forgers were lazy and never varied the place of issue of the visa from Belem.

Counterfeit U.S. alien register cards (I-151's in official parlance), which are valid for reentry into the United States, are made in considerable numbers in Mexico and may sell for as little as $150 each. Even a fake marriage certificate is valuable if it shows that the prospective immigrant is married to a U.S. citizen. Someone is always willing to lend his name to such a marriage of convenience, which is forgotten the moment the

148

client is safely on American soil. "Counterfeiting," admitted an official at the U.S. Immigration and Naturalization Service, "is big business."

Forgeries of complete passports are rare. The real art is in doctoring stolen genuine ones to make the description, photograph, and visa stamps tally with a new owner. This must be a highly professional job. An immigration officer may appear to handle a passport casually, but he can read it like a book; the jumble of visa stamps charts out a voyage to him in detail. He glances at so many in the course of a day, that he may detect an altered one because of some absurd little inconsistency. If the passport has been well used but the page listing the owner's personal details looks too fresh and clean, he will search for any telltale sign that the original page has been carefully cut out and a new one stuck in. After handling perhaps a thousand passports that are just right, the wrong one can stand out a mile.

There is no highly organized outfit specializing in coping with the needs of the criminal on the run or the odd couple bent on outwitting authority. They must simply find a contact into the amorphous market in stolen credentials, which, like a floating crap game, tries to stay one step ahead of the law. But there are three rackets in human contraband today which count their clients by the thousand and their annual takings in millions: the floodtide of over 100,000 Mexican "wetbacks" a year into the United States; the smuggling of illegal immigrants from India and Pakistan into Britain; and the infiltration of more than ten thousand Chinese into Hong Kong every year. The "wetback" traffic (originally named because the Mexicans got soaked crossing the Rio Grande) is nothing new, but it has mushroomed in the 1960's. The U.S. Border Patrol picked up just over 22,000 Mexicans in 1960 who entered the United States illegally; in 1967 they caught over 86,000. The number of "smugglers of aliens" (as the Patrol calls them) arrested jumped up from 330 to 1,219 in the same seven years. Head counting on the British traffic is less exact, and estimates range all the way from 1,000 to 10,000 a year. But the importance of this route is that it is quite new.

When the Conservative government passed their Commonwealth Immigrants Act in 1962, severely controlling the entry of Commonwealth citizens to Britain in search of work, few predicted that this act would lead to the most complex and perhaps most profitable of all international human-smuggling rackets of the 1960's. The act was passed at a time when immigrants from the West Indies, India, and Pakistan were pouring into Britain at the rate of over 100,000 a year. Their motive was quite simple—to earn more money. Few of them knew what to expect in Britain. A clerk in Bombay or Karachi earning less than fifty dollars a month heard that he could earn more than fifty dollars a week as a laborer in a British factory. Frequently the man came alone and either saved enough money in Britain to bring his family over after him or sent money back to them every week. The climate and the housing conditions in cities like Birmingham, Bradford, and Wolverhampton were often a rude shock and a sore trial for the immigrants, but that, apparently, did not diminish the appeal of Britain for those still at home—particularly in India and Pakistan. "If they could afford it or were allowed in, the whole population of India would come here in search of work," said an Indian community leader in Southall, the northwest London suburb where many of the Asians have settled.

The Commonwealth Immigrants Act limited the number of immigrants permitted to enter the United Kingdom each year to a comparatively small number of workers (in 1969 the quota was 8,500) plus their dependents. It was a sudden legal barrier to entry, but it did not change the urge of those who wanted to come. Indeed, it can be argued that, in line with all prohibition, it made Britain seem the more attractive. The temptation to capitalize on this circumstance was irresistible to a handful of racketeers.

But, curiously, it was only the Asians who took advantage of it. There is no evidence that West Indian or African Commonwealth citizens are entering Britain illegally, which does not mean none of them is, only that there is not an organized traffic. With the Asians, regrettably, the whole business is on an enormous scale; some unofficial estimates suggest as many as 50,-000 have entered illegally in five years. Since the premium over the normal air fare paid by most immigrants is up to $1,200, this means, if the estimate is accurate, a gross profit for someone of some sixty million dollars.

The business was first highlighted in the summer of 1967, when George Castle, the caretaker of some cottages near Sandwich, in Kent, saw eight men coming ashore around eight o'clock one morning from a pale-blue cabin cruiser anchored two hundred yards offshore. "I didn't take much notice at first," Mr. Castle explained later, "until I saw a dinghy lowered. Three men were then ferried to a groyne near the house. If they had been wearing gumboots, I wouldn't have looked twice, but it isn't every day you see a bunch of Indians or Pakistanis suddenly landing on these deserted beaches wearing nice new brown suits." He called the police. They picked up the eight men strolling along the road into Sandwich and took them to the police station. What were they doing landing on such a desolate stretch of coast so early in the morning? The Pakistanis were unperturbed. Quite simple, they said. They were all old friends, and they had decided to have a reunion. They had met at Dover at four in the morning, boarded a boat they had booked in advance, and sailed merrily along the coast to Sandwich, where they disembarked to have a picnic. The boat was going to return at three in the afternoon to pick them up. They were walking into Sandwich to buy food for the picnic when the police stopped them. Furthermore, all said they were resident in Britain but, alas, they had left their passports and other papers at home when they set off for the reunion. However, they gave their addresses and even named the firms in London, Oxford, Liverpool, and Bradford where they claimed to work. One or two could name their foremen.

It was a consistent, if highly unlikely, story with several puzzling points. For example, all the Pakistanis had some English money, but it was entirely in notes; they did not possess one English coin among them. After persistent questioning all day from police and hastily summoned immigration officials, one man finally conceded they were all illegal immigrants. The tale which then emerged showed they were just one batch of hundreds of Pakistanis and Indians who had been ferried the twenty-five miles across the English Channel from the Belgian and

French coasts over the preceding two or three years. Their particular trail led right back to a travel agent in Lahore, one of many in Pakistan who are charging anything between £50 and £1,500 for providing passports and making all travel arrangements for prospective immigrants. They are dispatched to Europe either overland in Dormobiles through Afghanistan, Iran, Turkey, Greece, Yugoslavia, and up to Germany and Belgium, or on cut-price air tickets direct to Europe. Provided they have a valid Pakistan passport, they experience no difficulty entering Germany, France, or Belgium as visitors in transit. Frankfurt, Brussels, and Ostend are the crucial staging posts. Here the immigrant waits for his sailing orders. It has become a common and depressing sight in Frankfurt and Ostend these days to see perplexed Asians wandering aimlessly around the streets with nothing to do. In Frankfurt they can be seen in the mornings holding little huddled conferences on the main railway station concourse near the newspaper stall, as they try to seek the latest word of future movements. They talk earnestly in a tight group for perhaps ten minutes and then disperse. They have little money and exist in cheap lodging houses in the back streets near the station. They lead an equally bleak life in Ostend, sitting in damp rooms in rundown hotels, waiting, always waiting.

The eight picked up at Sandwich had been hanging around in Ostend for several days until they were contacted by an Englishman who told them to meet him outside Ostend station late one afternoon. He took away all their baggage (which they never saw again) and bundled them into two taxis, which drove them sixty miles west along the coast over the French border to Calais. In the French seaport their English guide at first told them to be ready to embark at nine in the evening, but the weather deteriorated, so they were advised to take rooms at the Hotel Pacifique. During the night, however, the weather improved. The Englishman routed them out of bed and led them through the deserted streets down to the harbor, where they boarded the *Rhare*, a seagoing cabin cruiser which, it turned out later, had been stolen from Marseilles nearly a year earlier. The Pakistanis knew this Englishman simply as Norman, but he was, in fact, Norman Piper, who had lived in France for a number of years and was shortly afterward sent to prison in France for complicity in stealing the *Rhare* from Marseilles. Once aboard the boat, Piper, according to his passengers, collected all their passports and personal documents. During the tedious voyage to the Kent coast, he briefed them, between their bouts of seasickness, on the story they should tell of the reunion and picnic if they were caught as they landed in Britain. They were also instructed that a car would be waiting to pick them up near Sandwich. They never made that rendezvous before they were stopped by the police.

This shoal of Asians suddenly turning up on a quiet southcoast beach in high summer naturally caused a stir. If there was this boatload, had there been others? There had indeed. Norman Piper was not the only man along the Channel who was hard at work running an illegal cross-Channel ferry at dead of night. A veritable armada was at work, for many south-coast fishermen found that ferrying Pakistanis from France was much more profitable than a hard night's fishing. The pay was £50 to £100 for each Pakistani carried. One fisherman from Rye, Sussex, Michael Sharp, who was sent to prison for five years in November, 1968, for immigrant smuggling, boasted, according to the London *Sunday Telegraph*, that he had brought at least two hundred across the Channel. On one trip alone he claimed he transported forty. The business was so flourishing that once when Sharp brought his boat, *Carrick Lass,* into a lonely beach near Boulogne, he embarked someone else's load of Pakistanis by mistake before his contact man came up with the group he was supposed to carry. "This stretch of beach," said Sharp, "was just like a bus stop."

His contact man, who had first recruited him with a tempting offer of £750 to bring "some friends from the other side," was one Harry Carpos, more often known as Harry the Greek. Harry is an enormous man, over six feet six tall, who operated at one time from a flat in the Finchley Road in London. He was the middleman, the transport liaison officer, so to speak, for the Lahore travel agent behind the racket. Harry the Greek was responsible both for the Dormobiles on the overland route and for arranging the boats across the Channel. He was paid £250 per person, of which he gave £50 to Sharp.* The operation was crisply run. Carpos would either cross with Sharp or would be waiting for him on the far side of the Channel. Sometimes the pickup was made near Boulogne, at others on the shore west of Ostend. The Asians were kept below deck in the hold, cold and seasick. A car or van was always waiting to collect them as they came up the English beach to drive them to Southall in the suburbs of London, where they stayed for a couple of days before being taken north to Manchester or Bradford. They were well briefed before or during the trip on what to say if they were stopped by police as they landed. Until February, 1968, through some quirk of the law, the immigration authorities could refuse entry to an illegal Commonwealth immigrant only if they caught him within twenty-four hours of his arrival in Britain. If he could show he had been in the country more than that time—even though he entered illegally—he could not later be deported. It was all-important, therefore, to remain undetected for the first few hours. In February, 1968, however, this law was amended to allow the immigration authorities twenty-eight days in which to examine and refuse entry to the illegal immigrant. It was also made an offense to be in Britain except on the authority of an immigration officer, so that those who succeeded in evading detection for twenty-eight days could be prosecuted later by the police.

The smugglers do not appear to have found this much of a deterrent. Harry the Greek, indeed, was as active as ever. In June, 1968, he lined up twenty-nine prospective immigrants in Ostend and got word to Sharp in Rye to come over and pick them up. It was a wild night, but Sharp succeeded in getting them aboard and set off down Channel in a Force Six gale. Everyone, including Harry, was violently sick, but they managed to stagger ashore on the broad sandy beach at Camber just before dawn. There was considerable confusion in the dark, and an angler flashed a light at them, causing a stampede. Eventually most of the Asians were packed into a truck and taken to dry out at a nearby farm. Two of them were left wandering around the sand dunes. Soon after dawn they asked a local resident the way to the

---

* *Sunday Telegraph,* December 1, 1968.

nearest bus stop. He told them, but also called the police, who found them huddled for warmth in the bus shelter. They quickly put the police on the trail of the rest. Sharp was arrested and his boat seized. But there was no sign of Harry the Greek. His handsome flat in the Finchley Road, London, was empty. Apparently he had decided it would be wiser to retreat to the Continent for a while and direct operations from Frankfurt.

Although Carpos was lying low, the ferry was still active throughout 1968. Since coast-guard and immigration officials all around the Straits of Dover were on special alert for any launches puttering around on moonlit nights, the organizers were trying to recruit boatmen farther afield. One load came into Chichester harbor in late August, and fishermen as far west as Devon were agog with talks of Pakistani gentlemen coming down from London with high-priced propositions. One fisherman in Teignmouth, Devon, alleged that he had been offered in a pub £100 for every man he would bring across the Channel.

While Carpos was running a highly organized operation, the numbers of Asians stacked up on the far side of the Channel waiting for a ride tempted other south-coast boatmen to run over and see what they could pick up on their own. Norman Piper, who had brought that first ill-fated load into Sandwich Bay, had been scouting his own Pakistanis, as had another friend of his who has since found it prudent to move to Cannes. They had an informal headquarters in a Calais café, run by a woman, whose young son accompanied Piper on some of his voyages. This café, down by the harbor, is a meeting place for many of the other freelance ferry operators, all eager to garner the latest word on where to find Asians looking for a ride. These boatmen were often charging up to £150 in cash just for the trip across the Channel. One yacht owner, busy smuggling stolen gold out of England to France, was picking up a load of immigrants for the return journey to add to his profits. Few of these freelance operators bothered to line up further transport on shore in Britain. On one occasion three Pakistanis, wandering around the Folkestone area with no idea where to go, came upon the Hythe to Dymchurch miniature railway and gave themselves away by inquiring the time of the next train to London.

No one knows exactly how many Asians have made the uncomfortable twenty-mile journey across the English Channel. A senior detective, who kept a close eye on the racket, suggests four thousand came in 1967. It is known that one major Pakistani operator was responsible for dispatching at least twenty immigrants a week; he directed half these across the English Channel, half through southern Ireland. His racket alone, therefore, would account for five hundred a year on the cross-Channel route.

While the cross-Channel immigrant traffic has attracted attention as the most dramatic unorthodox way of entering Britain, even more illegal immigrants have been filtering through in ones or twos on normal scheduled air services, using passports and work vouchers obtained by bribery or forgery or by taking on completely new family relationships for the occasion. The section of the Commonwealth Immigrants Act which gives most room for maneuver concerns dependent relatives. This lets in wives, children under eighteen, and parents over sixty-five of Commonwealth citizens already living in Britain. In the slightly chaotic state of many Asian birth and marriage registers, ages and relationships are often hard to determine precisely. This offers marvelous opportunities to the fertile mind of the racketeer. An Indian woman busy in New Delhi making arrangements through a travel agency to fly with her children to London is asked to take an extra "son" along for the ride. A little astute forgery adds the "son's" name to those of her children in her passport; often a successful deception, provided the dates of birth of the children remain in a sensible sequence. One Indian woman was caught because, according to the entry in her passport, she gave birth to a daughter in July, 1952, and a son two months later. Another woman was detained because immigration officials thought she looked far too young to be the mother of two teen-age sons. An alternative system is for Asians already living in Britain to apply for their "son" to join them. A plausible family history will be concocted, the son's passport amended accordingly, and a well-briefed father shows up at London airport to greet his son. If they are questioned by the authorities, both of them will be brimming with the date grandma died or the name of the village where great grandfather lived. However, if the questioning gets tough and the immigration men start to detect areas of family history with which both are not familiar, then the father will disappear and leave his "son" to his fate of being sent back home on the next plane.

A variation on this theme is for an Asian resident in Britain to pop over to Brussels or Frankfurt (often taking out illegal currency with him) and return with two "sons" in tow, who, he will claim, are just arriving for a short visit with the family. Each son will have been lent one hundred pounds or more to prove that he is self-supporting. They are admitted as visitors; they return their loan to their temporary father and neglect to leave the country at the end of their holiday. It may be weeks or even months before the local police, alerted by the immigration authorities, go around in search of them. Invariably, no one at the address they gave on arrival has any idea where they have gone.

The variations are limitless. Old men arrive claiming they are over sixty-five, when, in fact, they have simply grown a beard and dyed it gray; spry young twenty-year-olds fly in pretending to be fifteen. One Indian youth of nineteen even tried to get through London airport disguised as a young girl in a sari. The immigration officer thought the traveler's shoulders looked a little broad for a girl and called for an airport nurse to take a closer look. The nurse found the "girl" was very shy. "At first," the nurse explained later, "she would not take off her clothes, but she was eventually persuaded. After lifting the trouser leg under her sari and seeing the hairy leg, we realized something strange was up." The girl's "father," who had turned up at the airport to welcome the child he claimed he had not seen since she was three, vanished rather hastily when told of this revelation.

The altering of passports is a thriving business. Not only the entry stamps are faked; photographs are switched; name, age, and birth details are altered; even whole pages are cut out and replaced with other ones. "They do a very craftsmanlike job with many of the passport stamps," an immigration official conceded admiringly. The most straightforward doctoring is to fake entry and exit stamps from Britain indicating the traveler has been a resident. Anyone who can prove he has been a resident of Britain within the last two years is freely readmitted.

The passports themselves are costly items. A United Kingdom passport will fetch over five hundred pounds in India or Pakistan. A cheaper alternative is a Pakistani passport, which the prospective immigrant can obtain on the excuse that he is making a pilgrimage to Mecca. This passport will be accepted in Europe, and he can then take the illegal Channel crossing, which calls for no documents at all. Alternatively, he can buy a stolen British passport on the black market once he is in Europe.

In the autumn of 1967, 450 British passports were stolen from the Passport Office in London. One of them was discovered three months later in the possession of an Indian named Prithvi Pal Singh, who was questioned at Dover by a customs officer about the amount of currency he was carrying (he had fifty-two pounds in cash instead of the permitted fifteen). He was traveling on a genuine British passport, but a second one in another name found in the bottom of his suitcase was one of the stolen ones. Singh claimed it had been given him by a Pakistani travel agent in Birmingham, who had approached him and asked him to take it to Munich as a sample and obtain orders for more.

Another batch of passports and passport stamps was discovered in the luggage of a Pakistani arriving at Karachi airport in the autumn of 1967 as he came back from Britain, where he had been a partner in a Birmingham travel agency. Travel agents, in fact, turn up at every twist of the illegal-immigrant trail. There was the director of a Karachi travel agency who flew to Frankfurt and set up in business at a hotel, selling passports to Pakistanis stranded in the city. He had an endless stream of customers for several weeks and was persuading them to get relatives in Britain to mail money for the passports. After a while he vanished one morning without paying his bill. Another passport conjurer in Frankfurt came unstuck unexpectedly when he mislaid a briefcase containing five Indian passports at the airport. The briefcase was handed in to lost property, who, naturally, opened it to try to discover the name and address of the owner. Instead they found, laid out neatly on top of the case, five Indian passports. The Indian came rushing up shortly afterward in search of his case, to find a warm welcome awaiting him from the airport police. The passports, apparently, had already been used by five Indians to enable them to leave India; in Frankfurt they had traded the Indian document for false United Kingdom passports, plus documents declaring each of them had one thousand pounds deposited with a bank in Britain and a job awaiting them. The Indian with the briefcase, who had engineered this shuffle at the airport, was planning to dispatch the passports home for resale.

A never-ending circle of altered passports and health documents also persists among the boatmen who bring the immigrants across the Channel. They collect all documents during the voyage and resell them back in France or Belgium, where they can be sold to more illegal immigrants, who in turn will later hand them over to another boatman who will . . . And so it goes on.

Forgeries run the whole gamut of health documents, employment vouchers, and even certificates guaranteeing entry into colleges. A Birmingham travel agency did a fast selling line in admissions documents to a technical college in the city—which would be grounds for admitting an immigrant to Britain—until someone spotted they were two years out of date. Official birth certificates, making the prospective immigrant much younger or much older, can readily be purchased in India or Pakistan. The problem is, explained an immigration official, "These fiddled ones often look much better than the authentic document. The real ones frequently have typing errors or spelling mistakes because they have been made out in a small village. The fake ones look immaculate."

Another turn on this merry-go-round of immigration dodging is through Eire. For this particular trick the immigrant normally has a Pakistani passport, which will get him into Ireland as a visitor. Once in Ireland, he meets a contact from Britain— often from Manchester, where this little racket was developed— who gives him an air ticket for Manchester-Dublin-Manchester. He discards the outward half and simply comes back to Manchester as an internal passenger who does not need a passport. Alternatively, he travels through Manchester or London in transit to Dublin and is joined on the last stage of the flight to Dublin by a friend who hands over the ticket. He thus arrives in Dublin initially as a visitor from Britain.

As the routes proliferate and the traffic prospers, it provides more revenue for other smuggling activities, from drugs to watches and gold to transistor radios. The link between the immigrant racket and drugs is twofold. First, some of the illegal immigrants bring a little on their own initiative, either for their own use or because they have heard it can make them a little easy money when they arrive in Britain. The amount involved, however, is small. Much more serious is the smuggling of drugs carried on by the organizers of the illegal-immigrant racket (see Chapter 4). They do not actually use the illegal immigrants to carry large shipments of drugs—the risk of entrusting several thousand dollars' worth of drugs to a man without a proper passport is simply not worth taking. The overlap is much more at the organization level rather than at the carrying level—although in at least one instance a large consignment of thirty-one pounds of cannabis was hidden in the spare tire of a car bringing immigrants overland from Pakistan. The immigrants, however, knew nothing of the cannabis; it was their guide who was the drugs courier, and he possessed all the right documents to ensure he had no problems at frontiers. But the accidental discovery of $40,000 worth of cannabis in a room of the Hilton Hotel in London in February, 1968, provided a much more direct connection. One of the men charged with conspiracy to receive this cannabis was an Indian who was working for a travel agency with offices in New Delhi, London, and Birmingham, which offered cut-price air tickets to prospective immigrants. He did not wait to stand trial. Although he had forfeited his passport, he slipped out of Britain while on bail and was last heard of back in New Delhi—still in the travel business.

Illegal-currency operations embrace not only illegal immigrants into Britain, but virtually all the legal ones as well, and provide the racketeers with sterling with which to finance their operations outside Asia. The currency business is quite simple. An Indian working in, say, Bradford wants to send money back each week to his family in Bombay. He could do this with a money order sent through the post office or a bank, but his family would be paid in rupees at the official rate of exchange (eighteen rupees to the pound in India, fifteen rupees to the pound in Pakistan). Instead, however, he hands over his money in England to one of the myriad of little unofficial exchange dealers who operate in all large cities in Britain where there is an Asian community. These dealers give him a much better rate of exchange, probably twenty-four rupees to the pound for India and twenty-two for Pakistan. Both sides find it an eminently satisfactory scheme; the family gets more rupees, the racketeer gets his hands on large amounts of hard currency outside Asia. Even the most respectable of immigrants living in Britain make use of the scheme. "I phone this friend," explains one of the leaders of the community in Southall, "and say, 'What is the rate today?' Sometimes I get double, although at the moment it is twenty-four rupees to the pound. I'm practical, and I work hard, and if I can get twenty-four rupees instead of eighteen, I'm going to do it. Once when I was there, two ministers from the Punjab, who were visiting England, were changing money at the same time."

The revenue from illegal immigrants adds to this sterling bankroll. Many of the immigrants contract to pay the money for their illegal passage once they reach Britain; they will hand over perhaps five or ten pounds each week until the debt is paid off. Quite apart from having to repay their passage money, the illegal immigrant is duty bound to remit any money home to his family by the illegal channel. In the first place, he does not want to draw attention to himself by sending it through official banking channels. Apart from that, the racketeers who brought him in can always threaten to denounce him if he does not use their currency-exchange facilities. A young Pakistani in Bradford who refused to hand over his wages to the agent who posed as his "father" when he arrived in Britain was reported to the police. The youth admitted he had come in on a false passport and told a made-up story to the immigration officer.

The tragedy of this flourishing traffic is that it makes officials hypersensitive to all Asian immigrants. They are looking so keenly for discrepancies in passport details or in immigrants' stories that they frequently make it hard on genuine arrivals.

What is more, potential immigrants, who do have grounds for entry and try to play it by the book, often get so frustrated by officialdom that they opt for illegal entry instead. A community-relations officer in Southall explained, "The honest ones are often turned away, while the racketeers get away with it. Asians sometimes come to me and say, 'I've played it by the rules, but I cannot get my son in. I don't want to do it illegally, but I will have to.' Others who have had difficulty with a relative the first time do it illegally the second time to save trouble." The unfortunate part is that illegal immigrants, whether they come by air or sea, are invariably well briefed on what to tell immigration officers on arrival; the genuine immigrant may have his papers in order, but no one has briefed him on what to say. He can easily become confused when questioned, and, in panic, tell conflicting stories. "The temptations to come illegally are very great," admits an Indian, "especially for the uneducated. Sitting in their village in India, they don't even know what the world looks like. They probably imagine London is a country. Then this professional agent comes along and says you pay me and I'll arrange it all for you. Just keep your mouth shut and do what I say." A great many of them do.

Now that the British immigration and coast-guard authorities are fully aware of most of the themes and variations of the illegal-immigrant business, things are tougher on the smugglers. During the 1968 Christmas holiday alone, fifty-five prospective immigrants were turned back at London airport. But greater vigilance by authority is not going to stop Asians wanting to come to Britain; the lure of a prosperous nation seen from afar has not dimmed. The prospect for the next decade is hardly cheerful. If British immigration laws get even stricter—and there is considerable pressure that the limited number of immigrants now allowed in legally should be reduced or stopped completely—then even more business is going to be directed toward the smugglers.*

By comparison with this intercontinental shift, the annual

* In the summer of 1969 new regulations were introduced by the British authorities requiring an immigrant to obtain an entry certificate for Britain before he left his home country. It was hoped this would cut down the number of bogus relatives turning up at London Airport.

shuttling of 100,000 or more Mexicans across the borders of the United States is little more than a commuter service. The Mexicans are frequently not anticipating settling in the United States; they just flit over for the cotton harvest in Texas in June and July or to help pick the fruit crop in California in July, August, and September. Most of them are unskilled. They work in the fields for a few weeks, then drift back to Mexico or are sent back by the Border Patrol, who tour the farms, sifting out the illegal from the legal workers. None of the illegal immigrants takes it very seriously if he is caught; he is bounced back to Mexico and is all set to try to crack the border again. One man established something of a record by being sent back to Mexico three times in one night. Not all Mexicans display the same enterprising talent. They show up in the border towns of Nuevo Laredo, Cuidad Juárez, Mexicali, or Tijuana, humping their belongings in an old suitcase or a string bag and looking lost. They are easy prey for the professional touts who hang around the bars and cheap roominghouses. Before they know what has happened, the touts have signed them up to pay $150 to be shipped across the border. The racket is not particularly highly organized; each little border town has half a dozen to a dozen men who dabble in the business. They are much less sophisticated than the narcotics smugglers operating in the same towns, but they prefer it as a less dangerous way of life which can, nevertheless, provide them with a nice little income. Some alien smugglers are so confident of their ability that they guarantee to get their clients over the border. If the chap is caught the first time, they will mount another border-running operation for free. Understandably, they prefer cash in advance, but since many Mexicans coming down from the interior of their country for the first time cannot muster $150, the smuggler will settle for whatever he can pay down and the rest later. He can always threaten to inform the U.S. immigration service if the man defaults on his payments.

The border-crossing techniques are not usually very subtle. A couple of Mexicans may be tucked into the trunk of a car and sent across during a peak traffic period when immigration has no time for detailed checks. More often, they are taken to a lonely spot on the border and either wade the Rio Grande on the Texas frontier or clamber over the eight-foot-high chain-link fence that strides across the border in New Mexico, Arizona, and California. The fence is topped with barbed wire, but the immigrants just toss a blanket or even a cardboard box into the spikes and scramble over. "The fence," a Border Patrolman concedes sadly, "is simply a deterrent for cattle." Once on the other side, if they are lucky and are dealing with a trustworthy smuggler, a car or a truck will be waiting to pick them up and take them to El Paso, Denver, Los Angeles, San Francisco, or even Chicago. Quite frequently, however, they are told, "Keep walking up that track, and you will find a truck waiting." It turns out to be an awfully long walk; the smugglers, having collected their cash in Mexico, simply neglect to line up transportation over the border.

Perhaps "wetbacks" should be thankful if the truck does not show up; they may be better off without it. On a scorching day in the summer of 1968 police in San Antonio, Texas, were summoned to a closed truck parked in the full sun, from which feeble cries and the faint thudding of fists could be heard. They broke open the locked back door, to find forty-seven Mexicans crammed into the broiling interior. One was dead, two more were dying, and fifteen others went to the hospital with heat prostration. Those who could still talk explained that each had paid one hundred dollars to be smuggled into the United States and taken to Chicago. They had forded the Rio Grande at night near Eagle Pass and been picked up by a driver who emerged from the scrub by the river. He took their money, locked them in the back of the rented truck, and drove off to San Antonio, where he abandoned them.

A much less hazardous and cheaper method of entry is the fraudulent use of the border-crossing card. These plastic-bound cards entitle Mexicans to unlimited entries into the United States for a stay of not more than seventy-two hours within a radius of 150 miles of the border. Small racketeers in the Mexican border towns make a nice collection of twenty or thirty of these cards and rent them out at ten dollars a time. The racketeer will shuffle through his cards until he finds one on which the photograph looks vaguely like his client. If that is impossible, the photograph is switched in a trice. All it requires is a razorblade to cut the unwanted picture out of its plastic covering and a hot iron to melt the plastic back smoothly over the new one. With the whole squad all set with their crossing cards, the smuggler then shifts them down to a border-crossing point at a busy time of day, and they all walk through bold as brass, flashing their little card as they go. The smuggler strolls through with his own legal card, collects all the phony ones, and heads back for the next batch of clients. The only real art in all this is a good, steady ironing hand for picture changing. Immigration officers often rub the card lightly between finger and thumb; after they have handled fifty genuine ones with the plastic quite smooth, a doctored card with a slight ripple where the plastic was cut and reironed is like a molehill on a bowling green.

The Mexican invasion accounted for almost ninety-seven percent of all surreptitious entries into the United States in 1967, keeping the Border Patrol in a constant scramble along the 2,013-mile border. A thousand of the Patrol's fourteen hundred men are stationed in the Southwest, but they cannot hope to keep pace. Much of the rough country on the California border east of Jacumba and all along the Rio Grande River is impossible to police effectively. The Patrol ranges through in jeeps and in dusty areas rakes a track smooth daily on the American side of the fence; this shows up the tracks of Mexicans coming over the wire and, in best Western tradition, the patrolmen are off on the trail. Mexicans who have clambered over on their own will often walk for miles to the nearest town. "They think nothing of walking for four days with a vinegar jar full of water and a couple of tortillas," says a Border Patrolman, "but we reckon to catch eighty percent of them."

The Patrol's latest anti-illegal-immigrant weapon is a seismograph plugged into a series of sensors buried along the fence. The sensors pick up footfalls of "wetbacks" sneaking across in the night. Each sensor will register a fifty-yard radius, and sixteen of them can be plugged into each seismograph. This is a splendid system over a short distance, but over four thousand seismographs with 64,000 sensors would be needed for the entire length of the border, making it an impractical proposition, at least for the moment. In the meantime, the Border Patrol sticks to it with their jeeps, planes, and the occasional horse, but it is a thankless task. Mexicans deported bounce back like Yo-Yos. In 1967 alone, nearly 28,000 of the 86,000 Mexicans caught for entering illegally had previously been expelled at least once. There is no real deterrent for smuggler or smuggled; the alien himself is sent back; the smuggler (if smuggling can be proved) will get a mere thirty days in jail. Then it's back to Mexico and business as usual.

Unofficially many farmers in California and Texas have always aided the traffic by sending their foremen down into Mexico to recruit labor and smuggle it in over the border. They were doing this increasingly in 1967 and 1968 to combat attempts by the AFL-CIO United Farm Workers Organizing Committee to organize migrant farm labor throughout the United States. The farmers, according to the union, were encouraging "wetbacks" to come across to strike-break. Quite apart from that encouragement, the pace of illegal entry is likely to quicken over the next few years. In the autumn of 1968 U.S. Secretary of Labor Willard Wirtz announced that Mexican laborers, who had been allowed into the United States at the rate of 400,000 a year for contract labor, were no longer needed—a situation which must make the alien-smuggling racket a growth business. If nearly half a million Mexicans who had previously entered the United States legally are suddenly denied entry, it is hardly likely they will sit back and starve in Mexico. The fence and the Rio Grande are going to be bustling with activity on dark nights over the next few years. The grass is always greener over that fence.

The same appears to be true in Hong Kong for thousands of Chinese living in Communist China and for many other Southeast Asians from Thailand, Burma, Laos, Vietnam, and the Philippines. The appeal of Hong Kong is partly that of political freedom, but rather more the prospect (not always fulfilled) of a good job or the reunion of a divided family. The traffic is known locally as the "snake trade," and the boatmen who carry the illegal immigrants are "snake heads." Since the majority of these immigrants to Hong Kong are from China, where it would be unjust to send them back, the Hong Kong government takes a liberal attitude toward people without the correct papers who turn up in the colony applying for identity cards. Indeed, between 1960 and 1968 as many as eighty percent of the Chinese registering for Hong Kong identity cards were illegal immigrants. The greatest exodus from China was during the famine in 1962, when 142,000 illegal entrants were granted permission to remain in the colony; the average for more recent years has been 10,000 to 12,000 a year.

The Chinese make their way down, primarily from the Canton area, either to Macao, just across the Pearl River from Hong Kong, or to one of the offshore islands dotted around the coastal waters of the colony. Then is it simply a matter of contacting a snake head for the boat ride into Hong Kong. His charge varies from 800–1,500 Hong Kong dollars (U.S. $130–250), according to the means, importance, and gullibility of the traveler. Regardless of price, it is an uncomfortable ride for everyone, battened down below decks in little junks and bumboats, along with cargoes of prawns, bean shoots, and rice. Frequently the passengers are packed in so tight that there is precious little air to breathe on the journey through the islands or across the forty miles of the Pearl River. Even when the snake boat pulls into the bustling typhoon shelter at Aberdeen or West Point, its illicit passengers may be forced to wait until long after dark before they can slip ashore. The marine police in Hong Kong constantly search the armada of small craft, checking for both people and drugs, but it is a frustrating and never-ending task. In one year recently they stopped and searched 43,981 boats. It really is like searching for a needle in a haystack—or, in this instance, a snake in the hold.

This traffic is, of course, of a very different character from the illegal migrations into Britain and the United States. Since Hong Kong rarely turns away an illegal immigrant who is caught, the real problem is getting *out* of China. Similarly, the crux of the matter in Eastern Europe is escaping *from* the Communist camp. The pressures, both on the traveler and on anyone who helps him, are thus much greater. The Pakistani who is caught attempting to enter Britain illegally and the Mexican sneaking into the United States are bounced back home on the next available plane or bus. Back home there are no repercussions. However, for anyone caught trying to escape from China or Eastern Europe the repercussions can be most uncomfortable. The groups who organize this latter traffic are either doing it from sincere humanitarian or political motives and accordingly would not dream of charging for their smuggling services, or are unscrupulous characters out purely for their own gain, with little concern for anyone they may leave in the lurch.

Many escapes from Eastern Europe are purely individual efforts, often without any aid at all from the West, or with the cooperation simply of a few friends or relatives who have been able to travel behind the Iron Curtain. Alongside them are the professional people—smugglers operating out of West Germany and charging fees, which may go as high as $2,500 per person, although more normal rates are from $100. The most direct methods have always been to hide the escaper in the trunk of a car, beneath a truck, or buried beneath baggage in a train. Tunnels have also been dug with considerable success right under the Berlin Wall from West to East Berlin. But Communist border guards are fully aware of these tricks and with little waste of time can prod the likely hideouts. In recent years the professionals have resorted to more uncunning—and often more unscrupulous —methods. A ruse used increasingly has been to send the escaper over the border flourishing the passport of someone who has already entered Eastern Europe quite legally. The complication, of course, is to find volunteers in the West who are willing to run the risk of being left behind in East Germany, Hungary, or Czechoslovakia without papers. In theory, at least, the scheme worked like this. The smuggler would find someone in the West, often a student, who, for sympathy or money, would agree to travel to Eastern Europe. There the volunteer's passport would be handed over to the potential escaper, who, after a quick switch of photographs, would be off and away over the frontier. After giving him a day's start, the visitor would rush to his local embassy or the police and explain that his passport had been lost or stolen. The embassy, according to the theory, anyway, would issue a new passport or temporary travel documents enabling him also to return home. In practice, the police in Eastern Europe are now alert to this little swap and in some instances have simply laughed at foreigners dashing in to say their passport has been stolen.

Two young Dutchmen and a Dutch girl who agreed to help out a professional smuggler in the autumn of 1968 were somewhat shattered to end up in jail. The girl was given a three-month sentence in Budapest after she confessed to the local police that she had given her passport to an escaper, while the two men were each sentenced to thirty-three months in East Berlin.

The tragedy of these rackets is that those who agree innocently to aid the smugglers are the ones who are often left to suffer when things go wrong. The smugglers do not warn these volunteers of the true danger, and never themselves make the mistake of handing over *their* passports to anyone else in Eastern Europe. These smugglers have to face the wrath of both the East European and the West German police, both of whom are trying to stamp out this kind of irresponsible racketeering. Unfortunately, several of the smugglers made their pile before the police caught on to the game. One West Berliner is said to have made $50,000 in two years through the passport-switching dodge. This kind of unscrupulousness also makes life more difficult for other groups with higher principles who are simply trying to do refugees a good turn in helping them escape and not aiming to grow rich in the process. Any investigation into racketeering inevitably makes their job that much harder; all they want is to be left alone to get the people out with the minimum of fuss.

INTERLUDE

Someone, Somewhere Is Waiting for a Cable from You

Someone, Somewhere Is Waiting for a Cable from You

The Hong Kong diamond dealer was in a dilemma. He had a stranger in his office when his assistant came in and inquired, "What about the cable to Antwerp? It's all made up, but what about the last two words?" The diamond man looked uncomfortable. "There's no hurry," he said. "It can go in half an hour." "No, it must go now to be in Antwerp when they get in in the morning [there is a seven-hour time difference]. How shall I finish it?" The dealer looked even more flustered. "How about 'When remitting?'" he ventured with an embarrassed laugh, hastening to explain to his visitor that this was often put on a cable from Antwerp to Hong Kong to determine when payment would be made. It was not, however, appropriate in this instance. Finally, almost in despair, the dealer said, "Oh, put 'All's well' on the end."

In any secret business, communication security is vital. Banks, diamond and gold dealers, and smugglers all have their codes, and they will go to any lengths to prevent them falling into unwelcome hands. The whole message may be in code, or there may be a password or catch phrase at the end of a cable to confirm its authenticity. Anyone cracking a code can have a field day. One group of gold smugglers in Hong Kong got the key to a Swiss bank code in 1967 and obtained over $200,000 through a fraudulent cable, which authorized the bank to pay one of their team.

Smugglers use both cables and international telephones extensively. The telephone, however, has its dangers, because it can be tapped; there are often long delays in calls from the Far East or Middle East to Europe, and local police departments make a nightly check of hotel records of all international phone calls made by guests. Since police intelligence files will almost certainly contain the telephone number of suspected international smugglers, it is all too easy to check if a guest has been reporting back that he made a delivery safely.

In Tangier in the 1950's the operations of the fleet of smuggling launches ranging out over the Mediterranean from the free port with cargoes of gold, cigarettes, and whiskey were directed by radio from the Rue Velasquez. Yet radio is an extraordinarily public method of communication once the authorities have detected the smuggler's frequency.

No method of communication can be one-hundred-percent safe, but one of the best is a code that can be understood only by obtaining a complete copy of the codebook. This may be a plain-language code in which a cable "Johnny has gastroenteritis hope you can come tomorrow" means to the initiated, "Courier with gold will be arriving on Pan Am at one tomorrow," or it may be a three-letter code based on one theme letter.

A three-letter code used recently in gold smuggling between the Far East and Europe was built around the letter b. There was a word to correspond to every combination, from "bbb" to "bzz."

In part, it read like this:

bbb – customs   bdb – jewelry
bbc – no market   bdc – gold
bbd – will arrive tomorrow   bdz – deliver to

174

bbe – consigned by air	beb – today
bbf – packed in wooden box	bfh – passport
bbh – money already received	bgb – suspect
bbi – kilo	bgz – from
bbj – flight number	bhi – pull out
bcb – Bangkok	bkl – alerted
bcc – Singapore	bmb – 1
bcd – Hong Kong	bmc – 2
bce – Geneva	bmt – 30
bcg – Manila	bne – 719

Thus the message "bmtbbibdcbbdbbjbnebgz-bcebdzbcg" is interpreted as "Thirty kilos gold will arrive tomorrow on flight 719 from Geneva deliver to Manila." Even more compelling, "bcdbbbbklbhi" means "Hong Kong customs alerted pull out."

THREE

The Luxury Trade

VIII

Diamonds

*You can carry enough diamonds on your
naked body to set you up for life.*

—Ian Fleming

The South African police colonel was a small, gentle man with
the air of a slightly puzzled puppy. He rolled a handful of diamonds across his desk amid a clutter of empty teacups like so
many peanuts. "This diamond," he said, picking up a gleaming
pebble between finger and thumb, "this diamond is ten carats and
is worth 2,131 rand [$3,000]." He selected a larger stone. "This
would cost 6,092." Casually he proceeded to unwrap a further
collection of stones from small screws of paper and scattered
them unconcernedly alongside the others on the desk. Another
detective picked up the 6,092-rand diamond, the size of a
cherrystone, popped it in his mouth, flicked it with his tongue
into his cheek behind his back molars, and carried on smoking
his cigarette. "You see," he said easily, "I can carry on talking to
you, and you don't know I have six thousand rand worth of
diamonds in my mouth. I once bargained with a diamond smuggler for half an hour, negotiating with him to buy diamonds.
When at last we concluded the deal, he plucked the diamond out
of his mouth. I honestly had no idea it was there."

The colonel agreed. "Hell, man, a diamond is so small, it's easy to hide anywhere. I could secrete a fortune now in the knot of your tie." Diamonds are a smuggler's best friend. He can hide them in his toothpaste or the ink of his fountain pen, in his cigarettes or the lining of his jacket; his ears, nose, mouth, stomach, and rectum are equally convenient. Ladies, of course, are even better endowed.

Whatever his motives, whether to avoid export duties in the diamond-producing countries of Africa or dodge import dues and profit taxes on cut and polished diamonds in America, Europe, or Japan, the smuggler is secure in the knowledge that the diamond, like gold, is effectively a universally accepted medium of exchange. The stability of diamond prices makes them a safe hedge against inflation, and everywhere from Indonesia and India to South Africa and the United States, they are an excellent way of skirting international currency restrictions. "A diamond," explained a South African dealer, "is an easy way for anyone to get money out of this country. If I took out twenty-five thousand rand [$35,000] in notes, I might be able to change them in Geneva, even in Paris, at twenty-five-percent discount, but if I buy rough diamonds here I can sell them anywhere." This convenience of the diamond in helping skirt normal banking channels and the prying eyes of the tax man has not passed unnoticed by the criminal looking for a secure investment for his ill-gotten gains. "We know," a London diamond man said, "that because the diamond has become such an excellent investment, the top people in crime—particularly in the United States—are investing their money in gemstones rather than banks." Obviously many people besides dewy-eyed courting couples take heed of all those romantic advertisements proclaiming "A diamond is forever."

It is hardly surprising, therefore, that the temptation to smuggle diamonds is universal. Recently those who have been unfortunate enough to be caught in the act have included an Ovambo tribesman arrested at Oranjemund in the diamond fields of South West Africa with $50,000 in rough diamonds sewn neatly into the hem of his blanket; some enterprising Russians working on a development project in Guinea in West Africa, who sent home industrial diamonds labeled as coffee beans; and an off-duty Lufthansa flight engineer, who was picked up in New York with $59,000 worth of diamonds in a tiny cylindrical package barely one inch in diameter and four inches long. Then there is the dean of diamond smugglers, Charles Travitsky, who recently served a three-year sentence in a U.S. federal prison for attempting to smuggle diamonds into the United States. He was first picked up in Miami as he came in from Venezuela. Contained within his body were several contraceptives containing in them cut and polished diamonds worth $47,330. While out on bail, he was arrested a second time when he flew into Miami from Brazil with industrial diamonds scattered like stardust among his clothes. Out on bail yet again, appealing a prison sentence, he had $12,000 in diamonds confiscated in Mexico City; while in Bangkok the Thai customs, acting on a tip, searched this globe-trotter's luggage as he came in from Singapore and sifted out $30,000 in diamonds, diamond watches, sapphires, rubies, and other jewels hidden in the walls of a corrugated box, in a record player, and in cans labeled "Fruit Salad."

Whether the smuggler is conveying rough diamonds mined illicitly in the alluvial diggings of Sierra Leone to Antwerp or a five-carat cut and polished diamond from Hong Kong to Tokyo, he will never be far from the protective umbrella of the diamond dealers' establishment. For the diamond business is a closed shop that would delight the most ardent trade unionist. Diamond dealing is a profession passed on in families for generations. Ask a dealer in Hong Kong whom he deals with in Antwerp, and he replies, "My brother has a diamond-exporting firm there." Well, how about New York? "I have another brother there—and my cousin is in Tel Aviv." "We are just like a small village," said a New York dealer, referring specifically to the New York diamond fraternity gathered together on 47th Street between Fifth and Sixth avenues. But he could have been referring equally to the international diamond community.

A member of any one of the narrow circle of diamond dealers' clubs in London, Antwerp, Amsterdam, Paris, Vienna, Milan, Tel Aviv, Johannesburg, or New York has immediate entrée to every other. "If I go tomorrow to any city where there is a diamond club," explained the New York dealer, "I have only to show my card and I am admitted." For anyone who is not a club member, the diamond business is likely to remain a closed book. The securely locked door of the club, with its spyhole through which a guard views visitors with an inhospitable eye, will remain shut.

Those who do break the hallowed circle find themselves in a world where diamonds worth hundreds of thousands of dollars are carried, seemingly casually, in little leather wallets tucked into a deep vest pocket and are spilled across the table amid the coffeecups for a fellow dealer to consider. Any deal is sealed with a simple handshake, and since many dealers are Jews, with the Hebrew blessing *"Mazel broche"*—"Good luck and blessings." The code of honor, discipline, and silence is strictly enforced. "Trust is vital," said the New York dealer. "I will trust with one hundred thousand dollars' worth of diamonds, someone to whom I would not give one thousand dollars' credit. And if someone does misbehave, it is over the wires in a flash." An erring dealer is blackballed not only by his own club but by the clubs throughout the world.

A tight code of ethics is essential in a business offering such spectacular temptations for theft or fraud, yet it acts also as a convenient mantle to shield from awkward questions the minority of dealers (who nevertheless are perfectly trustworthy within their own profession) who handle stolen or smuggled diamonds. Within the sheltered hub of a diamond club no one will question the origin of a parcel of diamonds. If a dealer has his own method of getting diamonds from Brazzaville in the Congo to Antwerp, from Antwerp to New York, or Hong Kong to Manila, that is strictly his business. Unlike almost any other kind of smuggling, diamond smuggling is largely conceived and controlled by legitimate diamond dealers. They may employ professional couriers to carry the diamonds for them, but the brains that engineer it all are within the diamond business. Consequently, the important diamond smugglers are rarely caught. Any investigation meets a wall of silence as complete as anything imposed by the Mafia. "I never knew what silence was until I went to Antwerp," one baffled diamond investigator admitted. "They would hardly admit they knew what diamonds were."

The dealers are not the only closed shop. The initial marketing of rough diamonds from the mines is, effectively, a monopoly —albeit a benevolent one. Since the 1930's up to eighty-five percent of the world's rough diamonds, excluding Russian production, have been sold through De Beers' Central Selling Organisation (C.S.O.). Not only does the Central Selling Organisation handle the production of De Beers' own mines in South Africa and South West Africa, but it also acts as a cooperative selling agent for diamond-mining companies in Tanzania, the Congo, Angola, and West Africa. The argument for the monopoly of diamond sales is that C.S.O., which has amassed large financial resources, can ensure a steady world price for diamonds regardless of the day-to-day demand. If the demand for diamonds falls, then the Central Selling Organisation will continue to pay the diamond producers but will stockpile the diamonds; a few months later, if the demand exceeds supply, C.S.O. can sell from stock to prevent wild price fluctuations.

Ten times a year the Central Selling Organisation holds "sights" at Number 2 Charterhouse Street, the London headquarters of the sales company, the Diamond Trading Co., at which dealers buy their diamonds. Advance notice of a forthcoming "sight" is sent to nearly three hundred international buyers, of whom about half attend every "sight" and the rest come three or four times a year. They have, however, curiously little control over what they buy. A "parcel" of diamonds will be made up beforehand by D.T.C.'s sales team for each dealer attending. The parcel will be tailored to his known requirements, but he must take the entire package or reject it outright. If he refuses, he must wait until the next "sight" before he has another opportunity to buy. He is not permitted to pick through the parcel, sifting out those diamonds he wishes to buy and leaving the remainder. Some dealers, like Harry Winston in New York, bypass D.T.C. for at least a part of their purchases by establishing direct contacts with the diamond mines. The majority, although they complain loudly on occasion that D.T.C. are high-handed in dishing out with the stones it thinks they should have, accept that it does give their business a stable price structure. "Of course dealers complain," a De Beers man conceded, "but most of them are very rich. A dealer from Antwerp can fly to a London 'sight,' buy a parcel of diamonds for sixty thousand pounds, fly back to Antwerp, and, if the diamonds are not what he himself requires at that moment, sell the whole parcel for seventy thousand pounds without even breaking our seal."

From its command post astride the world's main diamond pipelines, the Central Selling Organisation is in a unique position to view both the legitimate and the illicit diamond business. In 1953 they caught the headlines when Sir Ernest Oppenheimer, chairman of De Beers, hired Sir Percy Sillitoe, the former head of Britain's M.I.5, to found an International Diamond Security Organisation (IDSO) both to prevent illicit buying of diamonds (IDB) stolen from the De Beers mines in South Africa and South West Africa and to try to ferret out the men behind the flourishing diamond-smuggling syndicates.

At that time diamond smuggling was a thriving business to the United States, where diamond tariffs were high, and to Russia, which desperately needed industrial diamonds for sophisticated tool-making equipment in factories throughout the U.S.S.R., Poland, and Czechoslovakia. Sillitoe hoped that by providing his undercover detectives with lavish funds to buy diamonds in Liberia and Rhodesia, where many of the diamonds from Sierra Leone and Central and Southern Africa were being smuggled, he would penetrate the syndicates. The concept of IDSO as an international force of diamond detectives was a perfectly valid one, since diamond smugglers operate with complete disregard for the boundaries that restrict a normal police force. But its activities also attracted international publicity, which was hardly desirable for an undercover network.

Ian Fleming, captivated by the whole thing, wrote a nonfiction book called *The Diamond Smugglers*, based, much to De Beers' chagrin, on the indiscreet revelations of a former IDSO detective. Fleming was somewhat carried away by the idea of a sinister character, whom he referred to only as Mr. Big, running one vast international diamond syndicate. This, however, was bowing too much to the world of James Bond. There were— indeed, still are—a number of wealthy diamond dealers in Europe and Asia who blend black-market dealings with legitimate business. But the notion of one mastermind, his loupe screwed into his eye, poring over a hoard of smuggled diamonds as he spins an all-embracing diamond network, is a trifle too romantic. (Bond himself was duly plunged into the world of diamond smuggling in *Diamonds Are Forever*, in which 007 battled illicit diamond buyers in West Africa and smuggled diamonds to New York hidden inside his Dunlop 65 golf balls.)

The International Diamond Security Organisation had a short life. Well before Sir Ernest Oppenheimer's death in 1957, Sillitoe's team of globe-trotting diamond detectives was quietly disbanded. Since then De Beers' security has concentrated essentially on protecting its own mines and its diamond-selling organization rather than mounting an international crusade against smugglers. Its intelligence network, however, is still excellently informed of all the latest twists of the illicit traffic, of which there are two main facets. First is the theft of rough diamonds, whether from the mines or from alluvial diamond fields by unlicensed diggers, and the smuggling of the stones to friendly buyers. This whole operation is called illicit diamond buying (IDB) or illicit diamond mining (IDM), and is confined essentially to Africa, which produces ninety percent of the world's diamonds. Second, there is the smuggling of cut and polished diamonds from the main markets of Antwerp, Tel Aviv, and Hong Kong into countries which ban imports, impose high import duties, or levy such heavy domestic taxes that a dealer likes to duck as much as possible by carrying on at least part of his trade under the counter.

IDB and IDM

The temptation of seeing a fortune pass daily through his fingers can overwhelm even the most upright citizen working in a diamond mine. As a diamond buyer in Kimberley put it, "The most seemingly honest man will often admit privately that if a one-hundred-thousand-pound parcel of diamonds came his way at precisely the same moment as the coast was clear, he would take it."

Many men succumb to temptation. Between thirty and fifty million dollars' worth of rough diamonds are either stolen from the diamond mines and alluvial diggings of Africa every year and spirited back to obliging buyers or are dug up by licensed diggers who neglect to sell them at official buying offices and thus avoid local or export taxes. Illicit buyers, with a nose for a developing traffic, settle like vultures around the borders of any diamond-producing nation in Africa.

The homeland of IDB is, of course, South Africa itself, which is the second-largest producer of diamonds in the world and ranks first in the production of gems (a gem is any diamond which will polish into a recognizable jewel). Illicit diamond buying is as old as the mines of Kimberley. From the first heady days of the diamond rush in the 1870's, in which Cecil Rhodes, Barney Barnato, and Alfred Beit made their fortunes, the diamond fields were plagued with nimble-fingered workers who pocketed, palmed, or swallowed diamonds when the boss's eye was turned. In those early days, security was an unknown word; by the time it was introduced, IDB was already an ineradicable way of life. Surprisingly few South Africans seem to frown on it. Indeed, a man convicted of IDB can become a minor hero in his hometown. "There's a chap here, respectable local farmer," said a legitimate Kimberley diamond buyer, "who went to prison for IDB. Everyone looked on him as if he was Robin Hood."

The most skillful illicit buyers, who invariably combine their skulduggery with quite legal mining or diamond businesses, have amassed sizable fortunes. One Johannesburg trafficker of some repute recently bought himself a new mansion in the city for over $250,000. A leading Kimberley operator reinvested his profits in a hotel which he eventually sold for $225,000. But few can top the coup of a Johannesburg diamond dealer in 1962. He got word of a 700-carat diamond, as big as a plum, which had allegedly been discovered on alluvial diggings at Bells Bank in Northern Cape province (although some rumors said it originated in Angola) and was being offered around on the black market. The dealer (who, it turned out later, had a criminal record in Europe and a great smuggling reputation from West Africa) agreed to buy the stone. He actually took delivery in Lourenço Marques in Mozambique, paying $84,000 in cash. He flew to Antwerp, where he sold it for $480,000. His departure with such a prize was naturally somewhat hasty. He left his wife and children behind, but a few weeks later they joined him in Europe to begin a new life on the proceeds of the deal.

The profits of illicit diamond buying are rarely quite so handsome. However, in the twelve months from September, 1967, to August, 1968, the 123-man Diamond Branch of the South African police seized $140,000 in diamonds filched from the mines. The diamond detectives concede that if they are lucky they catch at the most ten percent of the illicit diamonds about which they *receive information*. There are many other transactions of which they receive no murmur from the underworld or informers. At the minimum, therefore, IDB is one and one-half million dollars a year; more likely it is twice as high. "An Antwerp dealer told me not long ago," a diamond detective admitted, "that by his estimate at least one million pounds' [$2.4 million] worth of diamonds are smuggled from South Africa and South West Africa to Belgium every year."

At first glance it is hard to see how so many diamonds can be stolen from the mines. Every South African mine is surrounded by a jungle of barbed wire; highly trained dogs prowl the fences; and diamond companies and police have informers among the European and African workers. The Africans, who form the majority of the labor force, are not permitted to leave the mine for the duration of their contract—normally a minimum of six months. When they do depart, they and all their belongings are submitted to intensive personal and X-ray searches. The Europeans, however, live outside the mine and can come and go each day. For health reasons an X-ray a day is impossible, but there is the deterrent of spot checks. The diamonds themselves are elusive; they are not scattered around like cake crumbs on the ground, but are embedded in "kimberlite" rock. It is only in the recovery plant, where the rock is crushed, sifted, and passed over grease tables, to which the diamonds adhere while the debris rolls on, that diamonds are revealed for plucking. The recovery plant is always staffed by a handful of carefully screened men; the average worker rarely sees a diamond. And yet the stones are successfully stolen.

Living under the microscope of security year in and year out can impel a man, sooner or later, to try to beat the system. "If you work in a South African mine or on the diamond coast of South West Africa," a security expert explained, "it becomes a game, a challenge. Your entire psychology shifts over to thinking how you can beat the restrictions. This is especially true among the Africans. Just as everyone in a concentration camp is thinking of ways to escape, so in a diamond mine everyone dreams of ways to get diamonds out."

The prize for ingenuity probably goes to the man who hit on the idea of hiding diamonds inside bolts from his car. He carefully cut through a bolt well down toward the end of the thread. Then he hollowed out the inside and packed the cavity with diamonds. He rewelded the two bolt sections together and screwed a nut up over the hairline crack where the cut had been made.

Within the mine it is usually the African who initially collars the diamonds, but he is often put up to it by a European agent of one of the main illicit buyers. This agent may have half a dozen or more Africans each working independently for him in the mine, all carefully briefed to leave their diamonds in different caches. The European can then pick up the diamonds once in a while, like a farmer going around to his henhouse searching for eggs laid by secretive hens, and arrange for them to be smuggled out of the mine. The agent himself will rarely do this; he will recruit another European. In the main mines of Premier and Finsch, where the European goes home from work each day, he can gamble that if he is searched and X-rayed in a spot check one day, he is safe to carry diamonds the next. Once the diamonds are outside the mine, they are easily passed to middlemen for the top illicit diamond buyers. These intermediaries hang around the bars and cafés near the mine. One café in Kimberley, run by a renowned diamond trafficker, is a favorite meeting place to debate terms. The actual transfer of the diamonds, however, will happen in less public places or even on the open road of the veld, where any trailing police cars will be uncomfortably conspicuous. The Indian quarter of Johannesburg, to the west of Market Street, is also an ideal transit point. It is a jumble of back alleys and interconnected houses. "It is very hard to arrest the runners with diamonds there," said a detective sadly. "You are sure a buyer is waiting in a certain house, you see the runner go in and are right behind him. But as you come in the front door, the buyer is out the back and away."

The important men are naturally remote from all this. They rarely touch the stolen diamonds; their task is to make sure the right man is in the right place at the right moment. Yet they make most of the profits. The intermediary, particularly the African, sees little of the loot. The African is seldom paid while he is still working on his contract at the mine, but is promised payment when he returns to his tribal area. He often has no idea of the true value of the diamond he steals and is in no position to bargain. His share of the proceeds is frequently nominal.

Priority, the moment the diamond is outside the mine, must go to getting it into the legitimate market as quickly as possible. It is an offense under South African law to possess a rough or an uncut diamond unless you are a licensed digger, buyer, or cutter; anyone, however, may own cut and polished diamonds. One secret, therefore, of a good IDB operation is to get the rough diamonds to a friendly cutter right away.

The main illicit buyers in Johannesburg, Kimberley, and Cape Town either have their own private cutting operation or employ an amenable licensed cutter to do a little moonlighting. Once the stone is cut and polished, it becomes perfectly legitimate, and there is no way of proving it was stolen originally.

An alternative way of "legitimizing" a diamond is to have a friend among the diamond diggers who still scour the alluvial diggings in the hard, red earth outside Kimberley or at Bells Bank with picks, shovels, and ancient sieves which appear to have seen service for at least a century. These old diggers (no new licenses are issued now) can "salt" their claim with diamonds stolen elsewhere. Provided they are careful not to salt it with a type of diamond found only five hundred miles away,

189

there is little chance of detection. The right care is sometimes lacking. When the Finsch diamond mine in Northern Cape province started production in the mid-1960's, the De Beers buyers, who make a weekly round of the old diggings, noticed rough diamonds with a greenish hue turning up for the first time in the finds. The only "green" diamonds in South Africa come from Finsch. The illicit buyers had quickly infiltrated their agents into the new mine and routed their haul to the ancient diggings.

Green diamonds from Finsch also turn up in the diamond production of Lesotho, that island of African independence in the midst of South Africa. They are smuggled over the border on horseback or in cars to a handful of dealers in Maseru, the capital of Lesotho, who are only too happy to register the diamonds as having been found in the African state. Here—and in the Republic of South Africa itself—there is often a feeling of triumph in such deals, because they amount to outwitting the giant De Beers, which has the diamond industry so firmly in its grasp.

The smuggling of diamonds into Lesotho is so widely known that many Africans turn it to additional advantage. They try hitching lifts along the road into the little country with their pockets full of fake rough diamonds cut from the bottom of old bottles. When a naïve traveler picks one up, it is not long before the African slips out a glass diamond. "You like to buy a good diamond cheap, boss?" he inquires hopefully. An innocent falls for the trick every day, believing he has stumbled on genuine diamonds being smuggled from South Africa to Lesotho. The initiated can detect the fake by rubbing the "diamond" between finger and thumb. A genuine rough diamond will feel slightly oily; a bottle-bottom diamond does not.

Whether the diamond thief intends to dispose of his haul in South Africa or Lesotho or entrust it to a courier to Antwerp, he is well advised to work for an existing IDB network. Although within a mine a man may operate as a lone wolf, it is essential for him to have the right contacts outside. The amateur, even if he can get in touch with an established illicit buyer, may find it very difficult to dispose of his stones. The buyer is bound to be wary of a stranger, for one technique used by the South African police to trap known illicit buyers is to send along a detective with a pocketful of diamonds from a special police cache which he tries to "sell" to the illicit buyer. The latter, therefore, will probably either refuse to buy from anyone he does not know or will offer an absurdly low price. The same would be true, of course, outside South Africa. Anyone without the right introductions who turned up in a diamond dealer's office in Antwerp trying to sell stolen diamonds would probably be shown the door. The diamond business, legal and illegal, is very exclusive.

Although South Africa IDB involves well over one million dollars a year, it could be curtailed only by enormously expensive security procedures. But there quickly comes a point at which security costs can outweigh the saving in stolen diamonds. In South Africa there is now an informal balance between security and IDB; it is at a "tolerable" level.

On the diamond coast of South West Africa, however, an acceptable balance between security and diamond thefts is much harder to achieve. This diamond field, four hundred miles northwest of Cape Town, has a romantic image as the "diamond desert." There on the bleak seaboard, where the Namib desert sweeps down to the Atlantic, is a narrow strip of rolling sand dunes clinging to the coastline between the sea and the Richtersveld Mountains. It is three hundred miles long and varies in width from two to twelve miles. The sand dunes, harassed by the southwest wind, often throw up a flurry of sand that blots out the landscape; the dunes themselves change shape overnight. Vegetation is virtually nonexistent. It is a rugged coastline that any sailor should avoid and any traveler overland should skirt— except for the lure of diamonds. For beneath that soft smother of surface sand are gravels peppered with the finest gem diamonds found anywhere in the world. Those gravels yielded $140 million worth of diamonds in 1967.

Diamonds were first discovered on the coast in 1908, when South West Africa was a German protectorate, but the South African invasion of this German domain in 1915 gave them control of the diamond fields. Sir Ernest Oppenheimer, who was just founding the giant Anglo-American mining finance house in South Africa, had visited the diamond coast before the war and realized its enormous potential. By 1920 he had skillfully won the approval of the South African government to an amalgamation of mining interests on the coast, bought out the assets of the German mining companies, and established Consolidated Diamond Mines of South West Africa. Half a century later Consolidated Diamond Mines (CDM) are still firmly entrenched along the diamond coast, which they rule as one of the most closely guarded private estates in the world. Few objects, let alone any person, enter or leave the coast without passing the thorough scrutiny of CDM's security guards. The main mining town of Oranjemund, with a population of three thousand, is owned and administered by CDM. They own all the property in the town and operate the schools, the library, the cinema, and all the shops on a nonprofit basis. The African employees live in compounds, the European employees rent their homes—and their furniture. There is a formidable list of items which may never be taken out of Oranjemund. They include most articles of furniture, bicycles, radios, pianos, refrigerators, and golf clubs. Slightly more leniency is shown to washing machines, baby-carriages, irons, and sewing machines. They are given export permits occasionally, but only if they are handed over to the security department at least fourteen days prior to departure. In addition, all clothing, books, clocks, baby's rattles, kettles, watches, cameras, and projectors may be exported only after an X-ray and physical examination. African and European employees and visitors are subject to X-ray examination. Visitors who arrive by car have to leave their vehicle on one side of the security check and pick up a CDM car on the other.

This fanatical security is not without reason. The diamond coast, unlike the conventional mine, offers unique opportunities for the nimble-fingered. The diamonds are sprinkled as casually as dewdrops over hundreds of square miles of desert. True, twenty tons of sand has to be bulldozed aside for every one carat of diamonds found, but once the gravel-bearing deposits are unveiled, every nook and cranny is picked over by hand and the bedrock finally swept with brooms. The alert broom wielder can pick up a small private fortune. "Those boys have eyes like hawks," admitted an admiring diamond man. The problem, the challenge, is to get those diamonds out. Between September, 1967, and August, 1968, for example, the security authorities caught seventy-two people who between them were trying to smuggle out $3,360,000 worth of diamonds. What really counts, of course, are the ones who get away.

Over the years a wild assortment of legends and barroom yarns to beguile the innocent visitor has evolved around the diamond coast. Everyone comes trotting out with his favorite. "Man, did you hear about the Ovambo who sent his guitar home to his wife asking her to have it repaired? She had it mended for him and sent it back. As it was checked in again, the security chaps found five rough diamonds taped inside. Stupid woman! She wasn't meant to send it back." Then there was the European who was picked up by security for a special search as he was going on leave one weekend. They found nothing. The next time he went on leave he made a special point of raising hell with the security officers. "Why pick on an innocent man like me last weekend?" he shouted. As he ranted, the policemen noticed him trying to slip out from under the table a diamond wrapped in chewing gum which he had stuck there when he was searched the previous week. Another chap, wracking his brains how to get a pile of stolen diamonds over the security fence, decided to build a rocket and orbit them out. All went well until launch time; then the rocket blew up on the little launching pad, scattering the diamonds for miles.

Peel off the added layer which each legend gains with every telling, and there is still no denying the incredible ingenuity of the diamond smugglers. One man who worked on the diamond coast for years carefully amassed a huge cache of diamonds hidden in a remote gully near the sea. Eventually he gave up his job and went to live in Cape Town. Some months later he hired a small plane and flew north to recover his loot. He landed safely on a lonely section of that windswept beach and loaded up with his diamonds. Then, as the plane zoomed down the beach ready for a takeoff, it hit a rock and pitched forward on its nose. A very disappointed diamond smuggler was discovered some hours later by a work party as he trudged over the sand dunes in search of civilization.

Many of those trying to beat the system are lone operators—although they sell to well-established contacts outside South West Africa. But there is some evidence of a more concerted diamond-smuggling operation. In November, 1967, two Africans from the Ovambo, who provide the labor force on the diamond coast, were arrested in Oranjemund. One of them, according to the police, had 250 diamonds worth $60,000 hidden in contraceptives sewn into the seams of a blanket he was taking back to Ovamboland. They were detected when the blanket was given a routine X ray and blips appeared on the screen. The second Ovambo had 142 diamonds worth $14,500. He had drilled a tiny hole in a tin of jam and inserted the diamonds. Then he sealed the hole with solder and replaced the label. Again the X ray caught him out. During the next few months the CDM security police kept the African compound under very close watch and made a number of snap raids. In the spring of 1968, nine Ovambos were charged with the illegal possession of 4,000 diamonds, weighing 8,500 carats and valued at over $700,000. The Africans all told the same story—they had been asked to get the diamonds by a local chief. Naturally he denied the whole thing. But the volume of diamonds and the consistency of the stories raised considerable speculation that this was a well-thought-out attempt by an organization outside South Africa to obtain funds for political purposes. The South African police, however, said that they had no evidence of such a plot and finally discounted the rumors.

Whatever the truth, the size of the nest egg of diamonds that those unfortunate Ovambos mustered on the beaches of the diamond coast indicates the rich prize to be gained by the successful smuggler.

Just to the north of the diamond coast, in Angola, everyone speaks openly of diamond smuggling to earn funds for African political and guerrilla campaigns. Angola is the world's third-largest producer of gem diamonds, which are scattered through alluvial diggings spread over 60,000 square miles of thick rain forest in the east of Lunda province, bordering on the Congo. This is the heart of the area where Portuguese troops have been fighting roving bands of African guerrillas coming in from the

Congo since 1961. Nothing is easier for the guerrilla, in between ambushes, than to shoulder a shovel and do a little diamond digging on a moonlit night. It is a highly profitable operation. One raid on a village in southeast Angola in 1967 netted over $300,000 in stolen diamonds. The diamonds are smuggled back along the forest trails into the Congo and are used eventually to purchase arms. "Their arms," admitted a Portuguese security officer, "are as good as, if not better than, anything we have. Their mortars are excellent." The African guerrillas are certainly using their diamonds to buy from the best source.

But the Angola diamond scene is tranquil compared to the chaos that has prevailed in the neighboring Congo Kinshasa since the Belgians withdrew in 1960. The Congo is easily the leader as the world's largest diamond producer (thirty-three percent, compared with South Africa's sixteen), although virtually all her diamonds are of industrial quality. Until 1960 the alluvial diamond diggings around Luluabourg, Bakwanga, and Tshikapa were controlled by the Société Minière de Bakwanga. Even then illicit diamond mining was relatively easy, as the diggings were scattered through almost impenetrable swamps and forests and anyone with a spade, bucket, and sieve could set up in business. But the Belgians kept some control, and the bulk of the diamond output was eventually passed up the marketing pipeline to the Central Selling Organisation in London. Congo independence and the ensuing civil war rudely shattered that procedure. Anyone and everyone not immediately involved in the civil war—and even a good many of the troops who were—turned diamond prospector and foraged through the swamps in search of a fortune. At the most conservative estimate, half of the Congo's production has passed into illicit channels in every year since 1960. In 1964 at least fifty illegal companies were wildly vying for the area previously controlled by the Société Minière de Bakwanga, and they spirited about twelve million carats of industrial diamonds into world markets. The following year the value of smuggled diamonds was put at twenty-two million dollars. The local diggers were selling the diamonds at fifty percent below the normal market price, but as no one had any overheads and no export duty was being paid to the Congolese government, the profits were ample. The government, of course, was losing not only the duty but also the precious foreign exchange, for the diamonds were all being sold outside the Congo. Overnight the little states of Burundi and Ruanda developed hectic diamond markets, although not a single diamond is actually produced there. At first it was the Lebanese and Arab traders who snapped up the industrial diamonds flooding over from the Congo, but the European buyers (including the Central Selling Organisation) were also soon entrenched to buy up the stones coming through jungle trails and across Lake Tanganyika. Antwerp dealers also established a bridgehead in Brazzaville, just across the Congo River from the city of Kinshasa (Léopoldville). The diamonds were easily spirited across in the jumble of small boats that ply the river. Congo (Brazzaville) suddenly became a major diamond "producer," bouncing into third place in the world-league table, although its own genuine diamond production is only a few hundred carats a year.

The Chinese Communists, already well established in Tanzania, also took advantage of the situation to snap up plenty of industrial diamonds from the dealers strategically positioned all around the Congo. In the 1950's it was the Russians who urgently required industrial diamonds and encouraged illicit diamond deals in Africa; the Chinese have an equal need today.

By 1967 the Congo began to settle down to some greater semblance of law and order, and President Mobuto tried to curb the diamond smuggling and steer the stones back into more normal market channels. He stationed troops at the diggings at Bakwanga and Tshikapa, declared the areas military zones, and instructed his men to shoot diamond poachers. All outsiders without legitimate business in the area were denied landing privileges at these towns and at Luluabourg. Mobuto hoped that, quite apart from controlling the poachers, the buyers, who often arrive by air with suitcases bulging with cash, would now be unable to get through. Anyone who tries making his way through the jungle laden down with cash will find it hard going. But everyone did not take the scheme seriously, and some of the soldiers sent to guard the diamond fields quickly traded their rifles for spade and shovel.

The Central Selling Organisation, however, set up in Kinshasa a new buying office, Britmond (British-Congo Diamond Distributors), with the full approval of the Congolese government and with exclusive rights to buy and export the Congo's diamonds. In the autumn of 1968 a second buying office was opened at Tshikapa in the Miba area four hundred miles east of Kinshasa, which is the main source of the Congo's gemstones. Britmond shipped all the diamonds to London, where the foreign exchange earned by the diamonds was quickly credited to a Congolese account.

This improved organization has slowed the illicit traffic, but at least half the Congo's production is still smuggled out. The trouble is that the export duty from Brazzaville is about one-third of the export duty from Congo Kinshasa. As long as that disparity lasts, the incentive to smuggle will remain. As one buyer put it, shrugging his shoulders, "We have to make the best of the Congo. It is still a comic-opera situation."

The Congo has almost capped Sierra Leone as the greatest center of diamond skulduggery in Africa. It was in Sierra Leone, a hot, wet little country of two and one-half million people tucked on the shoulder of Africa, that most of the postwar diamond-smuggling rackets started in the mid-1950's. Although Sierra Leone yields a mere four percent of the world's annual diamond production, it is the fourth-largest producer of gemstones. They are sprinkled liberally through gravel in the swamps of the interior, often less than a foot below the surface. The country is rugged, populated with mosquitoes and mambas, but here again any bold soul with his spade and sieve can reap a rich harvest in diamonds.

Officially one large slice of 207 square miles of the richest diamond diggings is licensed exclusively to the Sierra Leone Selection Trust mining group; the rest of the diggings are open to diggers in possession of a government license. It is an offense for anyone to hold rough diamonds unless he is a licensed digger or a licensed buyer, and all diamonds must be sold either to the Government Diamond Office, which is run by the Diamond Corporation of West Africa, or to four other exporters (three of them American) approved by the Sierra Leone government. No one seems to pay much attention to these rules and regulations. Many of the licensed diggers choose to sell their diamonds through illicit channels, while a marauding horde of up to eight thousand unlicensed diggers ravages through the swamps like a pack of beavers, many of them digging right in the heart of the Sierra Leone Selection Trust's exclusive mining areas. Their spadework is so energetic that they recently diverted a river through the middle of a village and virtually dug out the foundations of a disused Selection Trust diamond-recovery plant. "It's so hectic up there," reported one buyer, "that from the air it looks as crowded as the beaches on D-Day." Around the town of Koidu, in the heart of the Selection Trust territory, the illicit miners are so blatant that they wave cheerfully to mining-company helicopters circling overhead. On the ground the diggers will greet visiting government ministers, judges, or businessmen without any apparent embarrassment. Any mining-company security men who intervene are liable to be beaten up. "The police are powerless to do anything," a mining man lamented. "The law simply is not being enforced. It's quite out of this world. I've seen three thousand men mining illicitly around Koidu in broad daylight."

The chaos reached such proportions in early 1969 that the Sierra Leone Selection Trust actually published a booklet on illicit diamond mining full of photographs of the illicit diggers hard at work and stressed the enormous losses in revenue being suffered by the Sierra Leone government as a result of the uncontrolled and indiscriminate digging. In fact, it is quite feasible to patrol the area and keep IDM down to an acceptable level, given a peaceful political situation in the country. But after one military coup in March, 1967, and a countercoup in 1968, the main preoccupation of the successive governments has been to keep themselves in power; there has been no time for little local difficulties like IDM. Matters are complicated because some government supporters have been actively engaged both in IDM and in the buying of the illicit diamonds, and it has not been a prudent moment to curtail their activities. As a result, at least twelve million dollars in diamonds have been leaving Sierra Leone illegally each year.

The actual incentive for the smuggling is threefold: to avoid paying a seven-and-one-half-percent export duty to the Sierra Leone government; to obtain hard currency, preferably dollars, in return for the diamonds; and to dodge internal taxes by avoiding reference to the diamonds in a digger's or a buyer's books.

The diamonds are smuggled out of Sierra Leone on foot, by boat, and by air. Many a passenger on flights out of Freetown bound either for Europe or down the West African coast to Lagos takes along a little bundle of diamonds. Even a Harley Street surgeon from London is reputed to bring back diamonds after he has treated his Sierra Leone patients. The two closest freebooting centers to Sierra Leone are Monrovia, the capital of Liberia, and Conakry, the capital of Guinea. Both these towns have played host to illicit diamond buyers since the mid-1950's. When the traffic first began, local African traders handled the buying. But they have few overseas contacts, and they were quickly supplanted by Lebanese buyers from Beirut, who have dominated the illicit West African markets ever since. The Russians played an active part in getting these buyers well established. They were desperately short of industrial diamonds in the 1950's, not only for their own industry, but also for Poland, Hungary, and Czechoslovakia. They arranged for Sierra Leone's industrial diamonds to be smuggled back to Beirut, where the Soviet Embassy picked them up and delivered them to Moscow. The Lebanese buyers thus had a double market: The gems went to Antwerp or New York, the industrials to Moscow. Several Antwerp dealers established strong contacts with the buyers in Monrovia, many of whom operated from the Ducor Palace Hotel. One Antwerp buyer alone was sometimes flying back as much as $200,000 worth of rough diamonds in a single consignment.

At one peak period in the late 1950's over twenty-five million dollars in diamonds were smuggled out of Sierra Leone each year. There was then a period of relative calm until the coup of 1967 ushered in another period of widespread IDM.

Sierra Leone's neighbors have given a tacit blessing to the traffic, which brings them in a pleasant extra revenue. Liberia, through which at least five million dollars of Sierra Leone diamonds are smuggled each year, charges an export duty of two and one-half percent on diamonds passing through her capital of Monrovia, which is five percent less than the export duty charged in Sierra Leone.

The diamonds are actually collected in Sierra Leone itself by the licensed dealers, of whom half are African, half Lebanese. For the sake of form, they put some of their purchases through the G.D.O., but most of the diamonds from the illegal diggers are passed swiftly along the back roads to Liberia. There are two main routes: From the Sierra Leone mining towns of Bo, Yenema, Kenema, and Koidu they are either spirited through the back country, across the river Moa by ferry into Guinea and thence down the road into Liberia; or the smugglers make their way down to Melema, a tiny community ten miles inland from the sea on the Sierra Leone–Liberian border, pay a boatman to take them across the river, and hitch a ride up the road to Monrovia. The routes are so well charted that it is possible for a dealer to take a taxi to the border and ask the driver to wait while he nips over to Monrovia to dispose of his diamonds.

De Beers, with its customary persistence, makes the maximum effort to curb this traffic. Since 1956, when it set up the Diamond Corporation of Sierra Leone to do the official buying at the diamond diggings and then the Diamond Corporation of West Africa in 1959 to run the Government Diamond Office, it has dispatched eager young British buyers, trained in London, to trek through the swamps operating mobile buying offices for diamonds from their Land Rovers or tents. But for all their efforts, as long as countries around Sierra Leone charge a lower export duty—or it is possible to duck the duty entirely—they can have limited success. Any suggestion that the whole business could be stopped by force is laughed off. "Catch the Africans smuggling diamonds?" scoffs a buyer just back from the mosquito-ridden swamps. "I could move a regiment through the elephant grass on the Sierra Leone border without anyone seeing."

Those less adept at maneuvers in the elephant grass can always use the fishing boats flitting back and forth over the Gulf of Guinea. An American entrepreneur, based in Lome in Togo, operates an informal shuttle service all along the West African coast from Ghana to Guinea, picking up diamonds not only from the Sierra Leone fields but from Ghana, where production is also plagued by hordes of freelance diggers. His little smuggling fleet is reputed to run so reliably that anyone with a handful of diamonds filched in Ghana can count on there being a boat leaving Accra every Tuesday bound for Lome. Once there, the stones are carried out by air, either secreted on women couriers, who are being used increasingly in West Africa (because there are few, if any, women customs officers to carry out personal searches), or in the sacred immunity of diplomatic bags. Many of the diamonds from Lome go direct to the fast-expanding cutting and polishing center of Tel Aviv.

Whatever clandestine route diamonds take out of West Africa or the Congo, a remarkable number of them are eventually snared by the all-embracing net of the Central Selling Organisation. C.S.O. does not sit back and view the illicit traffic from a position of moral superiority. It pitches in wholeheartedly, trying to buy up as many of the diamonds as possible. Whenever a new market for diamond buyers opens up in Burundi or Brazzaville or Monrovia, a buyer from De Beers will set up shop alongside the more shady buyers. He often has the advantage that he can bid the genuine world price for the diamonds, while the "spivs" (as De Beers delights to call them) must offer a trifle under the going world price. Even if the diamonds elude the C.S.O. net in the immediate local market, many more of them will be purchased once they are back in London or Antwerp. "It amazes me," conceded a West African buyer, "just how little escapes De Beers—either in intelligence or diamonds."

Occasionally the adventurer-buyers who frequent the illicit markets of Africa delight in staging an elaborate rigmarole before they will dispose of their diamonds to a staid European buyer. One leading Antwerp dealer, who buys many stones which have been smuggled out of Sierra Leone, once traveled to Paris to appraise a parcel of smuggled diamonds. He was picked up at his Paris hotel, blindfolded, and driven by a roundabout route to a blacked-out apartment. There he viewed the diamonds, debated the price, was then blindfolded once more, and delivered back, with every courtesy, to his hotel. The majority of smuggled diamonds, however, arrive in the hands of the Central Selling Organisation or other established European buyers without such exaggerated cloak-and-dagger exercises.

Whatever the fun and games en route, every smuggled rough diamond ultimately finds its way to some little cutting and polishing room, lit by a north light, where a highly skilled cutter will spend hours, days, weeks, even months making it sparkle like all those gems in the "A diamond is forever" advertisements. Then, of course, the smuggling starts all over again.

The Smuggled Solitaire

A good ninety-five percent of customs seizures from smugglers are made on the basis of information received. Just once in a while a customs officer has a hunch or a stroke of pure luck. Take the time New York customs officers were proudly showing their commissioner, Ralph Kelly, up on a visit from Washington, D.C., how bright they were in sifting through the airmail coming into the United States. One of them picked out a bulky envelope from a pile. "We're pretty sure, Mr. Commissioner," he said, eager to display his wizardry, "that this little packet is full of pornographic pictures." Just to prove the point, he split it open. Out tumbled ten thousand dollars' worth of cut and polished diamonds, which had been packed neatly between two thin pieces of cardboard—giving the envelope the feel that it contained photographs. The envelope had been posted in Antwerp, Belgium, where a street called Pelikanstraat is the hub of the cut and polished diamond business. If the Central Selling Organisation is one bottleneck through which most of the world's rough diamonds pass, all roads in cut and polished diamonds lead to and from Pelikanstraat, Antwerp. It is to the diamond business what Wall Street in New York and Threadneedle Street in London are to the world of banking and high finance. This particular envelope, postmarked Antwerp but with no further clue as to who in Pelikanstraat had mailed it, was addressed to Brooklyn. For the next few weeks the New York customs kept eagle eyes open for any more letters for the Brooklyn address and shortly picked up thirteen, all stuffed with diamonds. The envelope invariably came via ordinary airmail, was not registered, and had no return address. After examining them, the customs men forwarded the letters for delivery in Brooklyn. The address there turned out to be an unoccupied leased store. Customs kept it under surveillance night and day, waiting for someone to come by and pick up the bejeweled mail. Finally, around two o'clock one morning a car driven by a woman, with a man sitting on her right, showed up and parked a few yards up the street. The woman got out, looked carefully up and down the street, and told the man it was all clear. He came over to the store, but just as he was going in, one of the customs men hidden in an alleyway nearby moved. The woman yelled, the man started running—and then customs agents came in from all sides. The man was a rabbi, with relatives in Antwerp, long suspected of diamond smuggling. Unfortunately, because the customs men had moved before he actually collected the mail, there was no firm evidence to charge him. All they could do was confiscate the envelopes of diamonds, worth in all $130,000. No one ever tried to claim them.

Americans, because of their basic prosperity and egged on by those loving-couples-walking-barefoot-by-the-pounding-surf advertisements, spend up to half a billion dollars a year buying almost half of the world's gem diamonds. Many of these diamonds arrive in the United States as rough diamonds and are not liable to import duty; but over $150 million worth a year are imported, mainly from Antwerp and Tel Aviv, already cut and polished. They are liable to duty. In the 1950's this duty was as high as ten percent on diamonds over one-half carat; by 1969 it was down to eight percent and will fall to five percent by 1972. This levy, especially in the 1950's, was high enough to make smuggling a most attractive proposition, particularly as sales tax and profits tax are also avoided on the smuggled stones. The close family and friendship circle of the diamond business also provided the essential bond across the Atlantic. Many Jewish diamond dealers who fled from the great European diamond markets of Amsterdam and Antwerp at the outbreak of World War II came to the United States as refugees and, perfectly naturally, continued their profession in their new homeland. When the markets reopened with peace, many of them did not return to Europe but the family associations remained, both with Antwerp, which has eclipsed Amsterdam, and with Tel Aviv, where the growth of the diamond-cutting and -polishing business has gone hand in hand with the emergence of Israel. Of course, only a handful of American diamond dealers smuggle; indeed, the Diamond Manufacturers and Importers Association of America, since its inception in 1932, has fought very hard against smuggling, but the vital alliance of trust and kinship exists for the minority who may be inclined to smuggle in a part of their turnover.

The heyday of diamond smuggling into the United States was in the 1950's and early 1960's, when the duty on diamonds was especially high. In its annual reports of the late fifties the U.S. Customs Agency Service invariably rated diamond smuggling, with 300–400 cases a year, as its number-two problem—exceeded only by the traffic in narcotics. The smuggling was extraordinarily well organized by a group in Antwerp who specialized in delivering diamonds to New York, and even guaranteed insurance. It worked like this. A New York dealer would travel to Antwerp and buy perhaps $100,000 worth of cut and polished gems from a fellow dealer on Pelikanstraat. Then in a bar or café nearby, he would make contact with an agent of the smuggling syndicate. The agent would take the dealer to an independent diamond appraiser, who would value the parcel of diamonds. The syndicate would then charge between five and seven percent of this appraiser's valuation as their fee for delivering the diamonds in New York. They undertook to accept all risks; if their courier was caught and the diamonds confiscated, they would reimburse the dealer in full for his loss. Many people, some in the diamond business, some outside, had a stake in the syndicate's kitty, and they could afford to stand the losses. So the New York dealer would leave his gems in Antwerp, fly home, and shortly thereafter be contacted by telephone and told where to go to pick up his diamonds. The syndicate's reliability was a byword. If the dealer said, "I must have my diamonds in New York by noon next Tuesday," they would be there on time.

The gems crossed the Atlantic in an infinite number of ways.

There was a Sabena airlines captain who took them in the specially hollowed-out heel of his shoe. Another trick was to bore holes two and one-half inches deep into the base of the neck of toy dogs, pack the cavities with diamonds wrapped in tissue paper, plug up the holes with plastic wood, sandpaper the surface smooth, and repaint the dogs. They were then dispatched to a post-office box number in New York. More than fifty of these diamond-laden pooches worth over 1.6 million dollars had been sent safely before someone in New York customs realized that the valuation put on the declaration accompanying each package was rather excessive for a mere toy dog. Only very careful inspection under an X-ray machine by a surgeon called in for his advice then revealed the diamonds.

The smugglers also had a field day on the Atlantic liners. They booked the same cabin both on inward and outward trips from New York. During the voyage from Europe the smuggler hid the diamonds in his cabin and on arrival in New York came through customs without a blush. When the ship sailed a couple of days later, either he or another member of the team checked into the same cabin and a friend came along to say a cheery good-bye. The diamonds were quickly recovered and handed to the friend, who walked ashore in the bustle as the "all-visitors-ashore" gong sounded and the paper streamers tossed by departing voyagers flew.

It was a gentlemanly business. The couriers or dealers who were caught accepted this fate with regret and resignation. "There was never any violence," says Lawrence Fleishman, the assistant commissioner of the Customs Agency Service. "None of them would hurt a fly." This is, of course, perfectly in keeping with the diamond business; its members are unstinting in business competition with each other but are otherwise the mildest of men.

In recent years they have quickly caught on to the widely used technique of undervaluing goods to duck at least a part of the duty. This indirect smuggling is much harder to detect, and the worst that can happen is that the customs will not accept the low valuation and charge duty on a higher value. The technique is a simple one. A dealer may buy two or three parcels of diamonds in Antwerp or Tel Aviv, each containing stones of a different size, color, and quality. If he imported each parcel separately it would be relatively easy for the customs appraisers to challenge his declaration of their value. So instead he commingles (as the trade calls it) good, bad, and indifferent gems in one scrambled parcel and shoots it through customs valued at, say, $75,000 instead of the true value of $100,000. Confronted with this diamond omelet, it is much more difficult for the customs to make an accurate assessment, and they may accept his low valuation. On a duty of ten percent (which applied until 1968) this would mean a saving of $2,500, or two and one-half percent of the true value of the shipment.

Commingling is also used as a subterfuge to bring diamonds which have been cut and polished in Russia and are liable to a higher duty into the United States. The Russian stones are parceled up with diamonds cut in Antwerp. Then the entire batch is listed as originating in Belgium. This little trick, however, has been spotted several times by the U.S. Customs' chief diamond appraiser, Leroy Pepino, a tall, bespectacled man who has an eye for diamonds rarely equaled outside the trade. The Russian cutting and polishing industry is still less than ten years old, and initially their diamonds stuck out like a sore thumb. "They cut a miserable stone," Pepino recalls. "It tended to be thick, with a small table and a high top. It was like a fingerprint identifying it as Russian." Now, however, the Russians, helped by Belgian experts, have improved their technique, and if their stones are mingled with gems cut in Antwerp, they are much harder to detect. "Their cutting now is most sophisticated," says Pepino, "and their polishing is beautiful. They are also creating stones which are not consistently the same." Nevertheless, the Russian stones can still be detected, partly by the cutting and also by the carbon occlusions, which differ slightly on Russian diamonds from those found in Africa.

These Russian diamonds traveling under a Belgian mantle are also backed up by a fake Belgian invoice. This invoice can normally be acquired from a cutter in Antwerp for about one percent of the price stated on the document he issues. The cutter justifies this in his own books by declaring that his wastage in cutting diamonds was, say, fifty percent when in fact it was forty-eight percent. This gives him an excess of merchandise on his books.

This growth of smuggling by paperwork has not, however, entirely eliminated the smuggler bringing in stones completely undeclared. Indeed, in 1968 the arrest in Laredo, Texas, of a lady with $37,000 of undeclared gem diamonds in her handbag when she came in from Mexico City led the customs men to a New York diamond dealer, in whose office they found papers indicating that a total of twenty-three shipments of diamonds worth $440,000 had evaded the customs by way of Mexico.

Although no other single country can afford to spend so much on gem diamonds as the United States (where eighty percent of the girls receive a diamond engagement ring), increasing prosperity around the world is creating new centers of demand, and duties and taxes being what they are, smuggling is never very far away. Even within Europe many jewelers in France and Italy, where tax avoidance is part of day-to-day life anyway, obtain a part of their requirements through clandestine sources. The fastest-growing market for diamonds, however, is in the Far East and is excellently serviced by the Hong Kong diamond dealers, who have happily watched their business triple in the last decade.

The Orient has always had a taste for precious stones, both as an adornment for beautiful women and as an investment. While the masses of Asia have always had a passion for gold, the wealthy prefer rubies, emeralds, pearls, and, increasingly, diamonds. "The whole Orient is diamond-minded," said a Dutch dealer who has worked there for thirty-five years. "A Chinese woman comes in, and she knows all about the purity, the cutting, and the value of a diamond. Her approach is highly informed. An American woman just says to her husband, 'Honey, isn't it wonderful; we'll buy it.'"

As for the Chinese dealers, "They are real maniacs about diamonds—and in this business you have to be a maniac, with an exceptionally critical mind. If you don't know the business, you had better not be in it. The Chinese do know it. They have the information from New York or Tel Aviv or Antwerp even before we do. And that's some achievement in such a closed, secret business."

Hong Kong, obligingly, has a free market in diamonds and is one of the cheapest—if not *the* cheapest—places in the world to buy cut and polished gems. The absence of import duties, the cheap labor, and the low taxes combine to keep the prices down. Even security is cheap. "People in Europe have to spend a fortune on alarm systems," a Hong Kong dealer pointed out, "but here if you walk down Queens Road past all those jewelry stores, you see they are wide open to the street. At the most there is an old chap with a shotgun sitting on a stool out front."

One of the colony's best customers, both for smuggled and legitimate purchases, is Japan. Indeed, Japan's annual investment in diamonds has gone up more than one thousand percent in ten years; she now buys over ten million dollars' worth of diamonds from Hong Kong each year through legal channels. De Beers, actively encouraging this enthusiasm for diamonds, has been busy buying space in Japanese magazines for pastel-colored advertisements of Japanese maidens adorned with diamonds, with the well-known slogan "A diamond is forever." But because the Japanese government chooses to charge an import duty of four percent plus a commodity tax of twenty percent on cut and polished diamonds, many of the diamonds are forever smuggled. "I can't keep count of the people coming down here from Japan to smuggle gems," said a Hong Kong dealer. "In Japan," added an inscrutable Chinese diamond merchant, "it is not polite to ask how diamonds arrive." A slightly less inscrutable European dealer volunteered, "Of course, there's lots of smuggling, not only to Japan, but to the Philippines, Indonesia, and Thailand, where the import duties are absurdly high. Hong Kong is a constant temptation, and plenty of fellows make it their business to come here, buy diamonds, and smuggle them back."

Hong Kong is a magnet throughout the Far East for anyone in search of diamonds. The wife of a Philippine millionaire, languishing beside her swimming pool and sipping a frosted tequila to combat the sizzling afternoon heat of Manila, explained how she and other wealthy ladies smuggle their diamonds from Hong Kong. "When I go to Hong Kong," she said, smiling over her

glass of tequila, "I wear an elaborate bracelet set with false diamonds. I declare the bracelet to customs here in Manila on the
way out, stating that it contains real diamonds. They give me a
reentry pass. In Hong Kong I go to my jeweler, who replaces the
paste diamonds on the bracelet with genuine gems. Then I take
the plane back to Manila. I declare the bracelet here but show
my reentry pass to prove I took the bracelet out with me."

In the Philippines, where the economy is heavily underwrit-
ten by American dollars, the diamonds are chiefly for adornment. In Indonesia, which is much less stable economically,
large, yellowish seven-carat diamonds are in great demand as a
means of getting money out of the country. Tight Indonesian
exchange controls and the poor rate of exchange for their
rupiahs abroad make it impractical for anyone to smuggle out his
nest egg in cash. Diamonds are an excellent and easily hidden
alternative.

Although Hong Kong is the hub of the Far East diamond
traffic, several of the European groups who are active in smuggling gold from Switzerland and Belgium to the Far East also
travel in diamonds. Both the main syndicates operating from
offices in Geneva have close associations with the diamond and
precious-stone trade. Indeed, one group is closely interrelated
with a diamond-dealing family with offices in London and Antwerp, which is also an active buyer of rough diamonds in Monrovia after they have been smuggled out of Sierra Leone. A few
of the most trusted gold couriers from Geneva, at the same time
as being given their solid-gold vests, have been asked if they
would mind taking along a toilet bag complete with soap, shav-
ing soap, and toothpaste in the luggage. At their destination they
hand over the toilet kit—and receive it back again, seemingly
intact, two hours later. This is one way of taking diamonds out
fast—or of bringing back diamonds or other precious stones in
payment for gold. Certain shipments of gold into Bombay have
been paid for with diamonds, smuggled back out to Brussels, and
then air-freighted quite openly to New York. One such shipment
of diamonds, worth $42,000, went awry in 1966 when it was
stolen between Frankfurt and New York. The diamonds had
been safely smuggled from Bombay to Brussels by a courier and

picked up there by the wife of a well-known gold and diamond trafficker. She delivered them to another member of the gang in Düsseldorf—and it was only after he had entrusted them to Lufthansa that they vanished. Even a diamond smuggler cannot win all the time.

IX

Gold

Gold smuggling calls for a great deal of stamina and costs a great deal of sweat. The favorite smuggling technique is to use a thin canvas or nylon corset, bearing thirty or more one-kilo bars of gold slotted neatly into rows all around the garment, strapped to the torso. Wearing it is a wearying experience. Suddenly it seems you are in a straitjacket, held down, restricted, unable to move—a latter-day Tutankhamen in a golden shroud. The weight of this golden corset is crippling: It grips you like a vise; the knees buckle slightly. Sitting down is not much relief; trying to stand up again, while maintaining a casual air, becomes a feat of strength. Walking becomes a deliberate effort with careful strides to maintain equilibrium. "Remember," says the man handing out the jacket, "that you can easily be knocked off balance if you are bumped or jostled in a crowd." Just to ram home the point, he comes heavily across the room on a collision course; it is all too easy to collapse ungracefully. Which could be most embarrassing in the midst of a busy airport under the eyes of the authorities. And always at the back of the mind is the story of the German courier with the golden vest flying from Geneva to the Far East who died of a heart attack, caused by exhaustion, at Athens airport when his aircraft stopped to refuel.

With so many physical hazards en route—quite apart from

the normal risk of detection by the authorities—gold smuggling has become, over the last twenty years, a specialized trade, second only, in terms of organization, to heroin. The main gold-smuggling syndicates operating out of Europe, the Middle East, and, to a lesser degree, Canada, handle between them 300 million to 400 million dollars in gold a year, a turnover which would put them in the top hundred companies in Europe or America if they cared to publish their dealings. In any event, their affairs are as well run as those of any giant corporation. Indeed, for most of the leading smugglers, gold is simply a profitable sideline to their normal business as well-established exchange dealers, import and export merchants, or travel agents. Of course, they have to be a little more discreet when it involves gold. As well as on the sweating couriers on international jets, the gold travels amid a clutter of goats and pilgrims on Arab dhows in the Arabian Gulf, or hidden in the engine casing of freighters outward bound from Hong Kong. One shipment of movie projectors into India in 1968 was ingeniously filled with canapé-sized bars of gold, while 560 cans of motor grease swung ashore in Yokohama docks were laced with over one million dollars in gold. Tins of condensed milk make an excellent hideaway because the thick white goo of the milk stops the gold from rattling. Best of all, of course, are golden nuggets shaped like a pigeon's egg, which cost around six hundred dollars, and can be carried internally. Women, they hasten to explain in smuggling circles, can carry twice as many of these eggs as men.

The two cornerstones of the world's gold market are London and Zurich. Until the gold crisis of March, 1968, which led to the introduction of a special two-tier price for gold (thirty-five dollars an ounce for monetary gold sold between central banks and official international monetary institutions like the International Monetary Fund, and a floating price for nonmonetary gold for jewelry, industry, private hoarding, and smuggling), the London market was supreme. It handled the massive yearly output of one thousand tons of gold, worth over one billion dollars, from South Africa, which mines seventy-five percent of the noncommunist world's gold. The second-largest gold producer, Russia, also sold most of its gold through the London market. Thus

London was the fountainhead through which gold was disseminated around the world, whether into the reserves of great nations or the jackets of smugglers bound for the Far East.

A large slice of the gold from London always went to the Zurich gold market, which is dominated by the big three Swiss banks—the Union Bank, the Swiss Credit Bank, and the Swiss Bank Corporation. Unlike Britain and the United States, Switzerland has a completely free gold market; anyone is allowed to buy, sell, import, or export gold as freely as cheese or chocolate. Switzerland has always been, therefore, an ideal haven for the private hoarder or the smuggler to buy his gold. Since the introduction of the two-tier market for gold in 1968, Zurich has come to dominate the nonmonetary slice of the market, and considerable quantities of South African gold are now air-freighted direct to Zurich in chartered DC-7's instead of going by sea from Durban to Southampton, England, by Union Castle liner, as had been the tradition for half a century.

This easy availability of gold, coupled with Switzerland's obliging laws on the solemn secrecy of bank accounts, has made it a natural sanctuary from which to direct the smuggling of gold. But all the gold passing along smuggling pipelines does not have to pass through Switzerland; a telex message or a cable from Zurich or Geneva can easily direct the gold from London to any one of half a dozen other strategic cities in the gold network around the world—Paris, Brussels, Beirut, Dubai, Vientiane, and Hong Kong. Official statistics of gold movements out of the London market are virtually meaningless because they often do not show the real destination of the gold. For example, the export figures indicate that London sends many tons of gold to Holland every year; in fact, this gold goes only to Amsterdam airport, where it is quickly redirected onto KLM flights to the Far East; its most likely ultimate destination is Saigon by way of Vientiane, Laos. But whatever the ultimate destination of the gold, virtually all new supplies pass initially through one of the two wholesale points of London and Zurich.

The gold sold by South Africa and traded at the monetary level between nations is invariably in the form of four-hundred-ounce "good-delivery" bars, each worth just over $14,000. A good-delivery bar must be at least 995 parts per thousand pure gold, contain between 350 and 430 troy ounces of gold, and bear a stamp and serial number from one of the forty-nine firms in fourteen countries which the London gold market accepts as reputable melters and assayers. Such a bar is somewhat cumbersome and expensive for many private hoarders or smugglers, so the markets supply gold to suit all tastes and the smallest of smuggler's pockets. The two most common small gold bars are the kilo bar (worth $1,390), which is the size of a pack of cigarettes and the ten-tola bar (3.75 ounces worth $160), which is little bigger than a luscious gold-coated chocolate and is the staple diet of smugglers to India. The markets can, however, oblige more exacting tastes. In Macao, just across the Pearl River from Hong Kong, the four-hundred-ounce bars flown in from London on orders placed by the Hong Kong gold dealers, are melted down into one-tael (1.33 ounces) or five-tael bars. The one-tael bar, which sells for $46.50, can be bought either in the form of a square bar the size of a postage stamp, or as a disc with a hole in the middle so that it can conveniently be slung on a piece of string round the waist. It is even available in a little nugget shaped like a slipper bath, which can be taped to the navel or secreted, like those solid gold pigeon's eggs, in more private places.

But why smuggle gold anyway? Logically, of course, the grip of gold in the hearts and minds of millions of individuals around the world is absurd. The metal has no intrinsic value. It is hard to imagine being cast up on a desert island with anything more useless than a bar of gold. But the basic motive for the ordinary man to hoard gold bars or gold jewelry is fear—and that at once casts logic aside.

The fear that dominates the gold hoarder may be of devaluation, of civil war or strife, of being kicked unceremoniously out of his country for political reasons, or simply, as in India, of losing face because he cannot deck out his daughter with enough gold ornaments on her wedding day. In Europe the greatest private hoarders of gold are the French. They have four billion dollars tucked away beneath their beds, in the cellars, or in safe-deposit boxes. Many middle-class people in Germany, Italy, Belgium, and Greece also like to keep a golden nest egg against evil days, for they still remember all too well how, within their own lifetime, invasion has made paper currencies valueless overnight. For these people buying gold is no problem; they are allowed to hold gold privately and can buy it through any bank or gold dealer. In Switzerland it is simple to buy a little bar of gold when you cash your traveler's checks at the airport or railway station *bureau de change*.

Around the world sixty-eight nations still permit their citizens to hold gold privately; the smuggler's market is the 145 nations that either do not or impose strict controls on the import of gold. In these countries fear can drive the black-market price for gold up to seventy or eighty dollars an ounce—twice the normal market price. The demand for gold in South Vietnam, for example, has escalated almost exactly in tandem with the expansion of the war; indeed, a completely new gold market was created in neighboring Vientiane, Laos, to cater for the black-market demand in Saigon. In India, which for centuries has been known as "a sink for precious metals," the import of gold has been forbidden since 1947, but the demand for twenty-two-carat gold jewelry, which means as much to an Indian as an American Express card and a life-insurance policy means to an American, has stimulated a black market which can absorb at least $150 million (at the normal price) in gold a year. The Indian passion for gold stemmed initially from the hazards of life in a small village. A farmer never knew when marauders might attack the village, burning his home and his crops; he could never be sure that the monsoon might not be late next year. So after each harvest he turned all his spare resources into twenty-two-carat gold jewelry, which was as freely exchangeable as any rupee. The village goldsmith became, in fact, an unofficial banker. From this beginning, gold became so entwined with the social structure of India that it will take a revolution to overthrow it. Every Hindu bride in India brings with her to the wedding her *stridhana*, a dowry in gold jewelry. The status of the family is judged on the size of the *stridhana*, and if the husband and wife are from different villages, it is the prestige not only of the family but of the village that is at stake. The Bombay Bullion

Association has calculated that if each of the 120 million families in India has a marriage once every fifteen years and a minimum of one tola of gold (.375 ounce) changes hands at the ceremony, the annual demand would be almost 100 tons of gold, costing $130 million at the normal market price; or nearly $250 million at the Indian price.

The one country with a healthy appetite for smuggled gold that is not stimulated by fear is Japan. Soaring prosperity has created a demand for ordinary gold jewelry that the country's own gold production of fifteen and one-half tons of gold cannot meet. Since the Bank of Japan places strict controls on the import of gold, the jewelry business has become an excellent client of the smuggling syndicates, paying some twenty to twenty-five dollars an ounce over the market price in Europe.

Catering to these black markets is no simple task. Quite apart from the physical problems of transporting gold illicitly, the financing of gold smuggled—with gold costing forty dollars an ounce, or well over one million dollars a ton—calls for reliable backing. Not only is the initial capital required to buy the gold, but the capture of one courier carrying up to $40,000 in gold could bankrupt any weak organization. Regular gold smuggling, therefore, is not a casual business; it is well financed, is run by men who understand the complexities of currency exchange, and is operated as a long-term proposition. Many people quite remote from the day-to-day smuggling activities will have a stake in a syndicate—indeed, it is rather like buying shares, except that they are not quoted on the stock market. Syndicates do not take kindly to newcomers trying to enter the smuggling business as rivals, but they will be quite ready to accept an initial stake of, say, $100,000 from a newcomer, in return for which they will keep the equivalent in gold moving along the smuggling pipelines on his behalf. Once a quarter or once every six months, he will receive an accounting. The syndicate will even split the risk; an investment of $100,000 may be spread over ten separate shipments, so that if one is caught the investor does not lose his entire stake.

People who have tried to gate-crash the gold-smuggling business without buying into an existing group have come spectacularly unstuck, particularly if they have tried to smuggle stolen gold. The syndicates buy their gold quite legitimately on the free market, and their profit comes from the black-market price half a continent away. Stolen gold attracts far too much attention from authorities around the world, whereas the sole hurdle that the true gold smuggler, who has bought his gold legally, has to clear is the customs in Bangkok or Manila, Bombay or Tokyo. He commits no crime in taking gold out of Geneva or Beirut. Anyone trying to set up in business with stolen gold may run a risk of being betrayed.

Indeed, the men who stole nearly two million dollars in bullion from a delivery van belonging to N. M. Rothschild and Sons, the London bullion dealers, in May, 1967, made a complete muddle of the affair, because of the problem of trying to smuggle stolen gold out of Britain with the authorities breathing down their necks. With so much attention focused on them, they placed themselves outside the normal protective code of the gold business and could not sell it through conventional channels. Some of it was ferried across the English Channel, but they got so desperate they even sold some to a Scotland Yard detective posing as a jeweler in search of gold.

The men who smuggle gold year in and year out are much more discreet. One group has even gone to the trouble to buy three regular, upholstered VC-10 airliner seats from BOAC so that they can train their couriers, bowed down with gold, to sit in them for hours on end without getting cramped and to be able to get up without appearing a cripple at the end of the journey. Another group has a courier-club tie which makes it easy for the courier to be identified either by a suitably bribed customs officer or by his contact man at his destination. The tie is wine-colored with black diagonal lines forming a diamond pattern; within this black diamond, silver lines form a smaller diamond pattern. Clearly a workmanlike job that any old-boy network or regiment would be proud of. Of course, tie patterns change occasionally; a wine-colored tie may be matched with a rosary carried in the hand. Frankfurt couriers working for a Geneva syndicate were using a red tie and a red bookmark during 1968.

Couriers come from every country in Europe and in recent

years have ranged from an out-of-work dancer from Cardiff to students from Stockholm; from Munich taxi drivers to Catholic priests from Milan (their robes are excellent for concealing gold). Women are equally welcome; they cannot carry quite so much gold, but they attract far less attention. Many couriers are wives, girl friends, even mothers-in-law of established smugglers. Others are recruited through carefully worded advertisements in the personal column of *The Times of London* or other newspapers which hint vaguely at rewarding travel opportunities.

Whatever his home country, the courier will normally pick up his golden shipment in Geneva or Brussels. Geneva is the command post of two important gold-smuggling syndicates; one has its offices in the Rue Mont Blanc, the other in the Rue de Lausanne.

One syndicate is run by two brothers who have had many years' experience in the exchange and currency business. As part of the informal agreement that seems to exist within the gold business, they specialize in smuggling gold to Thailand, Hong Kong, the Philippines, Indonesia, and Japan. The brothers never carry gold themselves and remain remote even from their couriers, few of whom know their name. Their task is essentially to make all the arrangements with their clients overseas, buy the gold, and then pass along a request for a courier or couriers to report to Geneva on a particular day, to be fitted out with his golden vest and pick up his tickets. Most couriers are treated to a night out on the town in Geneva before they depart, to drown any last-minute qualms.

The courier teams are well organized, particularly in Germany, where the Geneva dealers can call on eighty couriers in the Cologne area, about eight or ten in Frankfurt, and a further team in Munich. Many of these German couriers are taxi drivers who take the occasional week's holiday to smuggle gold, but the ring also includes students and young businessmen. In each of these cities there is a courier manager who is the link between Geneva and the couriers themselves. He is responsible for the recruiting of couriers and for dispatching them to Geneva to pick up each consignment of gold. For this he normally receives a fee of seventy-five marks (nineteen dollars) per courier. The couriers themselves are paid up to five hundred dollars a trip, with all expenses paid.

The link man in Frankfurt used to be a journalist, but after he was involved in a spot of bother with the Frankfurt police, he was replaced by a young man of about thirty who is to be found most afternoons quietly sipping lemon tea in one of two cafés in the center of Frankfurt. He sits impassively with droopy pouches under his eyes at a corner table with a good view of the door. He has one of those faces that never reveals what he is really thinking. He has a clipped beard, which grows well around his chin but is shaved into a thin line down his cheeks. He hardly cuts the figure of a dashing international gold smuggler; indeed, he seems a very moody, worried man as hc talks to two associates. He has some reason to be worried; a relation was arrested smuggling gold in the Far East in 1967. All his couriers appear to be either his relatives or close friends. He is, understandably, extremely wary of selecting unknown recruits. Some untried couriers have given him some nasty moments. There was the Frankfurt taxi driver, on his first gold run to Bangkok, who was so terrified by the time the aircraft touched down in Thailand that he could not face running the gauntlet of customs. In the transit lounge he hurriedly rebooked onward to Saigon. When he arrived there he was in such a lather of perspiration that he was immediately picked out by South Vietnamese customs. Meanwhile, back in Geneva and Frankfurt, no one knew of his failing courage; they had only an urgent cable from Bangkok that the courier was not on the plane. Had he absconded with forty thousand dollars in gold? The Frankfurt men hurried around to his apartment to intimidate his wife to try to learn the truth. However, once they heard he had been arrested in Saigon, they calmed down. Couriers who are caught are not penalized by the syndicate; only those who run off with the gold. The man's wife and family were given a pension of four hundred marks a month while he was in jail.

Couriers are expendable, but it can pay an organization with a turnover of perhaps twenty million dollars a year to look after its employees when they are in trouble. The gold syndicates are always at pains to stress that they are not criminal outfits, that they are merely supplying a commodity that is prohibited by some quirk of local economic regulations. They go to considerable trouble not to recruit people with criminal records and are most ethical in all their business dealings. One well-known international smuggler, operating out of Brussels, was double-crossed in Pakistan and lost a major shipment of gold, which he had obtained largely on credit. He went to great lengths to raise the necessary capital to pay off his debt.

Even couriers who have been caught are not necessarily blacklisted. Indeed, one Swiss courier had the doubtful distinction of being caught twice during 1968. He was first arrested by American customs in Seattle in February with thirty-two one-kilo bars of gold in a jacket beneath his shirt, when he was in transit from Vancouver, where he had taken delivery of the gold, to San Francisco, where he had a reservation on a transPacific flight to Manila. He was posing as a representative of a Swiss duplicating firm. Just months later he was arrested again, together with a Chilean, coming into Hong Kong aboard the SS *Tarantel* from Manila. The two men had eighty-four one-kilo bars of gold between them, which they had picked up in Switzerland, carried in jackets by air to the Philippines, and then tried to bring to Hong Kong by the highly unusual back-door sea route from Manila (smugglers coming into Hong Kong normally come direct by air). On both occasions this Swiss courier had a veritable deck of airline tickets with him. In Seattle he had two thousand dollars' worth of tickets and a routing of Geneva, Frankfurt, Nicosia, Istanbul, Beirut, Vancouver, Tokyo, Hong Kong, Manila, Djakarta, and Bangkok. He had two Swiss passports, one issued in 1965 and already completely filled with visa stamps; the other, issued in Hong Kong, was already being filled up fast.

The second syndicate operating out of Geneva trades under the guise of an import-export company with connections in India and Pakistan. It is a rather loosely knit outfit. Over the last ten years a number of important international gold smugglers have been linked with it from time to time, and it is often hard to fathom whether, at any one time, they are working on their own account or in a kind of friendly cooperative. The man who gives his name to the group is a former airline steward who was born in Paris. In addition to his gold activities, he has extensive contacts with the illicit-diamond-buying business in the Congo and West Africa. His principal associates are an Austrian in his late forties who has lived in the United States, Brazil, and Switzerland; an Englishman traveling on an American passport who has been responsible for recruiting many couriers, including airline crews; a forty-year-old American who splits his time between Los Angeles and Geneva; and a German in his mid-fifties who lives in Düsseldorf, whose main responsibility is the German couriers.

This group has always concentrated on the trade to India, and one of their most experienced smugglers, Jean Claude Donze, has had a checkered career with the Indian customs authorities. Donze first hove over the gold-smuggling horizon in 1959, when he was busy in Beirut taking air hostesses who were working on the route to India out to dinner and offering them expensive presents. In 1961 four couriers working under his guidance were arrested in Pakistan carrying gold worth $36,000 and Pakistani currency to the value of $54,000; Donze himself was not in Karachi. But he was arrested in New Delhi the following year in connection with a case involving an Englishman named Ronald Stanton, who was caught bringing $45,000 in gold into India. At that time Donze was traveling under the name of Pierre Carraud, and it was not until sometime after his arrest that the Indians learned whom they had really caught. Under interrogation Donze was alleged to have admitted traveling on at least twelve different passports of varying nationalities. He was sentenced to six months in jail.

Undeterred, he was back in India in 1966 with an American adventurer named Daniel Hailey Walcott, with whom, according to the Indian authorities, he was associated in a variety of gold drops from a light aircraft onto lonely roads north of Bombay. In 1966 the two men entered India on false passports via Madras and headed for Bombay. There they were picked up by the Indian police, quite by chance, after an alert detective on his nightly round of the hotel registers and the log of international phone calls by hotel guests noted that the guests in Room 503 had called a number in Colombo, Ceylon, which was on an Interpol circular. The two men were arrested and sentenced in Madras to five years for fraudulent use of passports, plus an additional six months for trying to break out of jail while awaiting trial.

Donze was perhaps a trifle unlucky. The other important members of this group, who have mostly confined their activities to arrangements at the European end, have come through unscathed. For a number of years many of their couriers picked up the gold in Brussels. The operation was run from an office in the Rue de Coligny, and a special flat for departing couriers was maintained in the Avenue Louise. The courier flew in from London or Frankfurt and collected the key to the apartment. It was an elegant pad with a pleasant view and a well-stocked refrigerator; the gold was hidden under a tile in the bathroom floor, and before leaving in the morning for his flight, the courier stocked up his smuggling jacket with gold.

Their couriers nearly always travel with at least two passports. Some of them, starting from London, will show one passport in their real name to the immigration authorities at Heathrow airport but show a passport in a false name on arrival at Brussels. At the outset the courier often has no idea where he is going. He is told to report to Brussels or Geneva on a certain day to pick up the gold. He will not be told his ultimate destination until he arrives at the airport, already burdened with gold beneath his shirt, to check in for his flight. This is a natural security precaution in case he gets drunk in a nightclub before departing and eager ears overhear him bragging, "I'm off to Bangkok in the morning with a load of gold." The flight reservation is also frequently made in another name; when the courier checks in, he will say, "You have a reservation for Mr. Smith; he can't come. I am Mr. Jones, traveling in his place." This makes it more difficult for airline security officials or customs authorities to check passenger manifests well in advance to sift out dubious characters.

Besides their European offices, the major syndicates also maintain "station managers" in the strategic cities along their routes, normally in Bangkok, Hong Kong, and Tokyo. These men are responsible for local contacts, for meeting the couriers, and, if necessary, for bribing local customs officials. There is invariably a great deal of casual talk among gold smugglers about bribing customs officers to turn a blind eye as those gold-laden couriers come staggering off the planes. In fact, there is good reason to believe that much of this "fixing" talk is pure bravado on the part of the station manager, who finds it a convenient way to pad out his expense account. One station manager reported he was paying Calcutta customs officers eighteen hundred dollars a month and Bombay customs nine hundred a month, but there was no way to check; he could hardly present a receipt.

It is a complex business to start bribing customs. One officer may be corruptible, but that is little safeguard for the smuggler. A dozen officers may be checking passengers off a particular flight, so, ideally, all of them need to be subverted, because it is impossible to predict which one will clear the courier. Also, the flight may well be late, and a new and perhaps unbribed shift will be on duty when it lands. The only real insurance policy is to bribe a sufficiently senior customs officer who can then let word filter down accordingly to his men. That is no easy task. The problems of reaching satisfactory terms were well outlined in a letter which was seized from a smuggler in the Far East in the autumn of 1968. It discussed first the smuggling of gold from Switzerland to various unnamed cities in the Far East. It then came down to the heart of the matter. "We must approach the customs and make a deal. We have not yet reached terms with the assistant preventive officer and other senior officials at the airport."

A very experienced customs officer can pick out a courier, unless the latter is very skillful. "You get an eye for them," explained an officer in Hong Kong. "Look for how they bend down to pick up their suitcase, see how they stand when they wait in line." One syndicate issues their couriers with tranquilizers to be taken just before landing to make them relax before customs inspection.

No one knows exactly how much gold is humped around the

world each year on the sweating backs of the couriers, but it is certainly at least fifty tons, worth nearly sixty million dollars. In one peak week early in 1968, just before the gold crisis and during the Tet offensive in South Vietnam, one Geneva group was sending twenty-five couriers a week to Southeast Asia, sometimes eight of them traveling together on the same flight. Assuming each of them carried at least thirty kilos of gold (a very strong courier can take up to forty kilos, but the average is between thirty and thirty-five), that means this syndicate alone was shifting nearly three-quarters of a ton a week. This is by no means a record. One Beirut smuggler likes to recall how he once went out to the airport to watch the Pan Am flight to Hong Kong take off with sixteen couriers aboard, with a total of half a ton of undeclared gold beneath their shirts. There was some speculation among the Beirut market as to whether or not the plane would get off the ground. It did.

For many years Beirut was a key center of the gold-smuggling world, with two main syndicates that began operations as far back as 1947. Over the years the personnel changed, but the strength of Beirut in the smuggling world was unchallenged. The gold flowed through Beirut like a stream in full flood and was dispatched to Kuwait, India, Hong Kong, and Japan. One Beirut syndicate is known to have sent 2.25 million dollars' worth of gold to Hong Kong alone during a period of three months. Most of it was carried by the couriers, but sometimes it traveled by more unconventional means. One trick was to secrete it in the engines of aircraft bound for Bombay, where ground engineers were paid three rupees per tola to fish it out while they were servicing the planes. One leading Beirut smuggler even investigated the possibilities of concealing gold in bales of cotton and sending them by sea to Hong Kong. He invested in a small cotton-pressing machine and made up some sample golden bales, but in the end he decided against the scheme. It was, he felt, too costly to have all that gold on the slow boat to China; he preferred a quicker return on his capital.

Airline crews were also subjected to constant tempting offers during their layovers in Beirut. Many of the crews stayed in the Bristol Hotel and frequented a bar just down the street. There they were frequently propositioned by one of the leading Beirut smugglers, who had an apartment nearby. The pressure was so intense that one major international airline persuaded the Bristol Hotel to open a fancy bar of its own in the vain hope that crews would drink there instead. The new bar was splendid, but the crews still preferred the smugglers' hangout down the street.

For a while the Beirut syndicates were so confident of success that one of them was able to take out an insurance policy on the smuggled gold. The gold insurance was arranged through a broker in Beirut, who placed it with one Swiss and three British insurance companies. It appeared to be an excellent arrangement. However, after a while the member of the syndicate who was responsible for the insurance decided that it was a waste of money paying the premium and terminated the arrangement. He did not, however, inform his partners, and continued to charge the premium against expenses. No one was the wiser until four couriers were arrested in Hong Kong; then the senior partner started an insurance claim—and was appalled to find the policy no longer in effect. The partnership was hastily dissolved.

The heyday of the Beirut smuggling groups was from the late 1940's until the early 1960's. In more recent years other new gold centers have opened up, giving easier access to India and the Far Eastern black markets, and far less gold has passed physically through Beirut. The syndicates there have, however, kept a stake in the trade, particularly in the business through Dubai on the Arabian Gulf. But the city itself is now most immediately preoccupied with smuggling gold into its neighbors in the Middle East—notably Turkey and Egypt. Until the six-day war in June, 1967, led to a tightening up of frontiers throughout the Arab world, Beirut's best customer was Turkey, which took up to $500,000 in gold a week. Since the war, however, the overland route through Aleppo in Syria has become very difficult, and most of the gold now goes up from Beirut by sea to the southern Turkish ports of Iskenderun and Mersin.

While Beirut declines, the gold-smuggling limelight has been stolen by Dubai, the tiny sheikdom at the southern end of the Arabian Gulf, which is well on the way to becoming the Hong Kong of the Middle East. For many years Kuwait, at the northern end of the gulf, was the center of a flourishing gold trade to India, but the discovery of oil enabled its merchants to sit back and relax without the perennial headaches of gold smuggling. Dubai, however, had no oil but was blessed with a three-mile-long creek that offered the best harbor within easy striking distance of the west coast of India.

Initially it was the Beirut gold market which provided much of the capital and expertise to establish Dubai as a springboard for gold smuggling. Dubai has had close trading relations with India for centuries, and the sleek dhows which moored in her creek have always plowed back and forth across the Arabian Sea carrying Muslim pilgrims bound for Mecca, rice, dates, and pearls, and the occasional shipment of hashish. Dubai and the other little sheikdoms of the Trucial Oman States even used Indian rupees as their currency until 1966, and many of the principal merchants were of Indian or Pakistani origin—so they had trustworthy friends and relations in India to help nurture the gold trade. At the outset the Dubai traders found the subtleties of the gold business, in which prices are calculated in quarter-cents, slightly confusing. "We used to make a nice little bit of cream from our sales to Dubai," one European gold dealer confided, "but not anymore. Those boys learned very fast."

Today a dozen Dubai merchants handle between them at least 150 million dollars' worth of gold business a year—the largest single smuggling market in the world—with expertise that tests even the most hardened London dealer. They have all installed telex machines, which keep them in constant touch with the latest fluctuations of the international gold market, and they are wizards at foreign-exchange manipulations. All of them, of course, are doing perfectly legal business in Dubai, which has a free gold market. The gold, always the chocolate-drop-size, ten-tola bars, is flown in direct from London on consignment from two dealers in the London market or from one Swiss bank. It is deposited initially in one of the local Dubai banks—the British Bank of the Middle East, the First National City Bank of New York, the National Bank of Dubai, or the Bank of Oman—which stand beside the gleaming white wind towers on the shores of Dubai's little harbor. And in the harbor are moored the flotilla of nearly fifty dhows which carry the gold on its twelve-hundred-mile voyage across the Arabian Sea. The round-trip voyage takes ten days. Most of the dhows are built in Pakistan, so they merge into the local sea traffic around the shores of the Indian continent, but they are all fitted with 320-horsepower marine engines, which give them a spectacular turn of speed, enabling them to outdistance the rather dilapidated pursuit craft of the Indian customs authorities.

At first glance there is nothing to suggest that this little fleet getting ready for sea in the Dubai Creek are really goldrunners. Their decks are cluttered with drums of oil and corrugated iron; sacks of flour or tins of paint are slung aboard; a group of Muslims returning from Mecca squat around a little brazier near the stern talking incessantly and sipping coffee from a communal cup. The gold itself will be picked up from the bank shortly before the vessel sails and quickly slipped aboard in the wood-fiber boxes sealed with strips of metal in which it is flown out from London. During the voyage it will be unpacked and slotted into the long, narrow pockets of smuggling jackets; each of these jackets, specially tailored to hold the canapé-sized ten-tola bars, can hold one hundred bars, worth over $16,000. Normally sixty to one hundred jackets will be filled during the voyage.

As the dhow sets off east across the Arabian Sea, a discreetly worded cable will be sent off to the Dubai merchant's "landing agent" in Bombay apprising him of the expected time of arrival, the rendezvous point, and the name of the dhow's *nahoda* (captain). The cable will be addressed simply to a post-office box at a particular building in Bombay. Five hundred people may live in the building, and all their mail comes to this one box. It is perfectly simple for the landing agent, even though he does not live there, to arrange with the caretaker of the building for this same post-office box to be used for his cables. The caretaker can never identify him; he is simply an Indian who wanders in off the street once in a while. If Dubai is dispatching a flotilla of four or five boats together, then the merchants will fly in a man in advance to warn the agent.

The agent will then contact one of the ten gangs in Bombay who specialize in bringing smuggled gold ashore and delivering it around the city. He will also alert a fishing boat from Virar, Dadar, or Bandra, one of the little ports near Bombay, to take him and one member of the landing gang out to meet the incoming dhow. The rendezvous takes place at night, usually just outside the Indian three-mile limit. The landing agent will flash a signal code to the approaching dhow. As the two boats draw nearer, a further recognition signal is exchanged; the landing agent calls out the name of the *nahoda;* the *nahoda* responds with the name of the landing agent. (This is partly to ensure they get the right shipment; there may be half a dozen dhows prowling around waiting to make contact on a dark night.) Then the transfer of the gold begins. The boats rarely come alongside; they heave to a few feet apart, and the jackets laden with gold are hauled across on a running line. The moment the delivery is safely made, the Dubai dhow sheers off out to sea to await a second secret meeting.

It is one thing to smuggle gold; it is quite another to be paid for it. The gold from Dubai is paid for in three main ways. The first way is by the underinvoicing of exports from India and the overinvoicing of imports. Underinvoicing means the official export documents on a shipment of, say, jute will declare there are ninety bales in the shipment; the exporting firm's book will record also payment in return for ninety bales. In fact, the shipment will be one hundred bales; the payment for the undeclared ten bales will be made to a separate bank account overseas and can be used as payment for gold or other illicit imports. Overinvoicing works in reverse; the Indian firm will pay for three thousand gallons of paint from abroad but will receive only twenty-five hundred gallons. The second method of paying for gold is through the currency black market. Almost any tourist to India will be approached by taxi drivers or hotel porters pleading with him to sell dollars or sterling at an exchange rate well above the official rate given by the banks. Instead of seven rupees to the dollar, the taxi driver may start bargaining at ten and one-half rupees to the dollar. The currency thus illegally obtained can be smuggled out of India. Alternatively, the unofficial currency-exchange system through which Indians working overseas can remit money to their families in India at a very favorable exchange rate (see Chapter 4) also provides a pool of foreign exchange outside India for gold purchases. The third method of payment for gold—and the main reason the Dubai dhow stands by for a second rendezvous in the night—is through the smuggling of silver out of India. The hoard of silver in India is as unfathomable as the store of gold. Since 1965 silver has been shipped out of India by the ton in the Dubai dhows to pay for gold and other smuggled goods. In 1968, after the price of silver on the world market had nearly doubled, more than sixty million ounces of silver, worth more than one hundred million dollars, was smuggled back to Dubai by the dhows, making India the largest exporter (albeit illegal) of silver in the world.

While the dhow waits for its silver cargo, the fishing boat laden with the golden jackets grounds on the beach. The jackets are slung ashore and stacked in a waiting car, which delivers them, after at least one change of driver, to a wholesaler. The landing gang's responsibility is now over. They are paid a flat fee of one rupee (fourteen cents) per tola for landing the gold. Since a single load may comprise anything from twenty-five to one hundred thousand tolas, this is a handsome reward. Out of it, however, they must pay all their expenses, including the fishermen, who usually get 3,000–5,000 rupees ($420–$700) per trip. Bribes on shore may cost even more. During 1968 one landing gang, made up of former opium smugglers, hit on the notion of bringing all the gold ashore at naval and defense installations in the Bombay area, on the very credible thesis that the Indian customs would hardly be looking for smugglers landing on government property. They made suitable arrangements with security guards at several of these establishments and started landing the gold at the Naval Coaling Depot, the Institute for Fundamental Research, and the Atomic Energy Institute. At one establishment, a security guard was bribed nearly fifteen hundred dollars each time he turned a blind eye. For a while the gang were landing twenty-five thousand tolas four times a month.

The wholesaler who receives all the jackets (and is also responsible for remitting payment to Dubai) will, in his turn, distribute the gold, a jacket or two at a time, to the local gold dealers in the Javeri Bazaar. If the prevailing market price is good, he may have disposed of all the gold within twenty-four hours; if prices are low, he will hold on to the consignment until the market improves.

The Indian buyer is always extremely conservative about the make of the ten-tola bar he will accept. It must bear the stamp of one of a handful of well-known gold refiners, preferably that of Johnson, Matthey, the London gold dealers and refiners who produce a major share of the ten-tola bars. Any new refiner breaking into the market may find his bars greeted with considerable skepticism. When Engelhard Industries, the American precious-metal company, took over the Royal Mint Refinery in London from N. M. Rothschild and Sons in 1967 and began exporting ten-tola bars emblazoned with the Engelhard stamp, the Indians quickly ran assay tests on the first bars to confirm they were genuine 999.9 gold.

The route from Dubai to India is so well charted that it would seem a simple matter for the Indian authorities to throw out a blockade and stop it. "I could stop Dubai just like that," said one Bombay customs officer. "Just give me twelve frigates, and I'll set up a blockade which will catch enough of the dhows to make smuggling unprofitable." The trouble is that the customs do not have the twelve frigates at their disposal. They have to rely on four vessels commissioned over ten years ago, which are no match for the Dubai dhows. Even so, they seize a remarkable amount of gold. In 1967 they caught 2,561 kilos of gold, worth over three million dollars at the normal market price and over five million dollars on the Indian black market. They estimate, very honestly, that they catch somewhere between two and six percent of the gold being smuggled into India. But the time is approaching when India will have to pay far more attention to the equipment of its customs service. The drain on India's meager foreign-exchange reserves due to smuggling of gold, watches, nylon yarn, transistor radios, and even lipsticks runs to at least a half-billion dollars a year; a small investment of five to ten million dollars could equip a customs fleet capable of stopping much of the smuggling from Dubai. The real hold-up is political. The Indians are at pains not to do anything to upset the

Arab world; relations could become strained very fast if Indian customs craft started shooting up fleeing Dubai dhows.

There is also the argument that the Indian passion for gold is so insatiable that if the Dubai loophole is plugged, others will quickly open up. Ten years ago gold was coming into India by land, sea, and air by every conceivable means; now at least ninety-five percent of the smuggled gold comes through Dubai. As long as it follows this single channel, both the Reserve Bank of India and the Bank of England can watch what is going on. If the Dubai traffic stopped, it would become much more difficult for the authorities to keep track of the gold movements. They almost prefer to have the illicit traffic effectively in the open, rather than go completely underground.

Although no other single black market can match the Indian demand for gold, the war in South Vietnam and the overall uncertainty on the political future of the whole of Southeast Asia have created a soaring demand for gold throughout Vietnam, Thailand, Cambodia, and Laos since 1965. Laos has conveniently developed a gold market to cater to this demand. The Laotian government, whose budget is normally balanced only through American aid, had the sense to realize that by allowing the Laotian capital of Vientiane to become a free gold market, in return for a modest duty (now eight and one-half percent) on the gold passing through, that they could substantially supplement the nation's income.

Thus Vientiane, a somewhat seedy, steamy town with one crumbling main street, became almost overnight a major gold market. It is a remarkably informal business. The gold is consigned to Vientiane by the Banque de l'Indo Chine and the Swiss Bank Corporation. It is flown out in kilo-bar form from Europe to Bangkok, normally by KLM. In Bangkok the gold is transferred to local flights of Thai International or Royal Air Laos for the four-hundred-mile hop up to Vientiane. Frequently the gold is simply tucked under the passenger seats of the Royal Air Laos DC-4's. On arrival at Vientiane's airport it is quickly bundled off the plane by a chain of sweating coolies and transferred into the trunk of the car of the local manager of the Banque de l'Indo

Chine. He drives the few yards to the customs shed, has the arrival of the gold duly recorded so the duty can be charged, and then dispenses the gold, almost as casually as candy bars, to his eager customers outside the customs shed. They stuff the kilo bars into shopping bags or battered suitcases. No one asks what happens to it after that.

In fact, some of it is swiftly melted down by Vientiane's goldsmiths into twenty-two-carat bracelets, necklaces, or solid-gold eggs and is then carried by "holidaymakers" bound for Saigon or Bangkok, where the price of gold is twenty dollars an ounce over the Vientiane price. Much more of it, however, remains as kilo bars and is spirited into Saigon by Royal Laotian Air Force or South Vietnamese Air Force planes on "goodwill" missions between the two capitals. They carry up to half a ton of gold a trip, with the full connivance of senior military officials. Everyone seems to be in on the racket. One Laotian prince, off on a visit to Europe, insisted on going first to Saigon in an official plane to deliver five hundred kilos of gold before picking up a commercial flight to Paris. It would have been much easier, but less profitable, to pick up the flight in Bangkok.

Payment for the gold is almost as unorthodox. Virtually all of it is paid for in American greenbacks smuggled up from South Vietnam through the little town of Pakse on the Laos–South Vietnam border. The favorite subterfuge is to wrap the dollar bills in polyethylene bags and conceal them in five-gallon drums of a fish sauce that the Vietnamese export to Laos. "Those notes smelled terribly of fish when they came into the bank," complained a local bank manager.

In 1967 more than fifty tons of gold, worth over fifty-five million dollars, passed through the Vientiane net and Laotian government coffers recouped nearly five million dollars from the gold tax. In 1968 they budgeted for a bumper year, hoping to reap 6.6 million dollars in taxes. But the Tet offensive and the introduction of the two-tier gold market suddenly caught the Vientiane market off balance. The most important gold dealers in Saigon were the Chinese living in the Cholon district, which was completely devastated by the Vietcong assault on the city in February, 1968. Their business was completely disrupted. Sec-

232

ondly, the fluctuating price for gold after March, 1968, has made it much harder for the banks in Vientiane to order large consignments of gold, because they can never be sure what the price will be by the time it arrives. They are unable to offer their clients a firm price; previously they could safely quote a price to the nearest cent, days in advance. As a result, the gold passing through Vientiane dropped in the first half of 1968 to 13.1 tons, compared with 38.7 tons in the second half of 1967. It looks remarkably as if Vientiane's splendid fling as a gold smugglers' lair has been short— but sweetly profitable while it lasted.

The rise of Vientiane threatened to eclipse the Far East's oldest gold market in Hong Kong, which had long been a center of smuggling operations. The Hong Kong market was always a rather curious affair, since legally there was no market there at all for newly mined gold. In theory all the gold in Hong Kong had been circulating there since the beginning of time, because Hong Kong, as a member of the sterling area, imposes strict controls on the import and export of gold. A neat sidestep avoids these regulations. The gold is ordered by three main dealers in Hong Kong, either from London or from Australia, which sells most of her gold in the colony. The gold arrives at Hong Kong's airport but is technically only in transit. It is moved by armored car to a warehouse in the Kowloon docks and then, about once a week, it is shipped over by hydrofoil to Macao, the Portuguese colony just across the Pearl River. Macao, like Laos, levies a tax on the gold, and fleshes out its budget from the traffic. Normally over fifty tons of gold a year is consigned to Macao, although in 1968 this dropped to twenty-two tons. Once the gold arrives in Macao in the form of 400-ounce good-delivery bars, it disappears behind the peeling facade of the Cambista Song Hong in the Avenida Almeida Ribeiro. Officially it never reappears. Macao admits to large imports of gold but not to exports, leading to the hoary joke "There are an awful lot of dentists in Macao." In fact, it is not the dentists hard at work with gold, but goldsmiths busy melting down those cumbersome 400-ounce bars into the more convenient navel-sized one-tael or five-tael golden nuggets. Since Macao itself has little direct communication with the outside world, the gold is smuggled back into Hong Kong either by passengers on the hydrofoils across the Pearl River or on the small armada of junks plying the river, laden with prawns, bamboo shoots, and rice.

This convenient Macao sidestep is handled by a company which trades under the formal name of the Wong Hong Hon Company. It is a consortium of leading Chinese businessmen headed by one Y. C. Liang, a charming man and a great Anglophile, who started his career as a bus conductor in Shanghai. Liang took command of this syndicate in 1965 on the death of Dr. Pedro José Lobo, who had been its leader for almost twenty years. Lobo had a passion for gold and classical music, and secured a succession of two-year contracts from the Portuguese administration to handle the gold. While he lived, the syndicate was never challenged, but in 1967, when the contract came up for renewal for 1968–69, Liang and his associates were met by a spirited rival bid from other Chinese businessmen. The syndicate managed, however, to fight off this threat to its long-standing monopoly in return for guaranteeing the Portuguese administration of Macao a minimum revenue of over nine million patacas (half a million dollars) a year from the gold tax, plus a contribution of $7,400 to the Social Welfare Department.

From the syndicate in Macao the gold filters back to the six main gold dealers in Hong Kong, and then, through them, to the two hundred banks and exchange dealers in the colony; thence to all corners of the Far East. In addition to the gold handled by Macao's Sindicato de Ouro, the Middle East and European syndicates use Hong Kong as a convenient transit point, where many of their couriers change planes or drop off the gold to await forwarding to Japan, the Philippines, or Indonesia by other means of transport. Several groups maintain station managers there. Their task is not always easy in redirecting gold. During 1967 one station manager, an Englishman, made something of a fool of himself by setting off to discuss a black-market currency deal and, breaking all the rules of the game, carrying thirty kilos of gold himself. When he tried to dispose of it in Seoul, no one wanted it and he had to bring it back.

Until the Dubai traffic to India became so clearly defined, much of the gold smuggled out of Hong Kong went by ship to

India. Today Hong Kong's main black-market client is Japan. The gold moves there by sea in freighters and by air in the couriers' jackets. Occasionally the Hong Kong Preventive Service picks up an illicit shipment going out. In December, 1968, they got a tip which led them to 660 five-tael bars worth $166,-000 hidden in the main engine casing of a freighter bound for Indonesia (another eager market for smuggled gold) and Japan. But the real chore of tracking down this traffic falls to the receiving countries. The Japanese, in particular, are most energetic at gold-smuggler hunting. During 1967 they seized 3,339 kilos of gold worth 6.5 million dollars on the Japanese black market. Assuming they caught a maximum of ten percent of the smuggled gold, this means at least sixty million dollars worth of gold was smuggled into Japan that year. The following spring the Japanese bagged their biggest ever single gold haul—560 one-kilo bars of gold, worth over one million dollars on the black market—concealed in the false bottoms of 560 cans of motor grease imported from Canada through Yokohama. This gold had been consigned initially from Geneva to Vancouver, where it was picked up quite openly from a bank—Canada permits the holding of gold by private citizens. It was then inserted into the specially made tins and shipped across the Pacific in freighters sailing from Vancouver and Seattle. The Japanese first caught one hundred one-kilo bars on an American freighter—after which they vetted every oil can coming into the country and, within a week, had found two more consignments of 460 bars, which were already on the high seas before the alarm went out to the smugglers that their ruse was revealed. However, the smugglers probably broke even on the deal. At least sixteen shipments involving over four thousand kilos were dispatched in all; the first thirteen got through safely. If the smugglers were working on a ten-to-fifteen-percent profit margin, they should have covered their costs.

Canada has become an increasingly important springboard for gold smugglers during the past few years, because there is a slight psychological advantage in gold arriving in the Far East from the American continent. Customs men in, say, Japan have become so accustomed to smugglers traveling on flights originating in Hong Kong or Zurich or Brussels that they are always alert. The same suspicions are not—or were not—aroused by flights coming from Vancouver, Seattle, Los Angeles, or even Mexico City, since none of these cities had any kind of gold market and in the United States the holding of gold is forbidden. It proved, therefore, most convenient for one syndicate, which has close connections with Las Vegas and Los Angeles, to arrange through Switzerland for gold to be air-freighted perfectly legally to Vancouver and shouldered there by couriers (or buried in the motor grease). The couriers could easily take domestic flights down from Vancouver to any city on the West Coast and board an American jet bound for the Far East.

Now that this bluff has been called, both in the case of the golden motor grease and by American customs, acting on inside information, picking up gold couriers as they came through the United States in transit, the smugglers are busy concocting other schemes. "Sooner or later," said a senior customs man in the Far East, "they are going to use a submarine."

But the gold smuggler had one serious setback in 1968, quite apart from his normal occupational hazard of being nabbed by authority. The fluctuating price of gold on the free gold market has made the costing of his operations much more difficult. Although ostensibly the smuggler always seemed to be doubling his money, in fact his profit is rarely more than ten percent by the time all his expenses and the cost of various foreign-exchange deals for payment are added together. This was acceptable as long as the price of gold remained within a few cents of thirty-five dollars an ounce, as it did until March, 1968. A daily price variation of two or three cents could be allowed for in his charges. Now, however, he may order his kilo bars from Zurich when the price is forty-two dollars an ounce, but find, by the time he is ready to dispatch his couriers, that it has fallen to forty-one dollars. Even more difficult is the issue of credit. "In the past," complained a well-known Beirut smuggler in the spring of 1969, "all I had to pay the Swiss bank was ten percent down. Now in Switzerland you must pay the whole price immediately." That is not the end of his troubles. "My couriers can still carry only forty kilos of gold, but the cost of those forty kilos has gone up eight thousand dollars. So I'm taking eight thousand dollars' more risk with every courier—those eight thousand dollars could have bought me an extra six kilos of gold under the old price."

There is no doubt that the smuggling market around the world has contracted during 1968–69, while the new two-tier gold system finds its feet, but it is hard to believe that it is more than a temporary pause. Gold will eventually be replaced by some more logical medium of exchange, but the emotions that it can release are a long time dying. "Man has not yet learned to trust man," says one London gold expert. "You tell me when man is going to change, and I'll tell you when the importance of gold will cease." In the meantime, the gold smuggler, whatever his temporary setbacks, can be sure of plenty of clients.

X

Watches

It is often hard to tell whether English thriller writers copy the wiles of the criminal, or whether the English criminal learns his plotting from his fiction reading. Consider for a moment the tale of a young Newhaven fisherman. Down by the quays a few years ago he was approached by a couple of lads who introduced themselves as Alf and Jim and confided to him they had recently had a bit of luck in winning eighteen thousand pounds on the football pools. They wanted to buy a boat with part of their winnings. They explained, however, that all these sudden riches had landed them in a spot of bother with the income-tax authorities, and would the fisherman mind if their boat was registered in his name? They would pay him ten pounds a week to run it. Delighted to help, he said. He admitted later he did think there was "something funny" in the offer, but, as he had heard other local fishermen were up to the same lark, he accepted.

The boat was duly bought for £675 in cash, and Alf and Jim invested in some fishing tackle, plus a radio direction finder. If the fisherman asked innocently what was going on, Jim would reply, "Cock-a-doodle-do, it's nothing to do with you." And in that cheerful vein the three men in their boat set sail one September night bound for the shores of France. They came into the French shore just west of Dieppe, homing on a red light flashing from the beach. Jim went over the side in a rubber dinghy and paddled away into the dark. Twenty minutes later he was back with three heavy bags, which he stowed in the fish lockers. The fisherman then turned the boat for home. As he told it later, it was all a pleasant night's boating. "They looked after me well. They brought me a bottle of Scotch, and we had that in tea and soup."

Just before dawn they slipped back into Newhaven harbor and offloaded the three bags into the trunk of a waiting Jaguar and piled in ready to take off. At that precise moment two men materialized out of the dark and opened the front doors of the car. "Good morning, gentlemen—customs and excise," said a voice with measured politeness. Alf, behind the wheel, did not pause to exchange the greeting. He put the car in gear and swept away, leaving the customs men in some confusion by the dock.

The escape, however, was purely temporary. Ultimately the fisherman was charged with being concerned in the fraudulent evasion of customs duty on 4,300 Swiss watches worth £23,000. Alf and Jim, together with three associates, landed up at the Old Bailey on a conspiracy charge, relating to the smuggling of £500,000 worth of watches. The trial lasted six weeks, and at the end of the long hearing the judge, glancing at the pile of confiscated watches on exhibit, remarked to the jury, "It is the habit, so far as I know, to reward long service with the gift of a watch. I am dissuaded from doing that in your case because I think if I did, the customs officials would immediately charge you with being in possession of uncustomed watches." His lordship did, however, exempt them from jury service for the rest of their lives, which was perhaps a greater reward; there are plenty of other places besides the Old Bailey to pick up a duty-free watch.

In Europe these days it is so easy to buy a watch duty-free that Alf, Jim, and the lads were among the last of the big-time smugglers who found it worthwhile to sneak watches into Britain. Now, with thirty million people heading south for the sun along the Mediterranean every year, it is easiest for each individual to select his own new watch in a duty-free shop at an airport or aboard a car ferry on the way. In Europe this is the age of the do-it-yourself watch smuggler.

But in many other parts of the world the professional has never had it so good. The beauty of the business is that, unlike gold, diamonds, or even drugs, which are purchased by a relatively limited market, everyone wants a watch. It is essentially an item of clothing—and perhaps the only one most people do not discard even when they make love. In developing nations, where import quotas may be low or duties high, a smuggled watch becomes a prestige article to be purchased at a premium and duly prized.

World watch production is rising at the rate of ten million a year, and in 1967 a record 141,241,000 watches and watch movements were produced. The Swiss, of course, leave everyone else at the starting gate. They manufacture almost half the world's watches. But three other countries are now coming up fast in the watch-making business: Russia, which is number two, and the United States and Japan, which are running neck and neck. But none of these countries, nor any other, can match the prestige of a Swiss watch. The problem is that in some countries, such as India, the import of assembled Swiss watches is either banned or on a strict quota system. Other countries impose high import duties. This creates ideal market conditions for a smuggler. He can buy his watches in Hong Kong or Singapore and sell them at four or five times the price in Japan, India, Indonesia, and even Australia. The profit margin into the United States is rather less, but the American watch dealer who buys smuggled watches not only dodges import duty ($2.25 on an average lady's watch or $1.80 on a man's watch), but avoids any reference to the smuggled watches on his books, thus ducking sales tax, income tax, and profits tax.

Although no one is publishing watch-smuggling turnover figures, a quick glance at Switzerland's official exports of watches gives some remarkable clues to the scale of the traffic. The largest single market for Swiss watches is, as might be expected, the United States. Almost twenty million watches and watch movements were exported to the United States in 1967. No surprise in that. But which country took second place? Hong Kong, population four million, took 6.3 million watches and watch movements. That means either that every man, woman, and child in the British colony buys one and one-half watches a year and is some kind of avid collector, or that Hong Kong is a handy entrepôt for watches destined for other nations. The third place in the list goes to Britain, again no cause for raised eyebrows, but fourth is given to what the Swiss call, rather charmingly, *Arabie Orientale*, that is to say, the Arab sheikdoms of the Trucial Oman States at the southern end of the Arabian Gulf. The population of this sun-baked stretch of sand is 130,000; between them these Arabs buy over three million watches a year, which is twenty-three watches each. In fact, the buying is even more intense than that, for the majority of those three million watches go to Dubai, the gold smuggler's lair, which has a population of sixty-five thousand. Half a dozen other nations or cities also seem to be inhabited by a breed of watch addicts—Mexico, Singapore, Kuwait, Lebanon, Tangier, and Panama. All of them import far more Swiss watches a year than could conceivably be worn by their population. Totting up the total for all these main smuggling centers reveals that among them in 1967 they imported over fourteen million Swiss watches (one-quarter of Swiss production) worth more than ninety million dollars. The smuggler's profits are not, of course, all of that ninety million dollars, but he will make at least one dollar on every watch or watch movement passing through, which means a minimum income of fourteen million dollars a year on the smuggling of Swiss watches alone. This may seem a small profit per item, but the watch smuggler is normally trading in the cheaper brands of watch, costing about seven dollars each wholesale, which have mass appeal. He orders, perhaps, twenty thousand watches or movements at a time.

The heart of the watch is always that delicate movement. Every year millions of Swiss movements are exported to be assembled with cases and straps in other countries. The United States, for example, imported over seven million Swiss movements in 1967; these went into cases made in the United States, Hong Kong, or Japan. Until the end of 1968 all Swiss watches and movements imported into the United States had to bear a three-letter symbol stamped onto the balance-cock bridge by the importer. One immediate way to identify a smuggled watch was to look for the symbol; if it was missing, then the watch had been smuggled. However, even if it did have the magic three letters, this still did not guarantee it as a genuine import. The first priority on every shipment of watches smuggled into the United States before the beginning of 1969 was to get a legitimate symbol stamped on.

The watch-smuggling business, like the illicit traffic in diamonds, is closely interwoven with the trade itself. This is not an indictment of every watchmaker or of every dealer. Half a dozen Swiss watch firms have a reputation, if that is the right word, for supplying much of the American black market. They may be perfectly innocent parties in that operation. If they receive an order for thirty thousand watches to be delivered in Mexico, and payment is duly made, it is not their responsibility if the fellow in Mexico then spirits them quietly into the United States. Although, when one of the leading smugglers, a Hungarian by birth, based in Tijuana, Mexico, also has a cousin working for one of the Swiss firms whose watches figure most actively in his trade, one may be forgiven for doubting its innocence.

But this, of course, is the essence of the watch-smuggling business, particularly into the United States. It is all between relations or old friends. The ethnic connection, so essential in many other facets of smuggling, is just as crucial in watches. "The importers smuggling watch movements in here are a very select group," explains a dealer in New York. "They all know each other very well. There are four really important ones. They are all former refugees, and they have a certain psychology which makes their activities perfectly understandable. Before they came to the United States, many of them were oppressed, chased over frontiers, thrust into refugee camps. Anything they got they obtained through outwitting the authorities—smuggling, if you like. It became a way of life. They smuggled from the day they walked; it became second nature. Having done it for so long, they are proficient. Now, suddenly, they are in America, where smuggling is a criminal offense, but they don't see that. They see nothing wrong in smuggling watches or diamonds." It is simply an obliging deal between two old friends or cousins, the one still in Europe, the other in America.

All these importers are, of course, in the legitimate watch business. Their technique is to order, say, fifty thousand watch movements through the legal channels and a further twenty thousand movements of the same make on the black market. The smuggling is almost entirely in seventeen-jewel Swiss movements, which are less bulky and weighty than the completed watch. The movement can easily be wedded to an American or a Japanese case once it is in the United States.

It is a cardinal rule to order the same make of watch movement through both licit and illicit sources. Fraud is then very hard to prove. If an importer's premises are searched, he can wave a customs receipt for duty paid on each make of movement in stock. It is impossible to prove he acquired some of them illicitly—provided, of course, he took the precaution of stamping a symbol on the smuggled movements. The sole danger is to get caught with seventy-five thousand movements when duty has been paid on only fifty thousand; but that can be avoided by intelligent ordering and swift disposal of movements once they arrive.

There is a twist to this technique which is widely used, particularly in South America. Once in a while the customs authorities will hold a sale of confiscated watches. A dealer scurries along and buys one thousand watches or movements. He gets an official receipt. He can then place orders through his black-market connections for unlimited shipments of that same make of watch, provided he never has more than one thousand on hand at any time. If authority asks awkward questions, he produces his receipt. "I bought these at your sale." "That was four years ago, and you still have 998!" "Yes, too bad, this kind sells rather slowly."

The Valiant Watch Company of New York once broke this rule. They were caught with a brand of watch which they had not also imported legally, thus giving the U.S. Customs their biggest-ever watch-smuggling case, involving twenty thousand watches and watch movements, twenty defendants, and a total of $82,-000 in fines. Valiant Watch was a well-established New York firm run by the four Katz brothers—Maurice, Zoltan, Israel, and Ludvig. They imported up to 100,000 movements at a time quite legally but developed a profitable little sideline of smuggling others up from Panama City through Miami and into California from Tijuana. On the California trail ten thousand movements a time were coming over the border in the roof of a car, which delivered them initially to Los Angeles. There all the watches were hastily stamped with the correct Valiant Watch Company symbol, SMU, to make them legal tender, so to speak. The movements were then driven on to New York, where they passed into the Valiant Watch Company's normal distribution channels. On the Miami route the watches came through by air from Panama City and were delivered to a local watch dealer for consignment to New York. And it was in Miami in June, 1963, that the U.S. Customs, who had been keeping a careful eye on Valiant Watch for over two years, got their first break. They seized four thousand unsymboled watch movements as a courier brought them in from Panama. Two months later they captured three thousand more movements in Miami as a courier handed them over to a local dealer, Jaime Posesowsky, who had close associations with Valiant in New York. The chain of evidence was building up. Three days after the Miami seizure, agents moved in on the Valiant Watch Company head office on 47th Street in New York. The raid revealed almost eight thousand unsymboled watch movements, together with over $100,000 in small-denomination notes stuffed into paper bags in desk drawers. Maurice Katz, the head of the firm, two of his brothers, and four other associates were arrested immediately. There was not sufficient evidence, however, to hold the fourth brother, Israel. He was released. Immediately Israel dashed out of the building, got his car, and raced to the home of brother Maurice. Customs men, hard on his heels, just caught him as he came running back out of Maurice's house to his car carrying two packages containing 1,050 more unsymboled Swiss watches.

Although ninety percent of the movements smuggled into the United States come through Tijuana into California, it is equally profitable to smuggle them across the Atlantic by plane. A courier can carry up to two thousand movements, worth at least thirty thousand dollars, in a smuggling vest, which is an excellent return on an Atlantic airfare and a courier fee of two hundred dollars. Inside knowledge of airline schedules can enable the courier to avoid the customs gauntlet entirely—a technique also used with considerable success by narcotics smugglers. The courier books aboard an American jet from Paris or Rome or Lisbon to New York, carrying watch movements either in a smuggling vest or in a briefcase. During the seven-hour Atlantic crossing he makes several trips to the toilet and conceals the watches behind the wash basin—an easy maneuver with a screwdriver. He then disembarks at New York and breezes through customs with a clear conscience. He will have found out, however, that the aircraft, with the watches still aboard, is due to fly on to Los Angeles or Detroit or Kansas City and that the following day it will be coming back through New York. He therefore takes another flight to the appropriate city and reboards the original aircraft for its return to New York. During the flight he goes to the toilet, lifts out the watches, and happily carries them off the plane in New York at the end of the domestic flight with no customs clearance.

It pays, however, to be careful how often you visit the toilet. On a flight from St. Louis to New York in 1965, a stewardess noticed that one passenger listed as S. Wile (in fact, his real name was Solomon Drummer) was making an extraordinary number of trips to the toilet; he was not airsick, and he looked perfectly healthy. She told the pilot. He slipped back to take a look—and found 2,700 unsymboled movements beneath the washbasin. He radioed ahead to Kennedy Airport, where customs met the plane and searched the restless passengers. Drummer, alias Wile, had two thousand more watch movements in his bag. It turned out that the watches, worth $32,879 and liable to duty of $15,393, had been planted the previous day during a flight from Zurich and Paris to New York.

Despite all this activity, the number of watches and movements smuggled into the United States is only a small percentage of the total U.S. watch sales, probably no more than two or three percent. This situation is dramatically reversed in other corners of the world, where import restrictions mean that virtually all foreign watches sold in a country are smuggled. India, for example, has a ban on the import of assembled watches, although she does permit the entry of about two million Swiss movements, which are made into watches in her own assembly plants. But that can hardly satisfy the demand from a nation of nearly five hundred million people. So between two and three million watches are smuggled into Bombay alone every year from Dubai, with a further estimated million coming through Madras and Calcutta from Hong Kong and Singapore. In Indonesia the situation is even more remarkable. At first sight there appears to be no shortage of Swiss or Japanese watches. They are boldly advertised in the newspapers. Yet officially Indonesia imported only 442 Swiss watches in 1967, which is hardly a generous supply for the fourth most populous nation in the world. The situation is the same in the Philippines. It is a hard fact of business life in Asia that firms which play by the rules and try to sell their watches legally are likely to go broke. "My firm," said an export salesman in Hong Kong, whose territory ranges from Japan to India, "can't do legitimate business in India, Indonesia, or the Philippines. We can't sell a single watch there in competition with the smugglers." Hong Kong watch agents learn quickly not to ask questions of their clients. One agent explained, "We get curious orders from local jewelers for one hundred and fifty watches of a special style—which is far more than he would sell here in two years. You just learn to play along."

Hong Kong itself is a Mecca of the watch business, where Swiss, Russian, and Japanese watches all blend together—indeed, one finished watch may contain parts from several countries. Switzerland exports just over one million finished watches a year to Hong Kong, but over five million movements. According to the Hong Kong telephone directory, there are 31 watchmakers and importers, 42 watch-case makers, 135 watch-strap makers, and 248 watch dealers in the colony. They have a glorious time putting together all kinds of watches, rather like a cook making an omelet with a chicken's, a goose's, and a duck's egg. The finished watch may well have a Russian movement, a Swiss dial (for prestige), a Japanese case, and a Hong Kong strap. And a word of warning about buying an expensive watch in the Far East: There are many floating around that purport to be of the very best Swiss makes, but nothing is genuine about them except the spelling of the name on the dial—and that may be a fake stamp. Even the most wary can be fooled. Not long ago the Indian customs seized from a smuggler coming in from Hong Kong one thousand watches of a highly reputable make. After the trial they sold the watches to the watch firm's agent in Bombay. A few weeks later he came back outraged. He had disposed of the watches, but his customers complained they did not run properly. He had checked and found the whole shipment were fakes. He accused the customs authorities of cheating him. "Not our fault," said the customs. "You can't expect us to know the movements were fakes; we don't smuggle."

The watches radiate from Hong Kong by air and sea. Frequently a group of seamen on a freighter will run their own informal syndicate. Each time they dock in Hong Kong or Singapore, they pool all their resources to buy watches. Then they can sell them off gradually through well-established contacts at other ports throughout the Far East. Some seamen work for a missionary in Hong Kong. He makes contact with sailors in his mission and then encourages them to smuggle watches—often counterfeit versions of a popular Japanese make—on their next trip. He does a good deal of traveling around the globe himself, but purely to look after his mission and make a few deals; he leaves the smuggling itself strictly to his seamen. Although his activities may be frowned on by authority, he is something of a hero among his friends. He plows all his smuggling profits back into his mission and into helping the poor. "He is," said an admirer of his skulduggery in Hong Kong, "a sort of Robin Hood."

Since no one can predict the adventures that may befall a watch on its journey from Hong Kong, most of them are sturdily packaged. Many of those that leave by sea are wrapped individually in polyethylene, minus the strap; then fifty watches in a batch are slotted into strips of strong plastic; finally, five thousand watches are packed neatly layer upon layer into hermetically sealed kerosene oil tins. Even if they have to be tossed overboard from a ship, the watches will remain undamaged; the only problem is to salvage the tin.

Such careful packing is equally important in the shipment of watches from Dubai across the one thousand two hundred miles of Arabian Sea to Bombay, for at the end the watches must be transferred at sea from a heaving dhow to an Indian fishing boat. Dubai's gold-carrying dhows (see Chapter 9) also carry many of the three million watches that pass through their little sheikdom every year, but the volume is so great that there are also some boats specifically to handle the watch traffic. (Dubai, unlike Hong Kong, trades entirely in finished watches rather than movements. Its role is purely that of staging post.) Although most gold smugglers concentrate their attentions on that specialty, some of them dabble profitably in the Indian watch traffic. That most renowned smuggler, the swashbuckling American pilot Daniel Hailey Walcott, who carried everything from shotguns and shells to gold into India before he began a long stay in an Indian jail in 1966, also carried on, according to the Indian authorities, a sideline in watches. On one memorable occasion, the authorities have alleged, he hired a twin-engined Riley 65 aircraft in London (his own aircraft had been impounded in Beirut at the time by the Lebanese, who had accused him of taking photographs of their military installations for Israel) and headed for India accompanied by a British copilot. Walcott, a tall Texan, was traveling on a British passport under the name of Peter Philby. In Cyprus the pair picked up a consignment of 675 Roamer watches, and a few hours later came skimming down for a landing on a quiet Indian beach at Murud, 150 miles from Bombay. The sand was unexpectedly soft, and the plane lurched to a halt with a broken nose wheel and bent propellers. Walcott did not turn a hair. He scrambled out and summoned up the head man from the local villagers who quickly surrounded the crashed aircraft. "Emergency landing," he explained. He told the head man he would have to go to Bombay and bring back a mechanic to make repairs. Meanwhile, said Walcott, he knew he could trust the head man to watch over the plane. He and his copilot picked up a couple of cases full of watches and set out to catch a bus to Bombay. They arrived there in the early morning and safely delivered the watches. Then they headed for the airport. Here was a slight snag; they needed to leave India in a hurry, but according to their papers, they had not arrived. This problem was soon overcome. By simply strolling around the back of the terminal building at Santa Cruz airport they got into the transit lounge and then came boldly through with the next planeload of passengers arriving on an incoming flight. They presented passports and smallpox and cholera certificates and thus entered India legally. Immediately they booked seats on the first outgoing flight and were up and away hours before the head man waiting patiently for them to come back to the beach with a mechanic began to wonder what was going on.

Not everyone has such a bold nerve in emergencies—or such good luck. There was the young Air India steward whom the Indian customs picked up at Santa Cruz airport, Bombay, one evening in 1967 as he landed from Hong Kong. He had 250 Swiss watches in his bag. At first the young man would not say a word, but the customs worked on him very skillfully. The interrogation was quiet and subtle. One officer interviewed him for a long while, going over the same details painstakingly again and again. Once in a while he reached out his hand and dinged loudly on a bell on his desk. Two other officers came in and popped several stern questions. They reminded the young man, "What will your family think of this? Realize the shame you are bringing on them." Then they retired, and the quiet talking continued. After one such sharp interlude the officer said, "In about ten minutes he will tell us everything." Sure enough he did. The steward had been recruited initially to smuggle £4,000 ($9,600) in sterling from Bombay to London concealed in a parcel. He had been given a telephone number to ring on arrival in London and a code word, "River Ganges," to identify himself. The parcel was speedily picked up from his hotel room by an Indian who did not volunteer his name but instructed him to call a certain number next time he was in Hong Kong and give the same code word. This he duly did and received the watches. He was then told to take them to a certain restaurant in Bombay at eleven o'clock the morning after his arrival, sit at a table on the right of the door, where he would be contacted and the watches collected —a rendezvous he was not able, of course, to keep. His pay for the two assignments was hardly handsome—600 rupees ($85) for taking the sterling to London, 1,000 rupees ($140) for the watches. In fact he was rather short-changed on the sterling. He should have received one rupee for every pound carried—but clearly as a newcomer to the racket he did not appreciate his own market value. What he told the customs was, of course, of very little value. He knew no names, he could give only a vague description of his contacts in London and Hong Kong, and he did not know who should have picked up the watches in Bombay.

This is the true measure of a good smuggling outfit. Even if a courier is caught and tells everything he knows, it will not incriminate anyone else.

Watch smuggling is perhaps one of the hardest of all smuggling rackets to crack, for almost every citizen with a watch around his wrist—and even more every citizen who wants one round his wrist—is on the smuggler's side. There must be few people who have not at some point in their lives been offered a watch "special offer going cheap." It is hard to resist. It probably seems no more immoral than trying to dodge some extra little bit of income tax.

As for the watchmakers, to them every watch sold is a little more business. It is not their problem if their product moves through black-market channels. Many watch firms are singularly unhelpful to the authorities and helpful to the smugglers. A remarkable number of Swiss watches are consigned to South America by air freight obligingly labeled "pens" or "machine parts." If a shipment goes astray en route the watchmakers prefer to forget the loss. In 1967 a package containing 1,075 ladies' watches, 605 men's watches, and 250 watch movements, worth in all around ten thousand dollars, was stolen while being airfreighted from Geneva to Buenos Aires by way of Frankfurt, where it was transshipped from a Swissair to an Aerolineas Argentinas flight. Frankfurt police began inquiries into the loss and telexed the Swiss makers for more details. Back came a curt message: "Just forget the whole thing." The firm did not wish to embarrass its clients in South America.

Watch smuggling into South America is rather like the latter days of Prohibition in the United States: Many people oppose the removal of the restrictions because they are making so much money while they remain. "It is really official smuggling," explained a Swiss expert who has made a study of the traffic. "There is even an authorized list of the people to be paid off." The easiest method of entry is for the watches to arrive under false declarations as machine tools or screws. Alternatively, they can be consigned to Santiago by way of Buenos Aires. They never get beyond Buenos Aires. The airline manifest, which showed Santiago as the ultimate destination, will disappear mysteriously during the stopover, and no one will ask any questions.

There is little point in getting upset about watch smuggling; it will continue just as long as there are import restrictions and high rates of duty. "There is," says an American customs man, "very little we can do about it. It's like throwing sand at the oncoming tide; you can't stop it."

XI

Art, Antiques, and Antiquities

The theft of art treasures is universally prevalent, and increasing numbers of criminals are realizing that an accredited work of art is a reliable form of currency, easily transportable and disposable in a world of monetary restrictions and instability.

—*Arts Review*, September 28, 1968

Someday a student of criminology ought to write a thesis on the literary tastes of criminals. It could be most instructive. He would find, for example, that one of the standard works essential for any good British thief's library is *A Guide to Marks of Origin on British and Irish Silver Plate from the Mid-16th Century to 1963*. He should also cast his eye over the shelves for S. N. Behrman's charming biography of that prince of art dealers, Lord Duveen of Millbank, in which Behrman notes, "Early in life, Duveen . . . noticed that Europe had plenty of art and America had plenty of money, and his entire astonishing career was the product of that simple observation." An observation not lost on the well-read criminal. Hard in the wake of the current art boom a remarkable traffic has emerged in the smuggling of antiquities from countries such as Italy, Turkey, and Iran, which are blessed with a rich archaeological subsoil, to America, which is not. Coupled with this has been an uncontrolled wave of robberies on the choice private collections of Western Europe of carefully selected art and antiques, which find a ready and well-paying market in the budding collections of America. It is impossible to set truly accurate values on the treasures involved, but it is estimated that between five and ten million dollars' worth of Etruscan and Roman antiquities are smuggled out of Italy each year, while art robberies in Britain alone now involve between five and seven million dollars a year. Early in 1968 Hart & Co., the London insurance assessors, was offering rewards totaling over half a million pounds (1.2 million dollars) for the recovery of works of art and antiques stolen in Britain; since rewards normally amount to ten percent of the value of the missing items, this implied a total of twelve million dollars in stolen art being handled by one firm of assessors alone.

Criminals' magazine and newspaper reading habits are also worth studying. *Country Life*, for example, frequently publishes excellent descriptions of private collections of art and antiques in English country houses and often provides a plan of the house. *The Illustrated London News* is a unique anthology of the latest archaeological discoveries from Haçilar to Angkor Wat; and the business-news section of *The Times* is running an excellent continuing series of articles on the rising price trends in the art market, put together by that newspaper and Sotheby's, the fine-art auctioneers. This *Times Sotheby Index* has shown that while the average United Kingdom share price tripled and the American average share price quadrupled between 1951 and 1967, the price of Old Master paintings and English silver went up six times, of Impressionist paintings nearly ten times, of modern paintings and Chinese porcelain fifteen times, and of Old Master prints eighteen times during the same period. More specifically, the *Index* has charted that prints by Peter Brueghel the Elder are up 2,400 percent, by Rembrandt 2,300 percent, and by Canaletto 2,000 percent.

Quite apart from the rising value of art, the expansion of the international art market has made it exceptionally easy to dispose of a painting or antique acquired or stolen in one country in half a dozen cities overseas. "A work of art today is as good as currency," said a member of Scotland Yard's special Art Theft Squad. "It has an international value." Indeed, in addition to the smuggling of stolen paintings in and out of Western Europe, there is also a lively international trade in paintings as a means of avoiding currency controls. It is quite simple to purchase a work by a minor Dutch painter for £1,000 in London, take it to Basel and sell it for 10,330 Swiss francs. Customs authorities pay little attention to works of art or antiques leaving —and, with the best will in the world, most customs men cannot hope to be able to appraise the value of a painting when they do see one. The London *Daily Mirror* put this to the test after one recent art robbery by dispatching a reporter to Belgium with a full-scale reproduction of the missing work. He accomplished the journey twice, once by air, once by sea; no one paid the slightest attention to him, least of all the customs men. Aside from the currency dodge, the motive for smuggling is normally either to avoid export control on antiquities or simply to escape detection in the movement of stolen property.

Nations whose soil is rich with relics of early man are understandably nervous of losing this inheritance to an army of overeager archaeologists or unscrupulous dealers, who can swarm through their lands like a horde of locusts digging up or buying up ancient treasures for museums overseas. Turkey has reacted by imposing a complete ban on the export of antiquities; other countries, including Iran, Italy, and Egypt, will grant export licenses only for a limited number of items and will sit firmly on any real prizes uncovered by archaeologists. While they have every right to do this, such controls only increase the frustrations of museums of other countries trying to develop their collections. Many of Europe's finest museums were able to build their collections in the nineteenth and early twentieth centuries, when the archaeologist or the traveler could return with whatever he found. Thus Lord Elgin was able to ship back to London aboard the British fleet some of the finest sculptures from the Parthenon in 1812. It could be argued in those days that he performed a noble deed in helping to preserve the marbles for posterity; the Greeks think of it as pillaging. Today a new American museum trying to establish a well-balanced gallery of relics of the Etruscans, the Trojans, or the Mycenaeans can find itself thwarted at every turn, even if it sponsors archaeologists on digs at the original sites. Since many of these museums are well endowed, they can afford to pay thousands of dollars for genuine antiquities. Preferably they will obtain them through legal channels; in the last resort, through illegal. A handful of dealers working in Italy, Turkey, and Iran have earned the undying gratitude of many American museums by spiriting across the Atlantic treasures which the museums despaired of ever possessing. "Look, there is no other way that a new American museum can build their collections," said an art expert in Rome. "Any dealer who smuggles is performing a valuable, albeit illegal, service."

It is also much easier for American museums to purchase antiquities from slightly shady sources. As an archaeologist explained it, "If the British Museum or a major European museum wants to buy something, they almost inevitably have to obtain the money through government channels—and governments want to know all the background before spending their money. But in America, a museum seeks out a millionaire who is striving for social acceptance and says to him, 'We can arrange for you to buy this treasure and present it to us, no questions asked about its origin or its price.' That puts the Americans in a very strong bargaining position."

Italy is the focal point of the traffic in antiquities, partly because of its own inheritance, partly because it makes a pleasant base of operations for covering the entire Mediterranean area. Under Italian law anything found underground belongs to the state, but if the government wishes to keep any article that is unearthed, it must pay the finder and the owner of the land fifty percent of the estimated value. The trouble is that this can take years of struggling with red tape before the authorities even decide whether or not they wish to purchase an item. Many Italians, therefore, bypass authority completely and sell their discoveries to an obliging American dealer in Rome, who has for years operated what is euphemistically called a "service" for American museums.

The richest area for these diggers is north of Rome in Tuscany, between the rivers Tiber and Arno, a region inhabited 2,500 years ago by the Etruscans. Here, before the rise of the Roman Empire, an extraordinarily cultivated civilization flourished, producing exquisite painted vases, terra-cotta figures, jewelry, and gold ornaments of high caliber. Fortunately, much of it has been preserved, for the Etruscans buried their dead in elaborate tombs, which were often entire underground streets of sepulchers cut out of rock and designed and adorned to look like the earthly homes of the occupants. These Etruscan tombs have been raided consistently for centuries by amateur archaeologists bent on improving their own collections and by plunderers in search of salable loot. Today these graverobbers, or *tombaroli*, are as active as ever, although they must now be a trifle more cautious. Their favorite method of operation is to build a hut of cane and reeds over the spot where they have located a tomb. They leave this decaying shelter for months or even years, until it seems a permanent feature of the landscape, then start digging inside the hut. Their finds are sold quickly, either through Rome or through an Italian-Swiss dealer, who works from the safety of Switzerland. The graverobbing is not limited to vases or figurines; it often includes whole frescoes. In August, 1963, thieves made off with huge sections of frescoed walls from Etruscan tombs in Tarquinia. They used an electric saw to cut into the stone and then inserted steel wires behind the frescoes and pulled them out. According to local gossip, a Swiss dealer paid the *tombaroli* eight thousand dollars for this fresco slicing.

There is little difficulty in spiriting these treasures out of Italy into Switzerland either by train, hidden among shipments of fruit, vegetables, or even cement, or by car. Italian customs on that border are more concerned with cigarettes being smuggled in than they are with antiquities being smuggled out.

At least in Italy anyone with interminable patience may obtain a license to export Etruscan vases or Roman statuettes. In Turkey there is a blanket prohibition on the export of antiquities, and, as a result, a steady illicit trade through Istanbul and Izmir. Even the casual tourist prowling through the bazaars, who is persistent in refusing the standard run of "antiques," may be lucky enough, if he mutters the word "neolithic," to be offered some genuine bronze stag from Alaja Huyuk or a goddess from Haçilar which the dealer will produce surreptitiously from his safe. And out at the sites of the ancient Hittite cities in central Anatolia or at Troy or Ephesus the discerning visitor can buy— for a price—a genuine figurine of a goddess or a seal depicting the weather god. Many Turks have built their fortunes by flocking like homing pigeons on the heels of the archaeologists and taking up the digging when the archaeologists shut up camp at the end of the summer. The best-organized illicit diggers, of course, do not rely on selling to the casual tourist passing by; they have good contacts with dealers in Europe and dispatch their finds by ship from Izmir or Istanbul or even by parcel post through the American Army post office. These shipments are often handled by specialist transporters who can slip anything from a tiny ring to four-foot-high statues out of the country. Payment for the smuggled items may be made in Turkey itself, but is most often into Swiss bank accounts.

The intrigue around the smuggling of antiquities out of Turkey has been heightened in recent years by the strange case of the Missing Dorak Treasure. This tale reads like a mystery Agatha Christie might have written after accompanying her archaeologist husband Professor Max Mallowan on one of his expeditions. It all began on a Turkish train between Izmir and Istanbul in the summer of 1958. A British archaeologist, James Mellaart, then assistant director of the British Institute of Archaeology in Ankara, found himself sitting opposite an attractive young lady who was wearing a solid-gold bracelet. Mellaart could scarcely believe his eyes; it was a bracelet found only at ancient Troy. The archaeologist, unable to restrain his curiosity for a second, introduced himself and inquired where she had obtained the bracelet. The girl, who later introduced herself as Anna Papastrati, explained it was part of a collection she owned. Mellaart, now thoroughly fascinated, asked if he might see the collection. Anna Papastrati agreed, and when the train arrived in Izmir took the archaeologist to her home. There she showed Mellaart an incredible assortment of gold and silver figurines, bracelets, and jewelry which she claimed had been excavated near the village of Dorak south of the Sea of Marmara. She

257

permitted Mellaart to make sketches of this 4,500-year-old treasure, but was highly evasive about exactly how it came into her possession. When Mellaart had finished his sketches, she said she would also send him photographs in a few weeks. The archaeologist returned to Ankara and waited for the photographs. They never came. Indeed, apart from one letter from Anna, which authorized him to publish his sketches, he never heard from her again, nor has anyone admitted to seeing or hearing of the Dorak Treasure since that day in the summer of 1958. Mellaart's sketches appeared in 1959 in *The Illustrated London News* and sparked off something of a furor among the Turkish authorities. Where were these treasures? Had they been smuggled out of Turkey? Inquiries at the address in Izmir at which Mellaart said he had stayed elicited the reply that no one had ever heard of Anna Papastrati, let alone the Dorak Treasure.

In the decade since then, speculation has been endless. The only really feasible answer seems to be that Mellaart was used as an innocent victim by a group of Greek smugglers (Anna Papastrati said she was Greek) to establish the authenticity of their finds, which were taken out of Turkey immediately after he had sketched them and then sold when publication of his sketches confirmed their historic importance. No one is letting on who bought them, but the rumor around archaeological circles is that they are sitting in the basement of a distinguished American museum.*

Across the border from Turkey in Iran the smuggling scene is just as active. Controls on the export of antiquities are extremely tight, with the Iranians displaying chauvinistic attitudes in insisting that what is discovered in the historical remains of Persia must be preserved for display in the museum in Tehran. This policy does not appear to prevent plenty of antiquities getting out. A recent congress in New York, attended by experts on Persian archaeology from all over the world, was, according to one museum man, "more like an Oriental bazaar. Everyone was coming up to you and slipping out a Persian lapis-lazuli figure from beneath his coat and asking 'Psst, do you want to buy?' "

* For the detailed story of the Dorak Treasure, see *The Dorak Affair*, by Kenneth Pearson and Patricia Connor, Michael Joseph, London, 1967.

The main traffic is in gold and silver bowls, vases, or plates, and jewelry, which can command much higher prices than simple pots. "The risks and the overheads are so high," explained an archaeology expert, "that it pays only to bring these things out." The trade is so well organized that in Iran there are two kinds of excavations—archaeologists' excavations and dealers' excavations. The tragedy of it is that dealers' excavations, like the sack of some ancient city, are concerned with sifting out only the really valuable finds; they ignore—and may well ruin—other artifacts which would reveal much more about the way of life of the people in these ancient civilizations. The dealers can bring so much pressure to bear that serious archaeologists believe that at one major site in Iran, legitimate digging was stopped and a most distinguished archaeologist refused permission to continue his research so that dealers could go in and loot the site. "It has sunk to the level of an industry," said a bitter archaeologist in London, "and many museums in the Western world see cooperation with the dealers as the only way to get these treasures for their museums."

Farther east, the Cambodians are fighting an even more severe struggle to prevent the pillaging of the treasures of the temples of the Khmer kings at Angkor Thom and Angkor Wat. Here the motive is not simply commercial; it is political. One quick way for guerrillas operating in Cambodia to raise money for arms and supplies is to raid one of the more remote temples deep in the Cambodian jungle and make off with carvings and relics depicting the exotic myths of the Khmer civilization. These can be smuggled over the border trails in Thailand and sold for dollars in Bangkok. From Bangkok they are shipped to London and thence to the United States. During the French rule of Cambodia very few treasures came out of the country to the markets of London and New York, but in the last three or four years London dealers have remarked how freely the sandstone carvings from the Angkor Wat region have suddenly become available through Bangkok.

The appetite for antiquities is so insatiable that dealers are bound to be close behind every archaeologist. Central and South America are just as deeply embroiled. Here Miguel Angel

Asturias, the Guatemalan writer who won the Nobel Prize for literature in 1967, has been campaigning to get the United Nations Educational, Scientific, and Cultural Organization to help control the systematic sacking of the remains of Maya and Aztec civilizations. But it is difficult for the U.N. or anyone else to take really constructive steps. Most of the Latin-American sites are in remote areas that are impossible to police effectively, and the authorities are always too occupied trying to stop the smuggling in of watches or whisky or diamonds to worry about a few pots going out.

The whole issue of the smuggling of antiquities is further complicated by the active sideline of fakes in everything from Etruscan reliefs, which are made in a little factory in Switzerland, to elaborate Persian gold bowls inscribed with cuneiform inscriptions in three languages. Many of the fakes are so good that even the most diligent of scholars can be taken in. The dealers, who often trade in the genuine item and the fakes, are in a strong position. An American museum in the Midwest that agrees to buy a smuggled Etruscan fresco from a dealer cannot probe openly into its history or get concrete proof from the excavation site without revealing that it is buying from undercover sources.

Even if persistent questioning does take place, it may well elicit inconclusive answers. In Iran, for example, the standard answer if a museum queries where an item was dug up is Ecbatanan in Hamadan province, just west of Tehran. It is known that after Alexander sacked the great Persian city of Persepolis in 330 B.C. he took the treasures of King Darius back through Hamadan. Thus in theory anyone digging in the cellar of their house in a village in the region might just stumble on part of the treasure. Anyway, it makes a good excuse.

Such excuses may at least help salve the conscience of museums buying antiquities through doubtful sources. The situation is, however, much more delicate when it comes to the sale of stolen paintings and antiques. At least it can be argued that a golden bowl dug up from the ground after two thousand years does not belong to anyone now; a painting pinched from the collection of a private house is quite another matter.

As it happens, leading museums or major art galleries are not normally faced with the worry of determining whether or not a painting has been stolen. The organized traffic in stolen art and antiques is in medium-priced works, which are essentially of interest to smaller dealers and private buyers. An illicit market in stolen Leonardos, Rembrandts, or Goyas is, mercifully, nonexistent. The notion that major art robberies are perpetrated to provide some new acquisition for the private collection of a South American millionaire is an enduring one, but nonsense. The majority of robberies of great works of art, of over $100,-000 in value, are either carried out by cranks with some kind of grudge or by thieves out to hold the insurance companies up to ransom. Three major art thefts took place in the south of France in 1960 and 1961. First, paintings by Braque, Picasso, Modigliani, Buffet, and Miró were stolen from the Colombe d'Or Inn at St. Paul de Vence; then fifty-seven Impressionist paintings were taken from the Annonciade Museum at St. Tropez; and finally eight Cézanne's were snatched from an exhibition at the Pavillon de Vendôme at Aix-en-Provence. These robberies were all the work of a French Corsican gang from Marseilles out to hold the insurance companies to ransom. All except two of these paintings were safely recovered, and it has always been rumored that ransom money was paid.

The problem, from the criminal's point of view, is that if he steals a well-known and valuable painting, it becomes too hot to handle. Every dealer will recognize it, and it can become very hard to dispose of. But if he steals a careful selection of pleasant paintings by minor artists or attributed to "school of," none of which is worth more than a few thousand pounds, the robbery will attract no international headlines and dealers will not be familiar with the paintings. John Sutherland, Witt Librarian at the Courtauld Institute of Art in London, in a letter to *The Times* in 1968, pleaded with all private owners to have their paintings photographed to provide a record if they are stolen. He argued, "Many of these paintings would be easy to sell again abroad, because, although valuable, they are often by artists, such as the Dutch seventeenth-century masters, who executed

261

many versions of one composition. Their pictures are thus difficult to tell apart and have not, for instance, the unique quality of a painting by Raphael or Leonardo."

Thieves indeed have a passion for Dutch and Flemish artists. In Britain alone the insured value of Dutch and Flemish paintings stolen in 1968 was over 4.8 million dollars, and in some raids only the paintings of these schools were lifted and the remainder of a collection left untouched. A gang that broke into the home of a London business executive at Redhill in Surrey in August, 1968, selected only nine paintings, all Dutch and Flemish. The most valuable was a Backhuysen valued at $4,800. The complications of identifying paintings in such a haul—even if they have been photographed—are immense. In one list of twenty-eight stolen Dutch paintings, five were described as peasants sitting around a table eating or playing cards, three were of winter landscapes with figures skating, three more were still lifes of fruit and flowers. Even a dealer with a photographic memory will have difficulty in picking out one of these skating scenes from perhaps a dozen others of almost identical description which he may view in a month.

The scholarship and selectivity displayed by the thieves indicates either that one of them is an art dealer himself or that they have done very thorough homework, reading gallery and saleroom catalogs. They are also careful to remove only small paintings which can be packed into the bottom of a suitcase, rolled in a newspaper, or tucked under the arm. In one list of sixty-seven stolen paintings, the largest was 36½ inches by 49¾ inches; the majority were less than twenty-five inches square.

The pattern with antiques, particularly the theft of silver from English country houses, is identical. Either through discussions with a genuine antique dealer or by looking through magazine articles, the thieves will pinpoint the next job. A quick browse through *A Guide to Marks of Origin on British and Irish Silver Plate from the Mid-16th Century to 1963* will confirm the marks to identify the most valuable pieces. "The thieves showed scholarship in what they stole," said one victim of a silver robbery, Lord Fitzwilliam, whose home at Milton Hall, Huntingdonshire, was raided. "They took only the best silver. Exquisite items like a pair of Queen Anne two-handled wine coolers with the arms of the Rockinghams and made by David Willaume in 1705. They are worth eight thousand pounds." The thieves paid no attention to Lord Fitzwilliam's collection of paintings by Canaletto, Van Dyck, and Stubbs—but they did leave behind a copy of *Country Life*, in which an article on Milton Hall had appeared a few weeks earlier.

This robbery was one of a series in the summer of 1967 which all showed the same skilled touch in the choice of antiques stolen. The thieves were clearly working in close liaison with an established antique dealer, who seems to have accompanied them on at least one of the raids. Police searching the grounds for clues found several unimportant items lying in the bushes by a window through which the thieves had entered. Apparently they had passed the silverware back to the expert in the garden, who made a quick appraisal and tossed aside any piece not worth taking. In each robbery they had also viewed the silver collection in advance, either by going around the house on visiting days if, like so many English country houses, it was open to the public at weekends, or by knocking at the door and posing as silver merchants and asking to appraise the collection.

The safest market for these looted antiques or paintings is abroad, for as long as they remain in Britain there is much greater danger of their being recognized. Many of the paintings are sold through dealers in Europe who will have no idea they are handling stolen property. Since Britain allows unchecked export of works of fine art over one hundred years old and valued at less than $4,800, there is no difficulty in taking the paintings out of the country. Several paintings stolen from English country houses have turned up in Vienna, Basel, and Milan within a matter of days of the robbery. The trail is very hard to follow. One painting, stolen on a Friday night, passed through the hands of three London dealers on the following Monday (none of them aware it was stolen, but each made a profit on the transaction), and four days later it had been purchased by a Swiss dealer in Basel. Although under British law anyone who buys a stolen

263

painting innocently can be made to return it, under Roman law, which applies in Italy, it is virtually impossible to recover a stolen painting purchased by someone in good faith.

This traffic between Britain and the Continent is two-way. Paintings stolen in Britain are best disposed of in Europe; paintings stolen in Europe are sold through the London art market. In either case, many of them eventually go to America, but they will acquire "legitimacy" before crossing the Atlantic.

Stolen antiques are exported with equal dispatch; some of them go through Dublin, which many British criminals find a convenient base of operations, as there are no language or currency problems and they are just out of reach of Scotland Yard. Dublin specializes in the distribution of stolen antique jewelry or gold, while much of the silverware goes direct to the United States, camouflaged among legal shipments of antiques. Even if the thieves do not have a friendly dealer standing outside the window to appraise the haul during the theft, they invariably work in close liaison with one. "There is nothing better than the antique business as a cover for almost any criminal activity," says a Scotland Yard man. "It gives you the excuse to explain away how you came by all kinds of strange things." A raid may well be timed to take place a couple of days before a dealer is exporting a genuine consignment of antiques, so that the "hot" items can be included. By the time a list of stolen property has been compiled and circulated, the antiques are on the high seas.

During 1968 one pipeline for stolen silver was through a dealer in the Brighton area, who had it crated up and sent along to Southampton docks to catch the next boat to America. Occasionally the silver was concealed amid horsehair stuffing inside Victorian chairs and sofas. Since crates of silverware may attract undue attention after a flurry of robberies, another easy ploy is to label the crates "Antique Pottery," on the assumption that no customs man is going to peek inside a load of old pots. Of course, even the best of theories can go wrong. One "Antique Pottery" crate going out through Liverpool was opened and found to be jammed with stolen silver. But most of the time the stolen goods are so well mingled with legal shipments that, unless every outward-bound crate is examined in detail by a skilled dealer, the stolen items can never be pinpointed.

No country in Europe escapes the attention of these internationally minded art thieves. Thirty pieces of antique jewelry stolen from the Valencia Museum in Madrid turned up shortly afterward in a London saleroom. Paintings and antiques stolen in Belgium are frequently shipped over to the London market in the luggage of passengers on the cross-Channel ferries from Ostend and Zeebrugge.

As for Italy, it is almost impossible to keep a count of the robberies. At least six thousand works of art were stolen in the ten years up to 1967, and a bare two percent of them were recovered. Many of these works of art, which have included in recent years Titian altarpieces, fifteenth-century carved doors from a palace in Florence, and thirteenth-century paintings of the Madonna removed from a church at Cossito in Umbria, have been smuggled out to Switzerland, through the same channels as the Etruscan treasures unearthed from the tombs of Tuscany. The Italian carabinieri has a special "art-rescue" squad responsible for tracking down stolen paintings, but most of the works of art are out of the country within hours of the haul, and the police success is inevitably limited.

And this is the crux of the problem. Police forces are hemmed in by their own national boundaries; the art thieves are operating internationally. A painting stolen in Florence today can be bought by a dealer in Basel tomorrow and be on view in a gallery in New York next week.

At the 1968 Interpol conference in Tehran a special secret session of the heads of delegations was held to debate how international police can coordinate to seek out and combat the experts who are organizing worldwide art thefts. The initial step has to be to organize much better dissemination of information about art thefts. Until now dealers in, say, London have had no way of knowing what paintings have been stolen in Italy or Switzerland or Norway and cannot be expected to recognize that a painting is stolen if it is offered to them. This is swiftly being remedied. Early in 1968 Scotland Yard formed a special Art Thefts Squad, attached to its Interpol section. One of the prime tasks of this team is to keep London dealers fully informed of paintings and antiques stolen anywhere in the world, and, through the Interpol Communications Center in Paris, to circulate quickly details of works of art stolen in Britain. Other European police forces, after hearing of the lead given by the Yard, are now planning their own specialist art squads.

Yet even this advisory service creates its own problems. "So much is stolen," explained an Art Thefts Squad detective, "that if we sent out complete lists we would swamp the dealers. So we prepare specialist lists for specialist dealers." The Yard has also enlisted the aid of the fortnightly magazine *Arts Review*. Since September, 1968, the magazine has been running a regular feature, "Reported Stolen," which lists details of stolen paintings and reproduces photographs of many of them. In the first three months details of over two hundred paintings were published, and at least four were recovered specifically because dealers recognized having seen them in *Arts Review*. One painting was traced to Switzerland, another to Vienna, and two more found in London.

This, however, is only a beginning; it is not a complete solution. The world of the art and antique dealer is almost as much a closed shop as the diamond business. Even though robberies and the ensuing smuggling are organized by someone in the business, with all the right expertise and contacts, it is exceptionally hard to prove complicity. It may be possible to apprehend the actual thieves, but not the dealer who selected what they should take and briefed them on how to distinguish a Georgian silver coffeepot from a Victorian one.

Along with all this criminal activity and the traffic in antiquities is yet another racket which is purely a by-product of political policy. The United States, with its phobia about anything emanating from Communist China, will not permit the import of any goods made there. Now, for generations before the Communists came to power, the finest Chinese antiques and jade carvings were bought and sold through the Canton market. But after the Communist takeover, this trade, at least as far as America is concerned, had to stop abruptly. No more fine antique Chinese screens or carved jade were allowed into the United States, unless they had a satisfactory certificate of origin to show they had been made in Hong Kong or elsewhere in Southeast Asia. It was an open invitation for fraud. The antique dealers from Cat Street, Hong Kong—the Portobello Road of the East—continued to make their twice-yearly visits to the Canton antique fair and returned laden to Hong Kong, where fake certificates of origin were issued. This little game worked splendidly until 1965, when the United States, fully aware of the subterfuge, put a complete ban on the import of carved jade backed by Hong Kong certificates. Then the smuggling really started. American dealers and tourists still bought happily in Hong Kong, but left their purchases with the dealer. He smiled knowingly and guaranteed delivery very shortly.

One obvious trick was to hide the jade inside other, unembargoed antiques bound for the United States. One Chinese dealer dispatched eighteen crates of teakwood and rosewood furniture by sea to New York addressed to his son who had an antique business in the United States. At the pier in New York, the customs, acting on a tip, decided to X-ray the entire shipment. Telltale blotches showed up on the X rays of two rosewood cabinets. The customs men pulled the shelves out of the cabinets and found behind hidden panels 580 ornamental jade plaques, each carefully wrapped in tissue paper. The plaques sold for around ten dollars each in Hong Kong but had a market value of over twenty dollars in the United States. This, in fact, is a modest markup. Since the embargo, the price of many Chinese antiques in the United States has risen to five times the Hong Kong price.

Another Hong Kong dealer adopted a more direct line. He paid U.S. airline crews one thousand dollars a time to hide jade and semiprecious stones in their baggage on flights through from Hong Kong to Honolulu, San Francisco, or Los Angeles. Once in the United States, all they had to do was pop the jade in the parcel post to the American dealer who had ordered it. American seamen visiting Hong Kong were also hired by a dealer who runs an antique business in one of the leading Hong Kong hotels to slip jade and semiprecious stones in through West Coast ports for California dealers. In 1967 one of these seamen-couriers was arrested in San Diego with twenty thousand dollars' worth of jade and semiprecious stones destined for a dealer in Coronado, California.

Alternatively, the jade has been passed through Japan or London, so that the certificates avoid any reference to Hong Kong. Since Japan has its own jade-carving industry, this little sidetrack is highly successful. A Los Angeles dealer flew to Hong Kong, made his selection, and arranged for the jade to be sent to Kofu in Japan, where the Japanese carving industry is centered. There it was repacked and dispatched to the United States as being of Japanese origin. Other U.S. dealers prefer to buy trunk loads of Chinese jade and antiques in Cat Street and have the whole consignment shipped to London. It passes through a London dealer and arrives in the United States with documents to show that it was purchased in London.

These roundabout routes are still used extensively, although since the middle of 1967 the United States has relaxed on Hong Kong certificates of origin and will now accept them again. There appears to be just as much fraud as ever. "Certificates of origin?" said a dealer in Hong Kong. "That's easy to arrange. No one pays any attention to the controls."

As for the Americans, who are on the receiving end of this floodtide of smuggled jade, stolen paintings, silverware, and antiques, their avid pursuit of art seems impossible to satisfy. As a New York dealer put it, "Prices have skyrocketed so much that even the most honest dealer will not ask too many questions. Can you blame them?"

XII

Cigarettes and Whisky

Sit at dusk on the broad terrace of a hotel in Lugano, guarded by a stately avenue of cypress trees stalking into the gloom, and gaze out over that pearl of Swiss lakes. The gray-green water is placid, misted here and there by the drifting drizzle from the multicolored fountains pluming lazily into the air in an evening spectacle for the tourists. The lights of the villas perched perilously on the mountains around the lake spark out cheerfully. Otherwise the hills are black, revealing no clue that a band of broadshouldered smugglers, bent under illegal burdens, are striding through the forests under cover of darkness toward the 11½-foot-high chain link fence capped with barbed wire that straddles the border between Switzerland and Italy.

Lugano is at the heart of the Italian-speaking Swiss canton of Tessin, which plunges down like a thumb into Italy between Lake Como to the east and Lake Maggiore to the west. No smuggler could ask for a more strategically placed haven. All roads from Lugano, with the exception of the main supply route back into the center of Switzerland up over the St. Gotthard Pass, lead into Italy. For every road, there are countless trails through the pine forests, and it is amazing how easily that chain-link fence yields to a pair of wire clippers. For generations the young men of both sides of the border—and particularly in the border towns of Chiasso and Como, have, metaphorically at least, cut their teeth on this wire. Indeed, the legend goes in Como that no Italian lady there will look at a young man until he has made at least one smuggling journey. "*Una consacrazione di virilità,*" they call it. From time to time the contraband slipping over the Chiasso-Como frontier may be fairly exotic—watches, gold, precious stones, works of art—but the staple commodities are less romantic: salami from Italy into Switzerland; salt, coffee, and cigarettes from Switzerland into Italy. And it is cigarettes, normally about fifteen thousand of them, made up into a neat little package called a *bricolla,* that these smugglers —*spalloni,* from the Italian *spalla,* for "shoulder," is the local nickname—are shouldering in the night.

Drive, an hour before midnight, south down the autostrada from Lugano toward the frontier, but turn off at the last exit before Chiasso and work slowly through a network of gravel side roads. Most of the lights in the houses are already out, but a spark of light gleams from a two-story white building about four hundred yards on the Swiss side of the frontier. Outside, curiously, hangs an L&M cigarette sign, for it is by day a small store. Now it looks closed, shut up tight for the night. But is everyone asleep? There is a light in one downstairs room. Reading late or waiting for someone? The frontier fence less than a quarter of a mile away is hidden in the darkness. At midnight all is quiet, but the light in the house stays on. Half an hour later two figures, walking fast from the frontier, loom up out of the gloom and, scarcely glancing around, tap at the side door of the store. A chink more of light as they go in. Five minutes later they emerge looking like hunchbacks, with packs strapped to their shoulders. Bending forward slightly under the weight, they retrace their steps toward the frontier. About a hundred yards before the fence they turn off the gravel road, walk through a field of tall rough grass, and vanish under a fringe of trees by the fence. A slight splashing of water as they ford a small stream on the Swiss side; then they are through the neat hole in the wire they had cut on their way into Switzerland, and they vanish into the darkness of Italy. There is no shout, no challenge, no shot from the far side; the men of Italy's Guardia di Finanza, who patrol the fence, are either farther up the valley or asleep. Another thirty thousand cigarettes safely through.

The motive for the smuggling is quite simple. The Italian government has a monopoly on the manufacture and sale of all tobacco products. Many Italians do smoke the "nazionale" brand made by the monopoly. This sells at eighty lire (twenty-nine cents) per pack and tastes akin to burning straw. Many others prefer imported American, Swiss, or British cigarettes, which may also be purchased at the government tobacco shops—at a price. They cost around four hundred lire (sixty-four cents) a pack. Yet just over the border in Switzerland these same cigarettes cost a mere eighty lire (thirteen cents). So naturally most people in Italy buy their cigarettes, not from the official stores, but from men who visit every factory and every office once a month with their briefcase or a basket stuffed with contraband cigarettes; they charge three hundred lire (forty-eight cents) per pack. Thus smokers save themselves one hundred lire (sixteen cents) per pack by buying smuggled; yet there is a tidy two-hundred-and-twenty-lire (thirty-five cents) margin to cover the smuggler's expenses and leave him a handsome profit. That makes everyone happy—except, of course, the Ministry of Finance, which runs the tobacco monopoly, and the Guardia di Finanza, who are charged with enforcing it.

Any estimate of the annual volume of cigarette smuggling is pure guesswork, although it has been suggested that for every Italian-made cigarette smoked in the land, *seven* are smuggled in. The seizures by the Guardia di Finanza do give some notion of the volume. In 1966 they seized over 241 million cigarettes, with a tax value of twenty-four million dollars. They arrested twenty thousand smugglers. Even applying the customs rule of thumb that they catch ten percent of smuggled goods (highly unlikely in this instance), this works out at 2.5 billion cigarettes entering Italy illegally every year. That is fifty smokes a head for every man, woman, and child in the country. Three-quarters of this infiltration comes from Switzerland.

The Swiss play a fairly passive role in all this activity. As far as they are concerned, nothing illegal is perpetrated in Switzerland, for the cigarettes, to benefit from exemption from Swiss tax, will normally be cleared for export with the Swiss Frontier Corps at Lugano, Chiasso, or some other border town. Once that formality has been complied with, the Swiss argue it is not their problem if the smuggler neglects to make a similar declaration on the other side of the fence. For the Guardia di Finanza, working all through the night to catch the smugglers, it is a sore point. "The Swiss think only of business," said the local Guardia di Finanza colonel at Como. But the Swiss are appalled at any suggestion that they should tip off their Italian colleagues. That would be interfering with Switzerland's export trade, and it might even, they hint darkly, be industrial espionage—a punishable offense.

The sole Swiss contribution to the traffic, therefore, is to provide the cigarettes (either imported American ones or, more often, American brands made under license in Switzerland) and package them neatly, ready for collection. Then the Italians provide the smuggling organization and the muscle. Milan, scarcely an hour's drive down the autostrada from Como, has both the well-organized underworld and the strategic position to make it the main distribution point for the cigarette syndicates. These syndicates are normally fairly flexible groups which emerge, flourish for a while, then die as their leaders get bored, caught, or move on to other things. In the summer of 1968 the grapevine indicated eight main groups were working out of Milan.

Techniques vary from group to group, but the basic pattern is always the same. The head of the syndicate takes a trip to Switzerland from time to time and calls on a Swiss cigarette wholesaler in Lugano. They agree on the size of the shipment, and the Swiss guarantees to have the cigarettes ready at a pickup point near the border on an appropriate night. The Italian drives back to Milan, taking great care that the Guardia di Finanza, who will most probably recognize him, have no excuse to detain him at the border—he *never* carries cigarettes. "Most of them don't even smoke," one Guardia intelligence man said cheerfully, "so there is no chance of them being caught with even one illegal cigarette."

Next step is to organize the *spalloni*. Most syndicates have a personnel man—a *basista*—who is responsible for recruiting the

spalloni. This is not an arduous task, for most of the farm workers on the Italian side of the border regard an occasional night
run into Switzerland as no more dramatic than strolling down
the road for a pint at a pub. Indeed, a Guardia di Finanza colonel guiding a visitor down the twisting gravel lanes on the Italian
side of the border on a warm summer afternoon will make an
expansive gesture with his hand: "This is the heart of smuggling
country. That man scything grass, those standing on the corner,
that one with the cart—all of them are smugglers. Everyone here
is." He does not seem particularly perturbed at the thought; it's
like a game of cat and mouse; sometimes you catch them, sometimes you do not. Does he rely on luck to catch them red-handed
with the goods, or does he get information? "Ah, we get no
information. It's just like the Mafia." Suddenly, as the unmarked
Guardia di Finanza Fiat sweeps around a bend in a cloud of
dust, he sees a black Alfa Romeo sports car with Milan license
plates pulling away from a small house on a side road about two
hundred yards inside the border. There are two men inside. He
gives a fast order to his driver. The Guardia car stops in a flurry
of gravel, backs up, and blocks the exit to the side road, halting
bumper to bumper with the Alfa. The Guardia driver strolls over
to the Alfa Romeo and asks the driver to unlock the trunk. He
pokes around for a moment inside—nothing except a spare tire.
He glances over the papers of both men, shrugs his shoulders,
and walks back. No luck this time.

Sometimes the *spalloni* operate singly or in pairs, but quite
frequently in long columns of a dozen, twenty, or even forty.
The economics of the business demand that if the organizer is
sending a truck up from Milan to pick up the cigarettes, he wants
a full load. Normally each of the *spalloni,* who are paid eight
dollars for the trip, carries up to fifteen kilos of cigarettes (one
thousand cigarettes to the kilo). There is a special reason for not
carrying more than fifteen kilos. If he is caught by the Guardia
with fifteen kilos or less, he simply has the cigarettes confiscated
(and that doesn't cost him anything, and he is paid even if he is
caught), and his name and address are taken. If he has over
fifteen kilos, he may be put in jail to await trial. In a long column
of *spalloni*, the two front men may not carry any cigarettes at all;

273

they act simply as lookouts. If they sneak safely through the fence, the others with the cigarettes follow. Once over the frontier, the cigarettes are dropped off at a house to await collection from Milan.

Occasionally the *spalloni* walk several miles with their burden, but in the heart of the smuggling country, which runs from the villages of Ronago and Maslianico to the east of Chiasso to Rodero to the west of Chiasso, the walk is less than a mile. A few houses are even strategically placed right on the border. The Guardia uncovered a tunnel to one of them a few years ago, which had been dug from a clump of bushes from the Swiss side, under the wire, and up into the cellar of the Italian house.

The smuggling is not limited to the energy of the *spalloni*. One smuggler, taking advantage of the fact that the border between Italy and Switzerland runs conveniently down the middle of lakes Lugano and Maggiore, built a homemade submarine which could carry one-third of a ton of cigarettes. The submarine looked like a primitive torpedo and had a small propeller at the stern which was powered by the smuggler himself, who sat inside pedaling furiously as if on an underwater bicycle.

The railways also provide splendid opportunities for cigarette smuggling on both passenger and freight trains. The toilets of the first-class carriages provide ample concealment in the ceiling ventilation for eighty thousand cigarettes. A whole freight-car load, suitably misrepresented on the customs papers, can carry five million.

Italy's most celebrated cigarette-smuggling case, the Case of the Contraband Friars, in the summer of 1965 demonstrated just how skillful (and occasionally careless) the cigarette smugglers can be.

The case really began at five o'clock one May morning when Prior Mario Milani of the little Capuchin monastery of San Francesco, perched high above Lake Albano near the Pope's summer residence at Castel Gandolfo south of Rome, telephoned the local police to announce, "I have a body in my garden." When the police arrived at the previously peaceful monastery, they found to their amazement that the heavy iron gates and part of an ancient wall had been completely flattened, that an assortment of thirty-six crates lay on the ground—and nearby was the body of one Pierino Scali, who was later identified as a well-known cigarette smuggler. The police quickly broke open the crates and found them full of seventy-two thousand packs of cigarettes.

Just as this discovery was made, a local hospital telephoned the police. A badly injured man had just been brought in by an ambulance from a local convent. A friar and two nuns in the ambulance had explained they found the injured man lying by the roadside, and they supposed he was the victim of a hit-and-run driver. The police made a few inquiries, which quickly established that the friar in the ambulance was none other than Friar Antonio Corsi from the San Francesco monastery.

Corsi and his fellow friars, challenged to explain all these sudden mishaps, offered a somewhat feeble story. They said that four men in two trucks had chanced to come by the monastery late the previous evening and asked the friars for a night's lodging. The friars welcomed them and later retired to bed. At one A.M. they were disturbed by screams, yells, and the revving of motors. They dashed out, to find their precious wrought-iron gates flattened, a dead man, an injured man lying on the ground, and no sign of their other guests or the trucks. It was hardly the most convincing tale.

Gradually the police and the Guardia di Finanza, who were summoned up from Rome as soon as the cigarettes were discovered, pieced together what really happened. Not only did the dead man have a smuggling record; the injured man turned out to be one Fermenegildo Foroni, a suspected smuggler from Lugano, Switzerland. Digging deeper, the Guardia discovered that some months earlier, the previous prior of the San Francesco monastery had moved to another Capuchin monastery at, of all places, Lugano. Shortly after this move, there was a noticeable rise in the living standards of the previously poor friars still living at San Francesco. Two of them even bought Fiats.

As Italy reveled in the press reports on the "scandal of the contraband convent," the station master at Capanello (home of Rome's main racetrack) happened to be looking out of his office window one day as he read the latest news and noticed, quite by chance, a remarkable resemblance between the crates full of cigarettes found at the monastery and a freight car loaded with crates labeled "Agricultural Machinery" parked in the siding outside. He called the police, who found thirty-six crates full of American and Swiss cigarettes, together with a bill of lading showing the full consignment had been 116 crates, containing 232,000 packs of cigarettes worth over $100,000 at the black-market price.

The cigarettes, it turned out, had originally been loaded at Lugano onto the freight car, which traveled first to Basel, then to Singen in West Germany, where it was hooked in with three other railway trucks. The crates on all the trucks were marked as electrical equipment bound for Haifa, Israel, via Genoa. Between there and Genoa, while the train was halted in Milan's Milan-Greco station, a railway employee who had been suitably bribed detached the truck containing the cigarettes, changed the labels and shipping papers to read "Agricultural Machinery," and addressed it to Commendatore Antonio Navone, Rome-Capanello station. He saw it safely hooked onto a Rome-bound train.

Meanwhile Friar Corsi, warned in advance that the shipment was rolling south, was frantically trying to rent storage space for nearly five million cigarettes. He asked the fathers at Oblate monastery nearby if he could rent a small storeroom for one night for the extraordinarily generous fee of $240. The fathers, somewhat suspicious, declined. Consequently, when the cigarette train rolled in, the only place to take the cigarettes until distribution could be arranged was the San Francesco monastery itself.

That evening Foroni, who had driven down from Lugano to supervise the operation, went to the siding at Capanello with three fellow smugglers from Rome and began unloading the crates of "Agricultural Machinery" into two trucks. The first truck, with thirty-six crates aboard, then drove to San Francesco, where it successfully negotiated the narrow gateway. A little later the second truck, a large red Lancia laden with forty-four crates, arrived. It was a tight squeeze to maneuver it through the gateway, and halfway in, the fenders caught in the gates. The driver revved up and tried to back clear—pulling gates and part of the wall with him. Scali and Foroni were caught by the collapsing masonry. In the ensuing uproar, the Lancia charged clear of the rubble and vanished into the night.

When the case finally came to court, Friar Corsi pleaded he believed he was handling macaroni. The judge was not amused. Corsi was sentenced to two years and eight months in jail and fined $440,000. Prior Milani was acquitted of smuggling, but four of Corsi's fellow smugglers were sent to prison and fined a total of two and one-half million dollars.

While the cigarettes flow from Switzerland as if on an invisible conveyor belt, Italy's five-thousand-mile coastline also presents the smuggler with a cheering panorama of deserted beaches and secluded coves. "We can't have a chain of men guarding all that coast," a Guardia di Finanza colonel admitted despairingly, "so the cigarettes come in by the ton from the sea." On the Adriatic coast the cigarettes are whisked across the Gulf of Venezia from Trieste in high-speed launches; farther south in the Adriatic the launches set out from Split or Dubrovnik.

The largest shipments, however, are offloaded from ancient tramp steamers just outside Italy's twelve-mile limit of territorial waters into fishing boats or launches. For many years these vessels picked up their supplies from Tangier and Gibraltar (which once boasted the largest wholesale cigarette business in the world), but after Tangier ceased to be a free port and controls in Gibraltar were tightened, it became easier to take on supplies in Lisbon, Rotterdam, and Antwerp. "It's a real common market in smuggling," the Guardia colonel said wryly; "there are no international barriers or treaties of agreement to worry about. Political differences mean nothing." He spread his arms wide. "Everyone in Europe is in it."

The smuggling can be so blatant that it even provides a spectacle for the whirring cameras of tourists on cruise ships. One tourist, happily filming the blue skies, the calm seas, and the bustle of deck tennis a few miles off Naples, suddenly swung his lens around to shoot a red launch that came skimming over the sea toward the side of the ship. As the camera ground on, the launch was maneuvered skillfully alongside the liner and a man swung himself up a rope ladder thrown down from an entry port on the lower decks of the liner. Five minutes later he scrambled back down into the launch, which circled once and took off for the horizon. Later two launches came zipping back and, in turn, took up station ten feet from the side of the liner immediately opposite the entry port. One man stood up in the stern, bracing his legs wide apart to retain his balance in the rolling boat, and gamely fielded a succession of cardboard boxes packed with cigarettes as they were tossed from the ship. Once his launch was full, the second moved up and repeated the operation; then they vanished toward Naples. The preliminary visit aboard ship had been to confirm arrangements and to prove that these were the bona-fide launches from the right gang.

Not all seagoing transshipments proceed so peacefully. In early 1968 a Guardia di Finanza patrol boat surprised the Panamanian cargo ship *Ster* as it was about to offload cigarettes inside Sicilian waters. When the Guardia vessel came up, the *Ster* turned tail and steamed at full speed for the horizon, trying to get outside the twelve-mile limit. But the Guardia boat did not give up; because she had caught the *Ster in flagrante* inside territorial waters, she was entitled to chase her anywhere on the high seas until she entered the territorial waters of another country. Every time the customs boat tried to close, the *Ster*'s crew pitched Molotov cocktails and iron cables over the side. Finally, eighty miles out at sea, the crew set fire to the *Ster* and took to the boats. The customs men succeeded in extinguishing the fire and found 378 tons of cigarettes aboard (over four hundred million cigarettes, or eight for everyone in Italy).

These ships, which may be used solely for smuggling cigarettes—with a little whisky to lace the cargo—are normally ancient vessels which the smugglers have bought up cheap on the ship scrapyards of the world. If the ships are caught and confiscated, they are no great loss. The profits quickly pay for a replacement. Assuming the profit margin of sixty lire per pack, the *Ster*'s cargo of twenty million packs would have yielded a profit of 1.2 billion lire (2.4 million dollars).

The main contraband importer usually buys his cigarettes for 80 lire (13 cents) a pack and sells for between 140 and 160 lire (22–27 cents) to a wholesaler in, say, Milan. This wholesaler in turn passes them on at 220–230 lire a pack. The price on the street varies from city to city. In Milan itself, the fountainhead, the price is as low as 250 lire (40 cents); in Rome the additional expenses incurred in transporting the cigarettes make the price 300 lire (48 cents).

At each stage the insulation of one group from another is complete. There are eight main stages between cigarettes being purchased in, say, Lugano, and being sold to eager smokers in a factory in Florence: (1) the chief buyer goes to Lugano and fixes the deal; (2) the wholesaler there places the cigarettes in a depot near the frontier; (3) the *spalloni* move them across; (4) they go to a preliminary depot in Italy; (5) they are moved to the main Milan distribution point; (6) they are bought by the main wholesaler in Florence; (7) he distributes in Florence to his network of salesmen; and (8) they are sold to the smoker. But at each level no one knows anyone of importance on the rung above. The wholesaler in Florence may telephone a contact in Milan; they will arrange to meet somewhere between the two cities to discuss the deal. Once agreement is reached, the Florence wholesaler is told to leave an empty truck on a specified country road at night with the keys in. He will either pick it up at the same point two or three hours later or will receive a telephone call telling him where to find it parked—full of cigarettes.

The Guardia di Finanza wage a battle against these smugglers with remarkable *esprit de corps,* considering the hopeless odds they are facing. Their forty thousand men, divided into eighteen legions, carry out their duties with a certain flourish. All their Alpine forces wear cheeky green feathers stuck jauntily into their hats. Since they are directly responsible to the Minister of Finance—whose department also receives all the profits of the state tobacco monopoly—the Guardia is, of course, always under considerable political pressure to keep hard at it. The tobacco monopoly yields some ten percent of all Italian revenues, so ministerial agitation if smuggling figures rise is quite understandable.

Spurred on by ministers with an eye on their treasuries, the

Guardia takes an almost childish delight in smuggler-chasing. Their official reports of establishment even list separately "motorcars for pursuit" and "motorcycles for pursuit" as distinct from the normal fleet of cars. They have teams of "antismuggling dogs" and a stable of thirty helicopters. The entire outfit is woven together with a radio and telex network. It all looks most impressive to the casual observer, but does not deter for a moment either the *spalloni* shouldering their burdens in the night or the flotilla of tired tramp steamers loading up with cigarettes at every major port in Europe.

In no other country is there such a concerted attempt by smugglers to offer a completely alternative supply of cigarettes to the legal outlets. High duties often provide the temptation to smuggle, but the cigarette running is normally limited to the odd boatload to supply a few bars or cafés in one town. In Britain the chief source of supply for cheap cigarettes is stealing or hijacking the trucks distributing them around the country. In the United States the cigarette smuggling is not international, but interstate. Differing local sales taxes lead to variations of from two or three cents to twenty to twenty-five cents per pack between one state and another, which is plenty of incentive if you are humping cigarettes by the ton—a one-cent price differential is equal to five hundred dollars on every ton of cigarettes. The most flourishing trade is from North Carolina up to New Jersey and New York, which is well supervised by the gangs in New York. The cigarettes are sold through garages along the New Jersey Turnpike and other main toll roads into New York and at bars in New York itself. Normally cigarette runners do not resort to much subterfuge; there is, after all, no reason to be suspicious of a truckload of cigarettes. But a timber truck was caught in 1966 with a load of twenty thousand dollars' worth of cigarettes hidden inside hollowed-out logs.

The only two areas, outside of Italy, where international cigarette smuggling reaches commercial proportions are between Sabah in North Borneo and the Philippines, and in the western Mediterranean and the Strait of Gibraltar.

Two ribbons of islands divided by the Sulu Sea stretch like stepping-stones from Sabah to Luzon and Mindanao, the two main islands of the Philippines. They make a perfect pathway for a myriad of small boats carrying cigarettes from the ports of Kota Kina Balu (formerly Jesselton), Labuan, Sandaken, and Lehad Datu into the Philippines. Smuggling is a major problem in the Philippines (see Chapter 1), where the government estimate they lose up to twenty to twenty-five million dollars in revenue a year on goods which evade the customs or which the customs agree may evade them. Cigarettes are a major item in this bill for lost revenue, and the traffic aggravates political differences between the Philippines and Malaysia. The former is constantly charging the Malaysians with permitting the smuggling through Sabah, their easternmost province, in an effort to undermine the Philippine economy. Indeed, one reason the Philippines is so keen to stake a claim to Sabah is to eliminate this convenient haven for the smuggler bound for its shore.

The cream of this cigarette traffic is in "blue-seal" American cigarettes—the blue seal to the pack indicating that they have been made outside the Philippines. Most of these cigarettes are made in Hong Kong or Singapore. Singapore alone shipped over three hundred million "blue-seal" cigarettes to Sabah in 1966. From Sabah the cigarettes are funneled into the Philippines by seven rival syndicates, one of them operating from Manila, the others directed from Mindanao and other more southerly Philippine islands. Many of their boats bring the cigarettes through Manila Bay right up the Pasig River to the quays in the heart of Manila. "What kind of cigarettes do you want to buy?" inquires the taxi driver, idling leisurely along the waterfront. "I can get you any brand you like."

Malaysia and the Philippines did agree to make some joint effort to curb the cigarette smuggling in 1967, when they signed a joint antismuggling treaty. But before any really practical steps could be taken, the political friction between the two countries nullified any useful cooperation and gave an extra fillip to the smugglers. But even with cooperation the smuggling would be hard to contain. "For these people on our southern islands, smuggling has been a way of life for centuries," says a senior economic adviser to the government in Manila. "They know of no other way of making a living. All the people on these islands across to Sabah are their uncles or their cousins or their aunts, and it's by way of being a family business."

It is almost as intimate around the western Mediterranean and the Strait of Gibraltar. The handiest staging posts for running contraband cigarettes are Ceuta and Melilla, two little Spanish toeholds on the coast of North Africa, and the Canary Islands. All these islands couple the advantage of being duty-free ports with a common language, social background, and family ties with Spain. Tangier and Gibraltar have also played strategic parts in this extensive traffic in cigarettes, whisky, and watches into Spain, but now, due partly to government controls and partly to friction with Spain, have been eclipsed by Spain's own nearby colonies.

A flotilla of ex-naval launches plies between all these ports and the beaches of southern Spain and Majorca. Until early 1968 their comings and goings were directed by a Spaniard known as El Canario, who, according to the Spanish authorities, was running cigarettes into Spain and smuggling currency out through Gibraltar, to be deposited in a Swiss bank.

El Canario's squadron of boats, operating mainly from the Canaries (hence his nickname) and flying Panamanian flags, were so well known in local waters that they would acknowledge the salute of Spanish patrol boats as they passed through the Strait of Gibraltar. Their boss had a pleasant understanding with certain Spanish customs officials, so there was no worry that his craft would be intercepted. Indeed, everything went smoothly for years, until El Canario, who owned a luxury villa just outside Madrid, made the mistake of falling out with a senior Spanish government official. He was arrested in February, 1968.

The traffic, however, continues unabated, run now by a young fellow known as Pedro, who learned his trade from El Canario. Pedro lives in Ceuta but flits regularly across the Strait of Gibraltar to the Rock and to Spain. Gibraltar's highly convenient location for smuggling has been hampered in recent years by the worsening political situation with Spain, which has resulted in very tight border controls; also by restrictions imposed by the British colony's own government on the reexport of whisky and cigarettes in an effort to minimize friction with Spain. However, four or five smuggling boats still operate out of Gibraltar, working in close cooperation with the smugglers from Ceuta and the Canary Islands. The Rock also provides a very central point for meetings to discuss future trips. Pedro and his colleagues rendezvous two or three afternoons a week in two bars in the main street of Gibraltar and sit sipping coffee or Fundador by the hour while working over schedules for the night.

Their cargoes, apart from cigarettes, include large consignments of Scotch whisky. Scotch is the most widely smuggled spirit in the world today, for the very good reason, as one manufacturer put it, "that you can make it only in Scotland. Palatable gin can be made in most countries, but not palatable Scotch. So everyone smuggles it." The active motive for smuggling is, of course, rather more mercenary. The price spiral on Scotch whisky is remarkable.

The whisky manufacturer back in Scotland receives about one dollar a bottle wholesale for his product; the whisky drinker who is lucky enough to be able to purchase his booze in a duty-free zone or shop, will pay around two and one-half to three dollars a bottle, while the unfortunate who pays the full price may be charged from six to seven dollars a bottle up to twelve dollars a bottle in countries where the duty is several hundred percent. It is the perfect margin to tempt the smuggler. In Tangier, for example, whisky is one dollar a bottle more than in Ceuta just along the coast, and the Scotch comes in over the mountains and by boat along the Strait of Gibraltar. In Spain it is at least two dollars a bottle more than in Ceuta, Gibraltar, or the Canary Islands. As a result, all these ports appear, from import figures, to be inhabited by alcoholics with an insatiable thirst for Scotch.

Gibraltar, for example, took over fifty-five thousand proof gallons of Scotch in 1966, which was two gallons per head of the population. Gibraltar's consumption has fallen since then because the tensions with Spain have complicated smuggling, but Ceuta and the Canary Islands have more than made up for any decline of "drinking" on the Rock. Ceuta's imports of Scotch doubled between 1966 and 1967, and the Canary Islands' imports almost doubled from 1966 to 1968. The Canaries are now taking more Scotch per head of the population than anywhere else in the world. In 1968 almost five hundred thousand proof gallons of Scotch went to the Canaries—which have a population of two hundred thousand. Now, this may not seem heavy drinking to the hearty Scotch imbiber; it is, after all, a mere twenty bottles a year per person. Yet Americans, who drink half the whisky exported from Scotland every year, each consume less than one bottle a year per head. In the other major Scotch markets, Australians, Frenchmen, Germans, and South Africans quaff less than half a bottle a year each.

So there is every reason to ponder on the eventual destination of the Scotch which is shipped to Gibraltar, the Canary Islands, and two other tax-free zones, the Netherlands Antilles and Panama, which all take more than a gallon of Scotch per person a year. Admittedly, part of this excess of whisky will be snapped up by tourists making the most of a tax-free paradise and by cruise ships replenishing their bars. But there is still plenty for the smugglers to distribute. And some kind of redistribution is clearly called for when you realize that the Spanish inhabitants of the Canary Islands buy almost as much Scotch as their thirty-one million cousins on the mainland of Spain. While that kind of inequality exists, Pedro and his lads have no fears of unemployment.

Across the Atlantic, in the Caribbean, is another strategically placed little clutch of islands enjoying a whisky boom. The Netherlands Antilles, barely fifty miles off the north coast of Venezuela, makes an ideal jumping-off point for contraband Scotch bound for the east coast of South America. The two main islands of Curaçao and Aruba in this Dutch colony, with a population of no more than 210,000, take as much Scotch a year as the home country of the Netherlands, with twelve and one-half million people. This whisky is redistributed through the ports of Willemstad in Curaçao and Oranjestad in Aruba by fishing boats going to Venezuela or coasters bound for Recife, Salvador, Santos, or Buenos Aires. The west coast of South America is equally well served by Panama, where one firm of ship's chandlers has an excellent reputation for seeing that southbound freighters are well loaded with Scotch as they leave the Panama Canal for Lima and Valparaiso. Captains and crews of these boats pool their resources in Willemstad or Panama and buy, perhaps, sixty cases of whisky. They can be quite confident of a good demand in any port they touch.

An alternative way of obtaining duty-free whisky in South America is to have a friend at an embassy and indulge in a little diplomatic smuggling. All embassies are permitted a quota of duty-free Scotch, and, as all diplomats must all be treated as equals, the quota is the same for every embassy. The quota must also be large enough to cater for, say, the American embassy, with a staff of seventy-five, which inevitably means that the embassy of a newly independent nation with a staff of two is vastly oversupplied. And one easy way to dispose of such an embarrassment of whisky is to sell it cheap on the unofficial market.

Obliging embassies and whisky galore from passing freighters cannot, however, always meet the local South American demand for Scotch, which is often officially curtailed by import quotas. So, to the dismay of the genuine whisky makers back in Scotland, there is also a considerable market in fake Scotch in South America. The true Scotch-whisky men argue of course that "Attempts have been made to copy the unique flavor of Scotch whiskies in many parts of the world, but with no success whatsoever." This pride is perfectly natural; without doubt the Scotch maker himself or the connoisseur among his clients can tell a phony bottle of Scotch at first sip. The trouble is that many millions of other drinkers cannot, particularly by the time they are on their third glass of whisky doused with ice and soda. For many years there was a steady demand in South America for used Scotch bottles, but after a while they got a little chipped and the labels became tatty; nowadays the local "Scotch" makers turn out their own fine clean bottles and smuggle in genuine labels, corks, and red seals from Scotland. The brew itself is made, according to a Chilean expert, "of good alcohol, coloring, and a little wood shavings for flavor. This whisky tastes very good with a little ice and soda."

The genuine Scotch manufacturers are in something of a dilemma over this outrageous misrepresentation. If they admit that some of the whisky on the market under their label is in fact made in the bathtub down the street, public confidence in an entire brand can be undermined in a moment. The situation is further complicated by import quotas; many firms are nervous at losing out on a quota if they start rocking the boat with complaints or lawsuits. They have little option, therefore, but to keep quiet and suffer. So they put on a cheerful front and hark back to the true definition of Scotch as laid down in the Customs and Excise Act, 1952, Clause 243 (1) (b): "Spirits described as Scotch Whisky shall not be deemed to correspond to that description unless they have been obtained by distillation in Scotland from a mash of cereal grain saccharified by the diastase of malt and have been matured in warehouse in cask for a period of at least three years." Quite remarkable credentials to fall back on in any emergency.

But perhaps the Scotch makers should be less sensitive about fraud or the smuggling of their product than they sometimes appear. After all, it is a great testimony to the quality of their product that Scotch whisky is the most copied and the most widely smuggled drink in the world. They might even try an advertising slogan: "Scotch—the whisky chosen by all discriminating smugglers."

FINALE

Anything to Declare?

Anything to Declare?

A Smuggler is a person who, though no doubt highly blameable for violating the laws of his own country, is frequently incapable of violating those of natural justice, and would have been in every respect an excellent citizen had not the laws of the country made that a crime which nature never meant to be so.

—Adam Smith

These days anyone can become a smuggler quite unwittingly. The quirks of the official mind make sure that sooner or later, somewhere or other, virtually everything the traveler packs into his suitcase or the importer wants to import is either prohibited entry or charged exorbitant rates of duty. The Arabs ban underwear with Marks and Spencer's St. Michael labels (Marks and Spencer is Jewish owned); the Americans try to keep out wigs made of human hair from Communist China; the Irish are worried about butter smugglers and pig runners from Ulster; while the South Africans make every traveler sign a declaration that includes the clause that he is not carrying bees, bee larvae, or beehive appliances. One does not hear much gossip about bee smugglers, although maybe there are some of these redoubtable fellows, who sneak up to the South African borders shrouded in magnificent bee-chasing veils and let loose a swarm to buzz over the border and home in on some honeypot strategically prepared by a fellow conspirator in South Africa. But if all is apparently quiet on the bee front, many other smugglers, running everything from pigs to parrots and butter to hormones, to say nothing of orangutans, are having a rousing time.

The heart of pig-smuggling country is the two-hundred-mile border between Eire and Ulster, a wilderness of purple hills and peat bogs, crisscrossed by a handful of well-guarded main roads and a patchwork of muddy byways known only to leprechauns and smugglers. The contraband-pig traffic across this desolate terrain takes advantage of a five-pound (twelve-dollar) price difference per pig between the two countries. In Eire the country's forty bacon-curing factories have been expanding business so fast that local pig breeders cannot keep up with demand, and the price has shot up. In Ulster, however, the price of pig meat is kept low by the annual farm-price review in London and is not determined by either shortage or glut. Officially, the Ulster farmer must sell all his pigs to his own pig-marketing board or face a £100 ($240) fine; unofficially, the Ulster farmers are selling up to three thousand pigs a week on the side to the pig runners southbound to Eire. Between them the smugglers and the farmers are raking in an extra £750,000 (1.8 million dollars) a year.

The smugglers set out from the little towns like Dundalk and Monaghan in Eire, fortified for the run by a Guinness or two. They drive up the main T1 or T15 roads toward the border, but short of the frontier post dodge off down some side lane that twists over the border at an unguarded point. Then they proceed direct to the farm to load up on their squealing contraband. Another Guinness or two or three to steady the nerves for the road, and they are off through byways again into Eire, with the pigs grunting in protest against the lurchings of the truck. Any customs man who happens upon this noisy contraband is likely to be given a good run for his money. Some chases have lasted for fifty miles down the back lanes. " 'Tis a rough business," said a seasoned pig runner; "the revenue men stop at nothing, and neither do we. If we hit trouble, we take to the hills and hope for the best."

Along with pig running, the other great Irish pastime is butter smuggling. As *The Times* put it charmingly not long ago, "The crock of gold at the end of many a devious Irishman's personal rainbow these days is yellow and brick-shaped—but soft—namely, Kerrygold butter." This buttery trail winds its way down the same lanes as the pigs and has an added, salty Irish flavor in that the butter smuggled in from Ulster has previously been exported from Eire itself. This somersault comes about because the government in Dublin pays a subsidy on butter exported from Eire, so that it can be sold abroad competitively. Thus Irish butter sells for 3/6d (42 cents) in Britain and Northern Ireland, but for 5/- (60 cents) back home south of the border, a difference too tempting to be overlooked by any self-respecting Irishman. So the butter runners nip over the border into Ulster, load up cars and vans with soft, golden Irish butter, and bring it home. Once back in Eire, it is swiftly repacked in either stolen or forged Kerrygold wrappers (Kerrygold is not the name that the butter is sold under in Protestant Ulster) and blended with normal butter supplies. The smugglers and shopkeepers who get their butter cheap find it a most rewarding venture. Some three thousand tons of butter are smuggled back into Ireland every year, yielding a profit of a half a million pounds (1.2 million dollars). With the pig business now added to the bargain, it is more than enough to keep every smuggler in Guinness and John Jameson twelve-year-old whiskey for years to come.

While the Irish run pigs, Mexicans run parrots. It is hard to decide which is potentially the noisier cargo, but at least the Mexicans have a fine way to silence their contraband parrots bound for the United States. They get them blind drunk on tequila, which may make the birds sing gaily for a while but soon sends them into a silent stupor. Then they are spirited over the border without any fear that they will try to chat up the customs man inspecting the car or truck in which they are concealed. It all works splendidly—until the parrots sober up. A parrot with a hangover can be a mighty unsociable bird. He will peck painfully at anyone within reach.

However, the profit to be made on parrots in the United States makes all the waste of good liquor worthwhile. A Mexican yellow-headed parrot costs a mere five dollars on home ground but can sell for nearly one hundred dollars in a department store in Los Angeles or Chicago. A smaller parrot, known as a Petz's Conure (which sounds like some Mexican's corruption of Pets Corner), can be snapped up for $2.50 in Tijuana, Mexico, but will cost twenty-five dollars in the United States. The real reason for the smuggling is to avoid a lengthy twelve-week quarantine if the birds are imported legally—and a parrot can eat an awful lot of birdseed in twelve weeks. So the parrots are smuggled on the scale of a bird migration. Mostly they are tanked up on tequila and put in the truck or under the back seat of cars (actually the tequila is hardly necessary, because any parrot popped into the dark will shut up). The record parrot carload was 832 live parrots in a specially built compartment beneath a 1965 Mustang; assuming a fifty-dollar markup per parrot, the profits of that little jaunt alone would be over forty thousand dollars. The bird smugglers are a determined lot. After one gang was arrested and charged with smuggling psittacine birds (as the U.S. Customs officially calls them), they were released on bail pending an appeal. They promptly organized another parrot foray to raise money for their legal fees. Parrot smuggling is by no means a genteel corner of the smuggling profession. There are spirited feuds between the Mexican birdmen, who frequently hijack each other's parrots. In one encounter, after all the parrots were snatched from a smuggler's car by rival parrot runners, the victim of the hijacking was handcuffed to the steering wheel of his car and abandoned in the desert. It was more than a day before he was discovered.

Parrots are at least plentiful; the tragedy of orangutan smuggling is that it is speeding their complete extermination. The orangutan lives only on the islands of Borneo and Sumatra, where there are now less than five thousand left. Another four hundred or so are in captivity in zoos, who are constantly in the market for more, and may pay as much as two thousand dollars for one. They prefer young ones, which are not only easier to transport but also more adaptable to zoo life. A young orangutan, however, is normally captured after killing the mother. As the female produces only one baby every four years, this slaughter speeds up the decline of the population. For years the mother orangutans on Borneo and Sumatra were shot by hunters and the baby orangutans shipped to Singapore dealers, who sold them to zoos. Frequently there were fifty or more orangutans at a time in the smuggling pipeline from Singapore to Europe and America. With each having a price on its head of up to two thousand dollars, it was a highly lucrative racket.

However, in 1962 Tom Harrisson, then director of the Sarawak Museum at Kuching in Borneo, and his wife, Barbara, who had made a detailed study of the orangutans living in the wild in Borneo, determined that the "orangutan crisis," as it came to be called, must be tackled. Through the International Union for the Conservation of Nature and the World Wildlife Fund, they persuaded the authorities in Singapore, Bangkok, and Hong Kong to enforce strict control on the movement of orangutans. Officially they may not enter Singapore now without an import license—and this is not granted without an export license from the country of their origin; reexport from Singapore is also illegal without a license. But, as in all things where a handsome profit is at stake, there are ways of getting around regulations. It is impossible to keep track of orangutans being smuggled into Singapore by sailors, who keep them on ships as pets until a convenient moment to slip them ashore. And unless the customs are particularly alert, they can be smuggled out again in batches of other monkeys. The real way to stem this traffic is to convince zoos not to buy orangutans; the most responsible, particularly in America, already take the orangutan crisis seriously. But a handful of zoos, notably private ones, are more difficult to bring into line. The dealers in Southeast Asia are now much more cautious of handling them, but the unscrupulous still run an orangutan when they can.

The crisis of the contraband orangutans is one instance

where authority is undeniably behaving reasonably. It would be a tragedy to see these cheerful apes exterminated, as Adam Smith, who was quoted at the opening of this chapter, would undoubtedly agree. This orangutan traffic does violate natural justice.

The contraband trade in human hair, however, although it may at first sound rather spine-chilling, does not seem to violate any natural law. The hair trade thrives because although American women prefer to wear their hair short most of the time, it is now fashionable for them to buy wigs and hairpieces for elaborate hair styles on splendid occasions. Chinese women grow their hair long and are willing to cut it off and sell it for a price. Which seems a fair exchange that can only enhance the prosperity of the Chinese and make American women more beautiful. But, unfortunately, hair, like everything else, can get caught up all too easily in politics. American political policy decrees that nothing from Communist China may be imported into the United States—not even hair. Nothing personal against Chinese women as a race, of course, but the hair shorn from any women living in Communist China must not enter American shores. On the other hand, the black tresses of any Chinese women living in Hong Kong, Singapore, or anywhere else outside the Communist camp are quite acceptable. The trouble is, how, by looking at a lock of hair, do you tell a woman's politics? Did she live in Hong Kong as a good little capitalist, or was she a neighbor of Chairman Mao in Peking? It is a sad reflection on the state of our society that grown men have to spend their lives trying to answer this question, instead of devoting their time and energy to more pressing and harmful rackets like narcotics smuggling.

When human hair first arrived in the United States from the Far East, it came with certificates of origin confirming it had been shorn from Chinese women living in Hong Kong. No worry about that. But as the hair came in by the ton and there were no reports from Hong Kong that the entire colony was suddenly close-cropped, it was quite obvious that some scurrilous characters were altering the certificates of origin. As indeed they were. The hair was cut in China and transported quite legally into

Hong Kong, which imposes no restrictions on hair movements. False certificates were then assigned. So in 1965 the United States refused to accept any more consignments of hair with Hong Kong certificates. "We soon sorted that out," said an international hair smuggler, calmly sipping his drink in the Dragon Boat Bar of the Hong Kong Hilton. "We send the hair from here to Indonesia, change the color of the ribbon with which the bundles of hair are tied, and send it on to the States with Indonesian certificates of origin." This diversion is known locally as "swimming hair."

Chinese hair has swum to all sorts of unexpected places. One Hong Kong wigmaker exported over $190,000 worth of wigs backed by false documents issued in Macao to Lisbon, where they were immediately forwarded to Fort Lauderdale, Florida, with Portuguese certificates of origin. Another hair trader shipped 6,600 pounds of Chinese hair worth $112,000 to a firm in Beirut, who repacked it and dispatched it by air to New York labeled as Arabian tresses. When that little subterfuge was exposed, there was an unexpected reverberation from the Communists. The manager of the exporting firm in Hong Kong was summoned up to Canton, where the Red Guards accorded him public disgrace for "not being clever enough in his business dealings and causing great loss to many people." He was replaced by a manager more adept in the wiles of smuggling. Contraband hair is obviously a priority item in Communist Chinese exports.

Indeed, according to a hair peddler in Hong Kong, "It is one of the biggest foreign-exchange earners for China." He might just be right. There are 150 wig factories and 314 wigmakers and dealers in Hong Kong, and they put through one hundred tons of hair from China *every month*. The going price for the hair is eight dollars a pound. At that price the Hong Kong hair trade earns over twenty-one million dollars a year for the Chinese. Since another one hundred tons a month is estimated to bypass Hong Kong and "swim" direct to Indonesia, where it fetches twelve dollars a pound, this puts the total Chinese hair earnings at fifty million dollars a year. Perhaps it is not surprising that an American customs agent trying to fight his way through this tangle cursed it as "the biggest racket of all." Clearly any American coiffeur who can create a new style of short back and sides for American women and convince them that wigs are now "out" is going to be the darling of the State Department and the U.S. Customs.

The only thing to top the tangle of the hair trade is the case of the contraband shrimp. This dastardly affair was touched off when the U.S. Food and Drug Administration, quite rightly, refused entry into New York to a shipment of frozen shrimp that was badly decomposed. The shrimp had been dispatched from Marseilles by a French firm, which had received them from a subsidiary in Hong Kong, which, in turn, had purchased them from Communist China. Studying the origins of these rotten shrimp, the authorities found that other consignments had followed the same route, but had always been accompanied by false papers, which declared the shrimp had swum initially into the shrimping nets of South Vietnam or South Korea; in fact, the whole lot had been caught by Communist shrimp boats. And, of course, Communist food along with Communist hair is prohibited entry.

The trouble is that expatriate Chinese living in the Chinatowns of San Francisco, Seattle, or New York often wax nostalgic for fat South China Sea shrimp, genuine Peking duck, birds' nest soup, or water chestnuts. They are not going to let a little matter of American foreign policy stand in their way. In 1950, when America first banned foods from Communist China, the imports of Chinese food into Canada went up six hundred percent. The business has been flourishing ever since. The food comes in through Vancouver and is then shifted down the West Coast. Once safely over the border, there is no real need for secrecy. Every Chinese store in Seattle and San Francisco has genuine birds' nest soup and lychees boldly displayed on its shelves. If any embarrassing question arises about how they came by such supplies, the answer is straightforward: It is from stocks already in the country when the embargo was imposed. Slow-selling line, that birds' nest soup; it has taken over twenty years to sell one case.

While politics precipitates the birds'-nest-soup racket, patent protection has fostered another in vitamin B_{12}. This vitamin, used in the treatment of pernicious anemia, is covered by a patent held by an American firm, but it has also been manufactured without license in Italy, a country with which the United States has no treaty protecting patents. The real attraction of vitamin B_{12} to the smuggler is its price. It costs around $22,000 a pound in the United States, which makes it more expensive than heroin, but in Italy it sells for $15,000 a pound—a disparity that can lead to only one course of action. Vitamin smuggling into the United States to avoid the patent controls has never been organized on a grand scale, but the smugglers have certainly realized the value of their contraband; one rented a safety deposit box in New York in which he cached it while he arranged distribution.

Because of its value and rarity, vitamin B_{12} is in heavy demand all around the world, particularly in India, with its enormous problem of famine and malnutrition. The vitamin is manufactured in India under license, but there is never enough to satisfy requirements. Since its import is forbidden, the alternative is to smuggle, normally through the smugglers' supermarket of Dubai. Indeed, smuggling is the only way in which Indian doctors can obtain adequate supplies of many drugs and medicines. "You can make yourself a five-hundred-percent profit by bringing in concentrated raw materials for all kinds of drugs," said a Bombay doctor. "There's a premium on everything from anticoagulants to hormone pills." While it is sad to see smugglers profit from illness, it can at least be argued that in this case the smuggling of drugs is ultimately beneficial.

This is Adam Smith's thesis on natural justice asserting itself again. Human nature has a remarkable ability for conveniently finding ways of bypassing the absurdities of officialdom. When there is genuine reason for concern, whether it be for the terrible dangers of heroin addiction or simply to save the orangutan from extinction, the basic reaction is to sympathize with authority. A smuggled pat of butter or a wig or a watch is another matter entirely.

A London newspaper suggested recently that history is

against the smuggler, that as the world shrinks and countries bring their economies more into alignment, the demand for his services will decrease. At the moment there is remarkably little sign of this happening; indeed, as economies develop, so do taxes and controls. When a bottle of whisky costs little more than two dollars in a duty-free shop and six to seven dollars with duty paid in London or New York; when gold retails at forty dollars an ounce in Zurich and seventy dollars in Bombay; when tight import quotas limit the flow of watches to Brazil or Indonesia; and while heroin fetches thirty thousand dollars a kilo in New York or Chicago and LSD commands two thousand dollars a gram wholesale, the smuggler remains safe with his motto "Profit for Sure."

Index